Tom has written one of the most thoughtful book:
act culturally. This helps us reimagine how to create
grain of who they are and their local distinctivenes
them strength and personality.

—Charles Landry, inventor of the creative city concept, one of the leading
thinkers on cultural planning, and author of *The Creative City* and *The Art
of City Making,* among others

Tom Borrup critiques the Eurocentric and colonialist assumptions often under-
lying city and cultural planning and calls for an anthropological understanding
of cities' diverse ways of life. He also addresses city planning's "often-invisible
cultural agenda" favoring "dominant economic, political, and institutional cultural interests." Anyone who cares about cities should read this book.

—Thomas Fisher, University of Minnesota

Borrup's decades of culturally based community work shine through, providing enriching insights on ways to incorporate culture into city planning. Often
overlooked, yet critically vital, cultural planning can empower more equitable,
socially just, and sustainable community development—and *The Power of Culture
in City Planning* is just the book that can help us better understand how to do so.

—Rhonda Phillips, FAICP, Dean and Professor, Purdue University

Tom Borrup is one of the most authoritative and seasoned voices in creative
placemaking today, and *The Power of Culture* is like having a meaningful conversation on the state of city planning and cultural planning in the Western world.
This book both inspires and challenges the planner (of cities, arts organizations, or cultural environments) to think deeply about their work. It should be
part of the reading list for courses on comprehensive community planning and
community-based arts planning. City planners and cultural planners should read
this book—preferably together—to see what they've been missing.

—Leonardo Vazquez, AICP/PP, Founding Director, The National
Consortium for Creative Placemaking, Director of Creative Placemaking,
New England College

The practice of planning stands to be enriched by a deeper engagement with
culture. Yet urban and cultural planning are often a world apart, leading to deficits in equity and social justice. A theorist and practitioner in equal measure,
Tom Borrup is the perfect guide to bring these disciplines into fruitful dialogue.

—Andrew Zitcer, Assistant Professor of Urban Strategy, Drexel University

The Power of Culture in City Planning

The Power of Culture in City Planning focuses on human diversity, strengths, needs, and ways of living together in geographic communities. The book turns attention to the anthropological definition of culture, encouraging planners in both urban and cultural planning to focus on characteristics of humanity in all their variety. It calls for a paradigm shift, repositioning city planners' "base maps" to start with a richer understanding of human cultures. Borrup argues for cultural master plans in parallel to transportation, housing, parks, and other specialized plans, while also changing the approach of city comprehensive planning to put people or "users" first rather than land "uses," as does the dominant practice.

Cultural plans as currently conceived are not sufficient to help cities keep pace with the dizzying impacts of globalization, immigration, and rapidly changing cultural interests. Cultural planners need to up their game, and enriching their own and city planners' cultural competencies is only one step. Both planning practices have much to learn from one another and already overlap in more ways than most recognize. This book highlights some of the strengths of the lesser-known practice of cultural planning to help forge greater understanding and collaboration between the two practices, empowering city planners with new tools to bring about more equitable communities. This will be an important resource for students, teachers, and practitioners of city and cultural planning, as well as municipal policymakers of all stripes.

As founder of Creative Community Builders, **Tom Borrup** is an international consultant and lecturer working with cities, foundations, and nonprofits to develop synergy between arts and culture, economic development, urban planning, and design. His book, *The Creative Community Builders' Handbook*, remains a leading text in the field. Tom earned his PhD in Leadership and Change from Antioch University and is Senior Lecturer and Director of Graduate Studies for the University of Minnesota's Master of Professional Studies in Arts and Cultural Leadership.

THE POWER OF
CULTURE IN CITY
PLANNING

TOM BORRUP

Routledge
Taylor & Francis Group

NEW YORK AND LONDON

First published 2021
by Routledge
52 Vanderbilt Avenue, New York, NY 10017

and by Routledge
2 Park Square, Milton Park, Abingdon, Oxon, OX14 4RN

Routledge is an imprint of the Taylor & Francis Group, an informa business

Library of Congress Cataloging-in-Publication Data

Names: Borrup, Tom, 1954- author.
Title: The power of culture in city planning / Tom Borrup.
Identifiers: LCCN 2020026978 (print) | LCCN 2020026979 (ebook) | ISBN 9780367347383 (hardback) | ISBN 9780367223762 (paperback) | ISBN 9780429327582 (ebook)
Subjects: LCSH: City planning--Social aspects. | Cities and towns--Growth--Social aspects.
Classification: LCC HT166 .B676 2020 (print) | LCC HT166 (ebook) | DDC 307.1/216--dc23
LC record available at https://lccn.loc.gov/2020026978
LC ebook record available at https://lccn.loc.gov/2020026979

ISBN: 978-0-367-34738-3 (hbk)
ISBN: 978-0-367-22376-2 (pbk)
ISBN: 978-0-429-32758-2 (ebk)

Typeset in Bembo
by SPi Global, India

Contents

Preface

This final essay was written in July 2020, in the midst of two very present and devastating phenomena, as well as a third phenomenon with even greater power just beginning to disrupt life and social order as it has been known. Their confluence highlights how such vexing forces are connected and can share common denominators. I write during the global COVID-19 pandemic, the United States' poor response to which caused inordinate health, economic, and social fallout. This is also written in the wake of civil unrest not seen in this country since the 1960s in response to persistent racial injustice and police brutality vividly and repeatedly displayed across the world on social media. Protests erupted May 25 a few blocks from my home in Minneapolis where police murdered a Black man, George Floyd, with the event streamed live on Facebook. Building on 400 years of injustice for people of African descent in the United States, and just the latest of many such videotaped police atrocities, deep-seated anger was set off, spreading to cities across the country and around the world. The other present and looming crisis is that of climate change which, like COVID-19 and racism, does not recognize city, state, or national boundaries. They all inordinately harm communities of color and the poor, and they are all fueled and compounded by the potency of culture, specifically White supremacy.

These present circumstances brought greater and much-needed attention to social, economic, health, and other inequities in the United States, a country long under the illusion that it stands for equality and justice for all. Racism and inequities are baked deeply into institutions, economic structures, policies, and practices—part of their "cultures." The need to change the culture of policing and police departments, for instance, is now more widely discussed. Of course, such ingrained cultures go beyond police departments to include such practices and institutions as city planning and the arts and cultural sector. These latter two are the focus of this book, along with how city planners and cultural workers have the potential to contribute to more equitable and sustainable communities. This book comes in response to these inequities and mounting crises. And, as I hope to make clear, these are cultural issues and must be addressed through cultural as well as political change.

American sustainability scholar Andrew J. Hoffman (2015), in his book, *How Culture Shapes the Climate Change Debate*, addressed why people see climate change differently. He wrote:

> Whether we like it or not, we have taken a role in the operation of many of the earth's systems. This brings a fundamental shift in how we think about ourselves and the world we occupy. Recognizing this emerging reality commences with a cultural shift akin to the Enlightenment of the seventeenth and eighteenth centuries.
>
> (pp. 87–88)

If Hoffman is right, dominant paradigms and ways of working must shift for humanity to survive and for any level of equity or fairness to prevail. To understand the damage humans continue to inflict on the planet, Hoffman (2015) concluded, "The debate over climate change in the United States (and elsewhere) is not about carbon dioxide and greenhouse gas models; it is about opposing cultural values and world views through which science is seen" (p. 5). His acknowledgment of the primacy of culture is critical, yet his analysis goes only as far as exploring why people disagree over science. In this book, I hope to push the discussion to another plane—to explore ways city planners can help people better live together through unprecedented changes unfolding in the early 21st century.

Wicked Problems Require Cultural Fixes, Too

Of a magnitude heretofore unseen, challenges facing not only the United States, but the entire world, are at once environmental, political, economic, and cultural. And, these shifts are making themselves more evident daily in the form of floods, droughts, fires, civil unrest, crop failures, massive and unpredictable storms, animal extinctions, and uncontrollable diseases, among others. This book was written with a sense of urgency, calling on colleagues in planning, community development, and cultural fields to do their part in addressing these challenges; to recommit to their fundamental purpose of building healthy, compassionate, sustainable, and just communities. To do so requires adopting new ways of working. Solutions to wicked problems facing humanity in the 21ˢᵗ century require significant changes to ways of living together—with the planet and with each other.

How local, state, and national governments, as well as communities of people themselves, respond to escalating cultural and social changes constitutes a vexing challenge beyond the physical impacts of the climate itself. During the May–June 2020 uprising in my Minneapolis neighborhood, many people were engaged in the protests, yet, at the same time, the community was devastated by looting, fires, and destruction of many essential local businesses that provide food and other necessities to largely working-class people of color and immigrants—the very people most abused by police. For over 48 hours, while the police virtually disappeared from the streets, fires ravaged the neighborhood. In this wake, hundreds of residents organized patrols to protect one another and local businesses that remained standing. In the days and weeks after, hundreds also showed up, many from outside the area, to sweep up and to organize food drives. Food pantries popped up daily every two or three blocks. A culture of mutual support and caring was evident in abundance—a level of social capital said to be lacking in multiethnic and mixed immigrant communities. I saw Latinx men wearing "Black Lives Matter" t-shirts volunteering at food tables serving Somali women, as just one example.

Worldwide climate upheaval, tragedies inflicted by COVID-19, and civil uprisings responding to racism hopefully provide many useful lessons. As we have seen, how people and governments respond to such circumstances determine the degree of harm they inflict. With climate change, damages the environment will inflict back on humanity—including the spread of novel viruses—and the inability of people to continue to live in places where they have lived, are only the tip of the iceberg. More communities will inevitably be displaced, and I fear it is not what the climate will do, but what people do to people—or do not do for them—that will be the most horrific. Impacts of climate, like viruses and racism, do not limit themselves within state or national boundaries.

Technical solutions to droughts, floods, storms, fires, crop failures, disease, and the like present enormous challenges, but I respectfully argue these critically needed interventions are not as complicated as the human and cultural challenges, for which city planners are less prepared. These range from the denial of science, as Hoffman (2015) discussed, to violence perpetrated against people appearing to be of Asian descent accused of spreading COVID-19. Culture and the capacities of people to live, work, recreate, and function in civic endeavors within culturally diverse environments are critical in the prevention of death, community devastation, and social and economic disruption yet to come. I hope this book makes a contribution to ways city planners and the cultural sector can find common ground and join forces to address these challenges.

Locating Myself

Writing this book involved both reflection on my own work and active learning. I draw on my experiences, research from scholars across a variety of fields, and observations of global affairs. As in any such endeavor, new ideas, stories, and developments arrive daily; thus, some of the material on these pages will be outdated by the time the proverbial ink is dry. In the text that follows, I simply hope to share some of my continuing journey and to contribute to critical ongoing discussions—especially those in city planning and cultural work. I was not formally trained in city planning and as such am an outsider yet have worked with, for, besides, and in the wake of many planners. As change and innovation rarely come from the center of any profession, my near-outsider status hopefully challenges and provokes in constructive ways.

In arriving at and presenting these ideas, I must own up to biases I know I bring—to my position of privilege in the world as a White, male Baby Boomer raised in a Christian tradition from a small town in Connecticut carrying an American passport and academic credentials. While of working-class roots, I have enjoyed many privileges, travelled widely, and, in spite of being a gay man, never experienced violence against my person. My parents endured the Great Depression and World War II, experiences surely engrained in my sense of frugality and civic responsibility. My mother was a nurse in an urban hospital and brought home a sense of compassion and fairness that impresses me long after her passing. My father, while a gentle man at home, was not so kind in speaking of others who were different. I have wrestled with this dichotomy throughout my life.

Relocating People and Cultures

When I began this book in 2016, a news story caught my eye about Shishmaref, an Inupiat community of nearly 600 people north of Nome, Alaska. *The New York Times* carried a story that leaders of the community voted to pack up and move their entire community, abandoning land, a part of the sea, and a way of life they had shared for at least 400 years (Mele & Victor, 2016). Coastal erosion and storm surge over the past four decades had already taken 2,500 to 3,000 feet of shoreline from their island. With the entire island now threatened, the choices they faced included: moving to nearby higher ground to try to maintain their way of life, but only for a short time; scattering to accommodating communities in Alaska where they could find familiar work; or trying to move together in an effort to retain their unique culture. Could they find a hospitable place that provides safety, livelihoods, and a place where they can live as a cultural community?

Assisting in the relocation of relatively small groups of people is not unique in city planning. How to assist in such relocations while considering the double-sided cultural dimensions is more complex. For this Inupiat community, retaining a cohesive culture when separated from ancestral lands is one side of the coin. Finding a welcoming place to resettle represents the other. For these 600 people, this will not be easy. Their way of life will be challenged, but they will likely survive.

This is not, and will not be, an isolated story. However, for many stories of *climate refugees* there will not be hopeful endings. In late July 2020, research presented in the *New York Times Magazine* focused on some of the social impacts of climate change. Climate patterns and their impacts on crops and living conditions have been the subject of much research, Lustgarten (2020) reported.

> Scientists have learned to project such changes around the world with surprising precision, but – until recently – little has been known about the human consequences of those changes. As their land fails them, hundreds of millions of people from Central America to Sudan to the Mekong Delta will be forced to choose between flight or death. The result will almost certainly be the greatest wave of global migration the world has seen.
>
> (para. 4)

Of late, the term *climate gentrification* has also surfaced (Keenan, Hill, & Gumber, 2018). Coastal lands in the United States close to shorelines have long been more highly valued. Property further from the water was historically relegated to poorer people. Such properties are now being scooped up by speculators or simply well-heeled, climate-aware residents seeking higher, safer ground, forcing residents to scatter to less-desirable, lower-cost locations or leaving them homeless.

In 2018, the Union of Concerned Scientists estimated that over 300,000 homes in the lower 48 states are at risk from rising seas over the next 30 years, and over 2.5 million by the end of the century (Union of Concerned Scientists,

2018). With droughts and wildfires rampant and increasing around the globe, how many flooded, parched, and fire-ravaged communities can governments relocate or bail out? Recently, the Union of Concerned Scientists (n.d.) predicted,

> By the end of the century, sea level rise alone could displace more than 100 million people. These migrations, as well as conflicts over increasingly scarce resources, will exacerbate existing political and social tensions, and significantly increase the risk of conflict and war.
>
> (para. 14)

The question, facing city planners in the United States is where will displaced people go? Who will welcome them? How much resistance will there be to their arrival—whether from South Florida, South Carolina, or South Asia? Are planners prepared to help people who are very different from one another live and function together in communities? Who knows how to plan for the kind of spaces and places in which diverse people can carry out their ways of life and livelihoods while finding productive ways of living together? Of course, these are not conditions uniquely resulting from climate change. They are already well-known questions in cities large and small.

Relocating the Work

This is not a book about climate change, global migration, xenophobia, or pandemics. These phenomena, unfortunately, provide the backdrop, the context in which the work described in this book intends to address. These global phenomena and the professional practice of city planning and cultural work are increasingly finding themselves face to face. This book is about ways professionals in those fields can make constructive contributions to mitigate problems those forces generate and reverse their negative impacts. Not to focus solely on the negative, cultural diversity and embracing creativity in communities has seen beautiful results. Spending a lifetime in such communities and in such work, I wouldn't trade them for anything. What I hope to share in this book are new ways of thinking and badly needed approaches I believe planners can use.

My decades in culturally based community work have been fueled by a commitment to working with professionals in city planning, community development, and cultural agencies in ways that contribute to greater equity and social justice. Through this work, I've advocated for changes to professional practices in cultural work, community development, and planning. The conjoined and accelerating challenges of climate change, globalization, and xenophobia, as well as economic inequities, make this work more relevant and urgent. Each of these phenomena are generating social disruption and anxiety at a steadily increasing pace and scale on every continent.

The denial of science that Hoffman (2015) described and the rising tide of nationalism, among other forces, are exacerbating these most difficult challenges of the 21st century. Hate-related violence has become too frequent to keep track of, and global tensions are increasing while the climate is literally turning up the heat. During the recent political era in the United States, federal government actions on the environment, as well as those relative to racial justice, were aiming to turn the heat up faster. This is less true on the local level, where most planners and policymakers deal with daily realities in more foresighted ways. It is thus of greater importance that city planners, community development professionals, urban designers, and local policymakers become better prepared for the cultural dimensions of their work.

The built environment, and how people use it, continues to cause massive environmental damage. Many planners and designers now admit complicity in enabling unsustainable development patterns including suburban sprawl, unhealthy lifestyles, and fossil fuel/automobile dependency. Some city planners are diligently at work helping their cities become more resilient and sustainable. These critical and sincere efforts are nascent, yet change is slow. While preparing for sea-level rise, warmer temperatures, and water shortages, among other challenges, city planners must also prepare for displacement, migration, and cultural connectivity. This means preparing space for people to practice their cultures and to share them while learning to adapt to new conditions.

The proposition I put forth in this book is that some of the techniques and approaches of city planning and cultural planning can create synergy to better address complex challenges facing cities of all sizes. I offer some ways city planners, policymakers, cultural workers and other activists can and must work together to foster places in which people can live in greater harmony.

Italian-born planning scholar Franco Bianchini (1999) teaching in Britain, observed, "Cities will not become more ecologically sustainable if we do not address how people mix and connect, their motivations, and whether they 'own' where they live and change their lifestyles appropriately" (p. 195). Similarly, Colombian anthropologist Arturo Escobar (2017) shone light on challenges confronting city planners, designers, and policymakers. He explained how dominant ways of thinking and relating to the natural environment are integral to yet often invisible in their work. Escobar described embedded ways of life that people from all corners of the globe adhere to and concluded, "It is, finally, about the cultural work that needs to take place for the creation of new futures" (p. 51). To be successful in contemporary and future planning efforts, planners cannot ignore cultural issues—how people live together and with the earth. To do so requires new ways of thinking and of carrying out their work.

The Force is with Us

Globalizing communities, or what Australian-Canadian planning scholar Leonie Sandercock (2003) called "mongrel cities," have long been part of the experience of city planners and policymakers in the United States and elsewhere. Sandercock coined the term to describe cities that have assumed a make-up and identity beyond a singular historical or established sense of ethnic identity to include a multitude of people. Migration seems to pose new challenges for cities and towns of all sizes across the United States, even though their populations have changed and grown repeatedly, sometimes radically, over the past two or three hundred years. Each incoming group continues to get the same cold reception as the last—or worse.

Has city-planning practice unwittingly contributed to darker, xenophobic forces that have risen in the face of growing diversity? Or have planners helped build physical and social capacities that enable people to live more harmoniously? What tools and approaches do city planners, designers, policymakers, and others employ to foster social connectivity? They may be quickly growing their toolboxes to address physical and economic aspects of climate change, but what do they have to help with the cultural challenges?

I have confidence that, given time, resource, and political will, the planning profession can lead and collaborate to mitigate and eventually reverse the physical impacts of climate change. Yet, I remain apprehensive about the cultural problems confronting humanity.

In the pages that follow, I explore and illustrate ways to understand and tackle cultural issues in the context of city planning. The book is addressed to city planners and policymakers, designers, and community development professionals, as well as to those involved in cultural planning, community arts, creative placemaking, and cultural work of all kinds—frankly, to anyone concerned with the future of humanity. It is my intention to advance thinking related to ways city-planning practices can move towards more people-centered approaches based in better understanding of human cultures and the ways people live together and with the earth. I hope the approaches examined in this book contribute to building greater equity, social justice, and more sustainable cities and towns for all who call them home or may want and need to call them home.

References

Bianchini, F. (1999). Cultural planning and time planning: The relationship between culture and urban planning. In C. Greed (Ed.), *Social town planning* (pp. 195–202). London: Routledge.

Davenport, C., & Robertson, C. (2016, May 2). Resettling the first American "climate refugees". *New York Times*. Retrieved from https://www.nytimes.com/2016/05/03/us/resettling-the-first-american-climate-refugees.html

Escobar, A. (2017). *Designs for the pluriverse: Radical interdependence, autonomy, and the making of worlds*. Durham, NC: Duke University Press.

Hoffman, A. J. (2015). *How culture shapes the climate change debate*. Stanford, CA: Stanford University Press.

Keenan, J. M., Hill, T., & Gumber, A. (2018). Climate gentrification: From theory to empiricism in Miami-Dade County, Florida. *Environmental Research Letters*, *13*(5), 054001. Retrieved from https://iopscience.iop.org/article/10.1088/1748-9326/aabb32/pdf

Mele, C., & Victor, D. (2016, August 19). Reeling from effects of climate change, Alaskan village votes to relocate. *New York Times*. Retrieved from https://www.nytimes.com/2016/08/20/us/shishmaref-alaska-elocate-vote-climate-change.html

Sandercock, L. (2003). *Cosmopolis II: Mongrel cities in the 21st century*. London: Continuum. doi:10.5040/9781472545527

Union of Concerned Scientists. (n.d.). *Climate impacts: The consequences of climate change are already here*. Retrieved from https://www.ucsusa.org/climate/impacts

Union of Concerned Scientists. (2018). *Underwater: Rising seas, chronic floods, and the implications for US coastal real estate*. Cambridge, MA: UCS. Retrieved from https://www.ucsusa.org/sites/default/files/attach/2018/06/underwater-analysis-full-report.pdf

Acknowledgments

A book like this is not a discrete project but an accumulation of decades of experience and learning. So, where does one begin in recognizing the people who provided intellectual, practical, moral, and other kinds of support? There are many cities and organizations over the years that entrusted me and my colleagues with facilitating planning projects with and in their communities. I hope we provided them with good results; I know they provided us with enormous learning. For anyone I inadvertently neglect in these acknowledgements, my apologies.

Colleagues over the years I had opportunity to work with and to learn from include Ta-coumba Aiken, Carrie Christensen, Craig Dreeszen, Christine Harris, Peter Musty, Leo Vazquez, Bob McNulty, and Penny Cuff. Thanks to my friend and assistant-in-chief, Lucas Erickson, and smart-as-a-whip data wrangler, Heidi Wagner. I also had opportunity to work briefly with both Greg Baeker and Charles Landry at different times, whose shadows I am honored to be in. Likewise, with Deborah Stevenson, whom I met only once but read voraciously.

Special thanks for enormous support and patience to my dear life partner and frequent collaborator, Harry Waters, Jr., an actor, director, and teacher of renown, who put to work his amazing talents at community dialog facilitation in dozens of projects we worked on together across the country. I also want to acknowledge my supervisor at the University of Minnesota, Ritu Saksena, for encouragement during this writing process.

A number of people provided material assistance in conducting research for this book including Lyz Crane, Craig Deeszen, Maryo Gard Ewell, the

Librarians at the University of Minnesota, and Pam Korza and Barbara Schaffer Bacon with Animating Democracy. Survey research on cultural planning was made possible by the direct support of Graciela Kahn and Randy Cohen at Americans for the Arts, and graphics were capably prepared by Elizabeth Taing. I also want to thank Celio Turino, author and former Brazilian Minister of Cultural Citizenship, who I spent a few days with while in Bogotá in 2018, for turning me on to the work of Arturo Escobar.

A number of people generously read and commented on chapters or the entire text at various stages. These include Benjamin Alfaro, Fernando Burga, Maryo Gard Ewell, Brenda Kayzar, Jason Kovacs, Hanna Mattila, Evan Plummer, and Andrew Zitcer. Last, and certainly not least, thanks to Norman Dale, who meticulously corrected my citations and formatting—and so much more—while catching many errors and inconsistencies, thus saving me from at least a few embarrassing oversights. Oversights of substance remain mine.

Much gratitude to my commissioning editor, Kate Schell, editorial assistant, Sean Speers, and Yassar Arafat, Natalie Hamil, and the rest of the editorial and production folks at Routledge for taking on this project and shepherding it to completion. The artwork of Eddie Hamilton, a Minneapolis artist, graces the cover of this book. His work speaks to or comments on how people live together in cities in such interesting ways. I thank him for his work and for allowing it to be reproduced.

I cannot conclude without acknowledging the welcoming and patient staff at Café a la Folie in Miami Beach where the majority of this book was written, revised, and edited. Thanks to Bertrand, Jeremy, Juan Pablo, Marie, Olivier, and especially Victor, as well as others whose names I never learned. The menu is delicious, the coffee excellent, and the croissants can barely be matched, even in France.

Introduction

Planning at the Intersection

The more urban—in other words the more heterogeneous, dense and large—the context we live in, the greater the need to define and constantly redefine who we are vis-à-vis others in our everyday life.

—Talja Blokland (2017, p. 107)

It is commonplace, but nonetheless valid, to speak of current times as turbulent, divisive, and uncertain to an unprecedented extent; amidst this, culture is a complex term with a no less complex role to play in calming, resolving, or further polarizing divided selves and societies. Is culture to be understood as being backward-looking, driving people into defensive enclaves in the face of hostility? Or can accentuating culture and celebrating differences, along with a more vivid appreciation of the diverse lifeways and creative practices of others, actually serve as a unifying force?

Dutch-German sociologist Blokland (2017) researched the formation of communities as a social construct and how that process takes place within urban spaces. As she advocated in the statement above, revisiting what constitutes community, especially under the pressures and benefits of globalization, must be a deliberate process and one that is ongoing.

For several decades now, professionals in many lines of work, including planners, have increasingly embraced ideas about culture as an ever-more-important focus of their work. In this book, I argue that planners need to open their thinking and their practice to better understand and include culture—or the ways of life of people—to find ways that people who are different from one another, can better live together. This is in step with a movement in the city-planning profession to refresh its core purpose and to bring greater diversity into the field, yet it goes further. This book addresses a rethinking of city planning and its younger cousin, cultural planning, and it illuminates how the two can work together to advance more just and equitable planning practices, and, in turn, more just and sustainable cities.

Unprecedented challenges of global climate change and xenophobic movements—described in the preface—on top of accelerated cultural changes brought on by technology, global economies, and human movement propel this work. I join calls to put *people*—their cultures or ways of life—at the center of planning and building of cities, towns, and communities of all sizes. This involves recommitting city planning to building healthy, compassionate, sustainable, and just communities and to incorporating new approaches. As British planning scholar John Montgomery eloquently advocated, planners should look at cities "from the standpoint of *users* rather than *uses* [emphasis added]" (1990, p. 20).

My proposition is to put the best practices of city planning and cultural planning into a new whole I call *just planning*. Combined, I believe these practices not only recognize and embrace growing diversity, but help individuals and rapidly changing populations live together better and live better together.

This book covers a considerable range of topics, and I hope I sufficiently show how they are related and integral to the work of city planners. In their training and in the demands of their work, city planners weigh and balance many factors and assess how those factors impact one another. Additionally, they think long-term. Folding culture into that mix—culture, in the broader, anthropological sense—is critical for planners if communities large and small are going to function and find and maintain quality-of-life, civility, justice, and sustainability through the changes in store in the balance of the 21st century.

Terminology Used

In this book I use the term *city planning* as the singular term inclusive of urban and regional planning as well as community, local, neighborhood, small-area, and town planning. The organized profession itself struggles to find a singular term and generally uses the word *planning*. However, in this book, to distinguish city planning from cultural planning, I use *city planning* and *city planners*. At times, simply the term *planning* or *planners* are used purposefully to include both city planning and cultural planning practices and practitioners.

The lesser-known practice of cultural planning—that I advocate needs to change—is sometimes known as *community cultural planning* and, less frequently in recent years, as *arts and cultural master planning*. In some parts of the world, it is referred to as *social planning*. The usage in this book is *cultural planning*. In short, as it has been practiced it is described as a municipal-level or community-wide endeavor that involves mapping, connecting, activating, and leveraging a city's or community's cultural resources, traditions, and creative activities. Cultural planning is generally led by public- or private-sector agencies, commissions, or councils concerned with promotion of arts, culture, and heritage. Cultural planning has been more akin to professional sector-based strategic planning and organizing. Its purposes on a local level, and what constitutes the arts and culture of a community, vary widely. More on that later.

The terms *cultural sector* and *arts and culture sector* are used to describe nonprofit arts, cultural, and heritage organizations of all sizes, as well as artists and creative practitioners across a wide range of disciplines. From community to community, who or what organizations are included in a local cultural sector may also vary widely.

I use the terms *arts* or *the arts* sparingly and with some ambivalence, as they are fuzzy, and in some respects have been weaponized. *The arts* is often used to mean Western or Eurocentric creative and cultural practices. Just as representations of the physical world, generated through dominant cartographic or mapping practices (see Chapter 7), have erased or marginalized Indigenous people in the service of White supremacy, many well-meaning promoters of the arts unwittingly do the same to "non-Western" or "other" cultures simply through an assumed understanding of what is and isn't art. Many traditional and everyday cultural practices and forms of creativity are thus erased or diminished, along with their practitioners. Often, the words *arts and culture* are combined as if they are the same, furthering the notion that worthy creative practices are confined within a specific cultural milieu (as in Eurocentric).

The term *culture* is used here in the anthropological sense, as in *ways of life*, unless it is associated with institutions that consider themselves *cultural* institutions or frame themselves as part of the *cultural sector*. Chapter 3 is entirely devoted to ways of understanding culture.

The term *community* is liberally used in reference to people sharing geographic space organized in neighborhoods, villages, districts, towns, and cities. *Community* is often used alternatively with those terms to describe such places. In some contexts, it refers to shared identity among people in a place; other times it refers to a place inhabited by a group or groups of people. In spite of the ubiquity and vagueness of the term, it remains useful and perhaps even hopeful in its connotations as it suggests a higher level of relationship among those sharing space.

I also use the term *placemaking* and *placemakers* in some chapters. I do so with reservation but because it is well-established in the practice of city design and activation of public spaces. The word **place***making* emphasizes physical place, following in the footsteps of land-use planning, rather than putting a focus on people as in a more holistic process of community building. *Place***making** also embodies a sense of denial that places (and people within them and their sense of belonging and meaning) already exist and therefore need to be "made." This recalls a colonial narrative. Native American colleagues object to the notion that people make places because it reinforces the subjugation of the earth or natural environment rather than appreciating the symbiotic relationship between people and place, or that people come from the earth, not the other way around. In the arts and culture sector over the past decade, the term has been adapted in the form of *creative placemaking*. This describes an arts-and-culture-infused set of activities to rejuvenate neighborhoods, towns, or cities through a combination of cultural, economic, social, and political strategies. As it is often practiced, creative placemaking adds a layer to the colonial narrative by suggesting creativity and culture need to be delivered or infused as if none existed. At the same time, it has often been usurped by those whose interests are largely in real estate profiteering. More thoughtful practitioners identify and build on the cultures and creativity already present and focus on organizing communities to advance self-determination.

Finally, I use the word *resident* or *community member* and intentionally avoid the word *citizen*, a word that is, unfortunately, commonly used in city-planning literature. *Citizen* excludes a great number of active community stakeholders. For instance, in my neighborhoods in both Minneapolis and Miami, many friends, neighbors, and shopkeepers I interact with daily are not citizens in the legal sense and feel excluded when hearing this word. Tens of millions of people residing and working in the United States are excluded by that term.

Planning Meets Culture

Canadian planning scholar Mohammad Qadeer (1997) provided an instructive description of cultural issues in planning that arise within diverse populations—what he called "spatial expressions of cultural values" (p. 481). Planners' efforts to foster equality through one-size-fits-all standards and criteria when applied in multicultural settings, according to Qadeer, "reveal the cultural biases embedded in the so-called universal standards" (p. 491). His marvelous example illustrates the complexity of diversity in planning:

> A tree can be the source of neighbourhood battles ... Italians and Portuguese like to keep trees short, allowing a better view of the neighbours. Anglo-Saxons want trees to be tall and leafy, blocking any views from and to neighbourhood houses. The Chinese believe trees in front of a home bring bad luck.
>
> (p. 481)

Official policy in Qadeer's city favors one treatment. He pointed out that "a seemingly neutral regulation about tree maintenance is in fact an embodiment of English/European preferences" (p. 482).

Cities are not monocultural landscapes where human needs and behaviors, and aesthetics are uniform. One-size-fits-all policies may strive for *equality* but do little to contribute to *equity*, or to the ability of all people to fulfill their ways of life. Treating everyone the same through approaches, such as providing universal spatial accommodation and design, does not necessarily achieve equity. As Qadeer (1997) observed, applying standards preferred by one group can be a disservice or disrespectful to others. Maintaining trees in one way might be an affront to cultural sensibilities for some as well as an incursion into their lifeways. In this context, however, is it possible for everyone to see their way of life or culture in the environment around them when people of many different cultures share neighborhoods and cities? Equality, in fact, can serve as the antithesis of equity. Ideas such as spatial justice, advanced by American geographer Edward Soja (2010), and aesthetic justice, as proposed by Finnish planning scholar Hanna Mattila (2002), are explored in Chapter 8.

Such conflicts, in fact, were part of my introduction to city planning in the 1980s. As a young homeowner in Minneapolis, I jumped into participating in neighborhood organizations. In one case, a committee was invited by planners to advise on a proposed highway barrier along part of an artery being expanded to speed traffic through the neighborhood in and out of the downtown, a direct line to the Minneapolis-St. Paul airport. The wall was to "protect" residents of an adjacent Native American housing project known as Little Earth. Some at the meeting advocated for the design of the wall and ornamentation to reflect American Indian cultures. Known in modern times as Hiawatha Avenue, the pathway served residents and travelers for hundreds if not thousands of years, connecting the convergence of two rivers or *Bdote* (Minnesota and Mississippi

Rivers) with the Falls of St. Anthony—"discovered" and named by Father Hennepin and French trappers in the 1600s—that is the site of the current downtown. Other voices at the planning meeting demanded the concrete panel wall be plain and white, or what they called "absent of any cultural influence," or what others call Scandinavian design. Are any aesthetic choices free of culture?

Around the same time, a meeting was called to advise on renovations to a neighborhood park. A vocal group of White residents attended to adamantly protest the continued inclusion of basketball courts. "Basketball attracts Black men," they declared, feeling no need to further explain or justify their racism and fears.

Like tree maintenance that not everyone appreciates or modernist- or neoclassical-designed public spaces that not everyone sees or uses in the same way, policies that regulate residential or commercial building standards do not recognize cultural differences, diverse needs, and a multitude of ways people live together (Hou, 2013; Pader, 1993). American social scientist Brady Collins (2018), in his research on southern California's ethnic enclaves, like Montgomery (1990), called on planners to revisit the "person versus place" or "users versus uses" debate. City planners see the physical realm first, sometimes ignoring inhabitants—or worse, seeing them as obstacles to achieve physical development.

Planning at the Edge

City planning has a storied history evolving significantly since its formal beginnings well over 100 years ago. According to Canadian urban strategist Glen Murray and cultural planner Greg Baeker (2002), late-19th-century Scottish biologist and philosopher Patrick Geddes, who is often credited as originating the profession, "believed that planning was more a human than a physical science" (p. 14). Geddes advocated that city planners need three types of expertise: to be anthropologists (specialists in culture), economists (specialists in local economies), and geographers (specialists in the built and natural environment). Most observers agree that a growing city-planning profession has deviated from these foundational concepts as well as from the field's early focus on public health and safety that grew in response to industrial expansion during the late 19th century.

By the mid-1900s, city planning pivoted to building automobile-oriented communities. The practice focused on helping people—those with the economic and social means to do so—escape cities in ways that ultimately and ironically worsened health and created unsustainable infrastructure. Central cities were also remade to be automobile-centric as public transportation in most cities was dismantled and denigrated. Cities then faced further challenges as they were physically torn apart by government policies that included so-called urban renewal, interstate highway construction, and home mortgage subsidies favoring detached single-family homes for White families. Exclusionary practices of redlining and restrictive deed covenants, among other strategies, reinforced racial segregation. Government and private disinvestment in cities, together with their own shrinking tax bases, continued through the 1960s into the 21st century (Grogan & Proscio, 2001). In recent decades, political and market forces, along with often felonious actions of police have, in fact, expanded racial and economic segregation after older tools to enforce it were declared illegal.

After clearing property through urban renewal, a widely discredited program that peaked in the 1970s, planners in central cities then focused on stabilizing values and trying to rebuild tax bases. In doing this work, city planners increasingly find themselves in untenable situations between the public interest and real estate markets. American planning scholar Samuel Stein (2019) in his alarming book, *Capital Cities*, traced the trajectory of city planning and its relationship with real estate interests. By the 1990s, many cities in the United States began to grow again. Investment and interest in urban lifestyles among the White middle class required another tact for city planning. As Stein described, planners' jobs turned to finding "creative ways to raise property values—either because they are low and landowners want them higher, or because they are already high and city budgets will fail if they start to fall" (p. 10). This contributed to the negative side of gentrification—dislocation of mostly elderly and poor residents who are inordinately people of color.

City planners and cultural planners, regardless of intentions or personal values, frequently find themselves in such compromised spots. As Stein (2019) detailed, city planners have been caught in the trap of serving landowners who are increasingly large financial entities rather than individual home and business owners, while the profession is buffeted by the political winds of the day. However, each of the overarching chores city planners faced since the beginning of the 20th century represents a heavy lift. They've responded constructively to social, political, environmental, and economic changes and learned new ways of working.

City-planning practice that endeavors to advance social justice goals also has a long history. Practitioners and scholars inside and outside the profession have devised and advocated many progressive approaches and theories dating from the origins of the profession. In 2018, I listened, along with 5,700 city planners assembled in New Orleans at the American Planning Association (APA) conference, to then-APA president Cynthia Bowen advocate the slow turn of the profession to consider its more human dimensions. She declared, "Social equity is the defining issue of our time." What that looks like, and how planners address this age-old but heightened issue, is indeed one of the profession's challenges. Added to the city planner's long list of everyday challenges, social equity, exacerbated by the dominance of big capital and xenophobia, remains at the bow of a big ship to turn. The profession, however, has proven responsive and resilient. City planners listen and learn while serving multiple masters. Balancing priorities is a well-rehearsed art. Together with the urgency of climate change, these challenges demand more aggressive efforts.

Escobar (2017) called on city planners and designers to envision "a transformation from the ecologically and socially devastating model that has been in place for over a hundred years to a codesign process for the construction of a life-enhancing pluriverse" (p. 5). He used the unusual term *pluriverse* to describe multiple ways of understanding and seeing the totality of the world. He asserted that the concept of the *universal,* into which everything and everyone fits, is part of a colonialist narrative and not constructive in efforts to build more inclusive global communities. Codesign processes, which I describe in Chapters 6 and 8, can incorporate multiple ways of working and understanding. Including broad-based community engagement, these represent practices focused on generating solutions rather than confrontations over expert-driven proposals.

Cultural Planning Emerges

Cultural planning is also rife with contested outcomes. British planning scholar Graeme Evans, who has written extensively on local cultural policy, saw "the very idea of planning for culture as inherently instrumental in maintaining cultural and growth hegemonies—both market and state-led" (Evans, 2013, p. 223). In other words, both city planning and cultural planning are generally in service to the agenda of dominant economic, political, and institutional cultural interests. As such, both practices can be tools of White supremacy, out of sync with basic human needs and/or "majority-minority" populations.

While standard contemporary approaches to cultural planning remain worthy efforts to coordinate and mobilize creative and cultural sector resources of communities, I advocate the practice also take a more expansive approach. It can offer more to communities and to the broader enterprise of city planning. In upcoming chapters, I describe select elements of cultural planning that are empowerment-based, as well as some creative practices known since the 1970s as *community arts* or *community-based arts.* Techniques from these practices can also be adopted within city planning practices to bring people and their ways of life into more central consideration.

In Chapter 1, I describe cultural planning that first appeared as a formal practice at the end of the 1970s and that has begun to mature and demonstrate ways it can address a wider range of cultural and community concerns. However, my assessment is not uncritical. Cultural planning, sometimes found among the sub-plans for an overburdened city-planning profession, is usually low on the list. Part of the reason, as I describe, is that cultural planning has frequently limited itself by primarily serving the concerns and interests of an institutional arts and culture sector. The practice thus has little value or interest to those outside the sector. And, to boot, it tends to serve a narrow slice of the cultures present in a city to the exclusion of so-called minorities who sometimes comprise the majority of the population. Institutions, such as symphonies and museums representing Eurocentric cultural practices and ideas, receive the preponderance of public and charitable resources, as well as the spotlight, while cultures of communities of color and recent immigrants, among others, are denied resources or even recognition (Sidford, 2011, 2017).

It is no coincidence that over the past 40 years, British settler states in particular have been the most commonplace sites of cultural planning. Only more recently have countries in Europe, Africa, and Asia begun to adopt cultural or what some call social planning. Origins of the formal cultural planning practice are traced to the United States, where it has largely been practiced as cultural colonialism focusing on and advancing the interests and practices of politically and economically dominant cultures. Change is being seen in cultural planning, but it is slow. The specific cultural planning practices advocated and described later in this book are those that attempt to decolonize the practice and to promote empowerment, cultural equity, and grassroots democracy.

In the initial 40 years of cultural planning, as I describe in Chapters 1 and 4, the first generation of the practice paved the way for local cultural sector players to see that by working together, they could leverage more resources, build new facilities, gain political influence, and collaborate on their work in education among other areas. This account reveals cultural and institutional leaders beginning to focus on building their collective capacities and applying their joint resources to impact tourism, downtown and neighborhood revitalization, and local economic development, along with a growing list of other civic concerns. Not all progress in cultural planning, however, has been positive. Its intersections with city planning stagnated, and it failed in making substantive contributions to cultural equity.

In spite of this critique, I assert that cultural planning can be—and sometimes is—practiced in more equitable and holistic ways. Practitioners have developed some unique strengths and approaches that can add great value to city planning. Later chapters explicate several of these approaches and why and how they can serve city planning and communities in important ways. A central thrust of this book is that culture, in its broadest sense, provides an essential lens through which city planners can better understand people and their concerns. A better-informed and more inclusive approach to culture, and greater cultural competency, can help city planning build more just, healthy, and sustainable cities. Such an understanding, along with the employment of creative practices described in later chapters, brings city planners fresh insights and provides new tools.

City planners are pulled in many directions and called upon to solve many problems. The intention in this book is not to add cultural planning as another task for city planners, but to add more tools to their toolboxes and bring more partners to the table. Australian planning scholar Greg Young, in his 2008 book, *Reshaping Planning with Culture*, appealed for what he called the "culturalisation of planning." He asserted a rationale for the importance of culture in planning, and asked, "is it possible to develop a workable system to increase the authentic integration of culture in planning able to produce beneficial outcomes regard-less of the value conflicts of a postmodern world of cultural diversity?" (p. 5). Simply understanding differences (and similarities) among people living in today's cities surely is a challenge. Retooling city planning is another. I hope this book builds on arguments by Young, Baeker, Montgomery, and many others who make similar appeals to the planning professions.

Embracing Culture

The complexity, misunderstanding, and multiple uses of the word culture, dis-cussed in Chapter 3, remain part of the challenge for planners. When it comes to thinking about the meaning of culture in a city, most planners and their employ-ers have tilted towards the narrow concept of Eurocentric "high arts" produced and experienced within institutional frameworks. In city planning, the formal or institutional cultural sector has attracted increasing interest during the past few decades while the cultures of people and some communities have been invis-ible. To confuse matters, city planners and policymakers are bombarded with advocacy-based research related to the social and economic value of "arts and culture" and, more recently, creative placemaking. These research and/or advo-cacy materials are generally designed to promote and extoll the virtues of the arts in all manner of community, economic, social, place-based, and educational development. Unfortunately, these pleas typically conflate *culture* with *the arts*. Diverse ways of life remain in the shadows while a spotlight is shone on specific exemplary (read Eurocentric) creative practices. While I don't dispute many of the virtues of these practices, this book is not meant to advance the interests of the arts or the arts and culture sector, per se. My goal is to broaden thinking about culture; "broadly" as in examining existing and evolving ways of life among people in communities. This book is about the role and power of culture in city planning and ways it can become an asset and a vehicle to strengthen the practice.

Culture has, in fact, not been well understood, nor has it been a significant concern in city planning or in a variety of social justice movements. The word itself triggers an association with what has been called "opera house culture" (see Chapter 3). Not having the tools or language to talk about cultural differences among people, some professionals adopt the flawed notions of "color-blindness," or of universality that diminish real and important differences based in experience, values, origins, or upbringing. Asserting that everyone is equal or the same, pushes aside real cultural, ethnic, and developmental differences that define people and comprise their sense of identity and connection to one another. Cultural recognition and identity have long been ignored in such movements, and yet unrecognized and misunderstood cultural differences represent the major cause behind most local, regional, and global conflicts.

In addition to the many challenges cities now face, planners are called on to manage involvement of more and different people in their work through public engagement. Skills related to such involvement are usually absent from the technical and analytical training most city planners receive. As such, asserted Australian planning scholar Paul Maginn (2007), city planners and policymakers often set up planning processes and local partnerships with insufficient knowledge of local cultures.

Diversity and Cultural Competency

Growing ethnic and racial diversity that brings different culturally based ways of working, different relationships to government, and different uses of public spaces, among others is clearly a challenge facing city planners. Diversity both complicates and enriches planning work. Sandercock (2003, 2004) noted that city planners need more ways to foster dialogue and creative problem-solving as the environments they work in become more complex. The goal in public process is for community members, planning practitioners, and other public officials to come together in deliberative environments, as American planning scholar John Forester (1999) described, "to learn together and craft strategies to act collaboratively" (p. 4). Before this can happen, these parties have to achieve basic trust and confidence in the process. This is complicated, Forester explained, "when they distrust or even detest one another, when they inherit painful histories of eviction or terror, racial hatred or sexual violence" (p. 4).

Providing such deliberative environments is hindered by city planners' lack of cultural competence, argued American urban planner Leo Vazquez (2009, 2012). He described how city planners lack reflective understanding of even their own cultural practices and biases, let alone appreciation and understanding of the cultures and practices of others. Cultural competency—also known as *intercultural competency*—in city-planning education is one needed tool to work through racism and troubled histories. American planning scholar Julian Agyeman and planner Jennifer Sien Erickson argued that "recognizing, understanding, and engaging difference, diversity, and cultural heterogeneity in creative productive ways requires cultural competency" (Agyeman & Erickson, 2012, p. 358). They built on Vazquez's definition, describing it as "the range of awareness, beliefs, knowledge, skills, behaviors, and professional practice that will assist in planning for, in, and with 'multiple publics'" (p. 361). This enables people to appreciate difference, to work in cross-cultural situations, and to proactively engage with diversity and promote intercultural dialogue.

Sandercock (1998) similarly argued that in city planning, the cultures of communities (as in ways of life) are all but invisible. This includes the practice of colorblindness or treating everyone as if they are the same (Young, 2008). Some may claim this reflects a profession dedicated to equality, but it means practitioners are uncomfortable or consider it inappropriate or irrelevant to discuss race, gender, and other human characteristics. Given that the city planning profession is overwhelmingly White, and, until recently, predominantly male, this is not unexpected. Robin DiAngelo, in *White Fragility*, pointed out, "Given how seldom we [white people] experience racial discomfort in a society we dominate, we haven't had to build our racial stamina" (DiAngelo, 2018, pp. 1–2). She observed that for White people, the slightest stress around race is intolerable, where "the mere suggestion that being white has meaning often triggers a range of defensive responses" (p. 2).

For a city planner to develop an awareness of their own cultural vantage point and biases is at least as critical as learning about others (Agyeman & Erickson, 2012). This impacts "how their own conscious and unconscious assumptions, beliefs, knowledge, and desires affect their ability to listen well and understand other cultures" (p. 359). However, city planners need to understand more than just the people in the neighborhood or in the room. They need to understand the cultural specificity of existing structures and processes they employ and how their attitudes towards nonprofessionals impact experiences of different groups (Maginn, 2007). Like everyone, planners are captive of their own biases and experiences, and pull from a limited vocabulary of aesthetic choices, land-use patterns, and ways of involving people in civic dialogue.

Motivating engagement of those who feel—and actually have been—excluded requires more than impressing on them the importance of choices about street widths and zoning variances. "Deliberative practice and participatory processes will fail," wrote Forester, "if planning analysts pay so much attention to technique or 'substance' that they ignore and dismiss the history and culture, the self-perceptions and deeply defining experiences, or the citizens involved" (1999, p. 245). When codesigning and leading such processes, as I describe in Chapter 6, I have found that artists demonstrate remarkable abilities to evoke unique experiences, honor histories, bridge differences, and move people to construct things together, even if symbolically.

Challenges of Globalization

In cities of all sizes, as well as suburban communities and even many smaller, rural-based towns, globalization and the influx of immigrants present daily challenges and bring opportunities. Living among people speaking different languages, practicing different customs and beliefs, eating different foods, and behaving differently in public spaces is intimidating for some people. Some feel their own culture or way of life is threatened by someone else practicing theirs. For others, such spaces are energizing and educational. As people from different parts of the world form and reform communities in places from Los Angeles to Willmar, Minnesota, city planners find that skills to address the social dimensions of communities, along with the physical, are not in their training or job description.

This ongoing process of defining identity and community described by Blokland (2017) at the beginning of this introduction needs to be recognized by city planners and can be facilitated through spatial design and cultural and civic programs. Culture does not sit still but changes constantly. Young (2013) asked, "How, for example, is it possible to draw on a useable concept of culture for planning and governance as the velocity of culture keeps increasing and cultures themselves continue varying in seemingly infinite and breathtaking ways?" (p. 398). This presents city planners with another challenge. Without the tools to fully appreciate the impacts of globalization and ever-evolving cultures, many city planners have succumbed to relying on off-the-shelf solutions and allowing market forces to homogenize places. The proposition is that such forms best serve everyone. In reality, however, they serve the interests of capital first and foremost (Stein, 2019).

In some smaller cities, such as Willmar in rural central Minnesota and in nearby North Dakota, fueled by an oil boom, jobs are more plentiful than workers. People who come from different parts of the country or the world and who bring new languages, faiths, foods, skin tones, and ways of life are not always welcomed. Willmar, in fact, is one exception. Leaders there have worked hard over decades to create a welcoming community. In other cities like Willmar, badly needed farm, food processing, and manufacturing workers, as well as teachers, medical professionals, and IT and marketing professionals, are not always made to feel comfortable. As a result, economies suffer, as does social and cultural enrichment from the varied cultures and life experiences migrants bring. These are instructive microcosms for the country as a whole.

Xenophobia seems only to have grown, or at least grown louder and bolder, over the past decade. Incorporating newcomers who supply labor and critical skills, and who look for a better life, represents a complex challenge, but it is not new for cities or small towns across the United States. Why has welcoming newcomers and learning about cultures, languages, and different traditions not become part of the fabric of American life?

Diversity, equity, and inclusion served as the theme for the 2019 APA convention in San Francisco. As a profession-wide call for change, this represented a priority that is neither new nor entirely clear. Cultural diversity is complex, and yet cultural uniformity is often hidden deep in the practice itself—not just in the color of faces carrying out the work. Within the context of APA, the call for diversity was grounded in bringing people of color into the profession. Although an essential step, this remains a limited response. Achieving diversity and equitable planning practices is complicated by the structures and methods of city planning themselves that are historically based in colonial expansion and seeing humans and the natural environment as separate and even at odds. These are among the cultural dimensions of planning itself that also require change.

City Planning as a Cultural Practice

Critics such as Stein (2019) have targeted city planning's underpinnings in regulating land use for contributing to built-in injustices and consequences on the climate. Libby Porter (2016), a British planning scholar who researched frictions between planners and Indigenous peoples in New Zealand, described how tenets of land-use planning grew from colonialist practices to perpetuate patterns of power imbalance. She noted "a suite of regulations, accepted procedures, institutions and actors that together perform systematic cultures of space that are by definition, by their very existence, constitutive of colonial relations of power" (p. 150). She explained how "planning's own genealogy is colonial and its work a fundamental activity to the ongoing colonial settlement of territory" (p. 12).

Most planners don't see their work as colonialist, nor would they call it a cultural practice, yet planning is a cultural form and a cultural activity involving the management of people and space, a form that in itself has an internal culture and an often-invisible cultural agenda. The DNA of city planning is steeped in culturally based ways of understanding human–environment relations. Planning, L. Porter wrote, "arises as an activity and set of practices from a locatable and cultural world-view" (p. 44). The very process of spatial ordering reflects this particular view that she described as a "colonial process of producing space for certain ends, to favour certain people (their cultural lifeways and economic systems)" (p. 46). For Indigenous peoples, relationships to land are fundamental to ways of life—the heart and the wellspring of culture. These relationships are not based in concepts of ownership or control. In this context, for Indigenous peoples, land-use planning as a practice represents not just a physical taking of land, but a cultural assault.

Libby Porter (2016) recognized the "cultural artifact of colonialism" (p. 16) evident in planning. She argued that in settler societies, "the structures of meaning and authorities of truth that give planning agency in the world are drenched in colonial historiographies, and so the colonial relations of domination and oppression are ever present" (p. 16). These colonial histories live on and shape places, planning practices, and institutions. This is true for both city planning and cultural planning.

At the turn of the 21st century, city planners began to give more attention to the cultural sector, mostly because of its economic impact based on its capacity to attract people and enliven spaces. Creative cities, creative economy, and the creative class (see Chapter 9) ramped up in importance to city leaders and local communities. Creative or cultural districts, and later, creative placemaking, became tools for planners, developers, and policymakers trying to gain traction in revitalizing disinvested city and town centers and neighborhoods. Some suburban communities got into the act as they matured and began to seek ways to establish unique identities and a heightened sense of place to distinguish themselves and promote a sense of belonging and civic pride. Australian cultural planner Colin Mercer (as discussed by Baeker, 2002) observed what he called a *cultural turn* in city planning in his part of the world, where both city and cultural planning focus more on meaning and place identity. Baeker (2010) wrote, "This manifests through positioning and marketing of towns and cities, in itself, a response to the profound implications for how cities work and survive in the context of two major forces: globalisation and the new economy" (p. 15).

Neither city planning nor cultural planning have yet succeeded at making equity and social-justice concerns central to their practices. As some of the scholarship—and my own research—highlighted in this book demonstrates, both planning practices have served the expansion of social, cultural, economic, and spatial inequities. Further, their practices have facilitated the maintenance of existing social, cultural, and economic hierarchies. But that is not always the outcome, nor does it have to be.

How This Text Unfolds

This book unfolds through nine chapters that begin with foundational knowledge of cultural planning, its evolution, and its awkward and inconsistent relationship with city planning. It moves through ways to consider culture in city planning and looks at several means by which practices developed through cultural planning can contribute to city planning. These include understanding attachments to place, applying creative practices within public participation, mapping the cultures and meanings of place, approaching planning and design in ways that promote democracy, and focusing on more equitable economic development through a creative economy based on a local or vernacular approach. Ways of addressing culture and integrating practices from cultural planning, as described in this book, are based on practices that seek more inclusive, equitable, and sustainable solutions to everyday and long-term challenges city planners face. These methods come with no guarantees but represent ways of working that bring greater humanity to the process, more productive public engagement, and more equitable and people-centered outcomes.

Chapter titles allude to science-fiction films, not to diminish the serious nature of this work, but in the spirit of using the imagination and bringing a small amount of levity to community work that, when successful, brings joy.

In this book, I made the unconventional choice to identify cited authors by their country of origin and/or residence and primary professional field as well as gender in most cases. In 2018 at the annual conference that I attended of the Association of Arts Administration Educators, a compelling presentation by Yuha Jung, a Korean-born arts administration scholar teaching at the University of Kentucky, urged educators to examine the ethnicity, gender, and other biases of authors they cite and assign as reading (Jung, 2018). For a book addressing culture and its contemporary complexities, this felt an appropriate choice.

The following briefly describes what each chapter addresses.

Chapter 1—Inception: Purposes, Beginnings, and Promises. The first chapter introduces the practice of cultural planning, reviewing the history and evolution of this younger cousin to city planning. Cultural planning gained traction in cities and towns across the United States in the 1980s, propelled by private and municipal arts agencies looking to expand their influence and resources. Evolving as a practice mostly apart from city planning, cultural planning has about one-third the lifespan of the city-planning profession. The practice grew in different ways in other parts of the world, notably Australia, Canada, and the United Kingdom. I review early visionaries as well as scholars and contemporary practitioners who see still greater promise in the practice.

Chapter 2—Close Encounters: What Keeps City and Cultural Planning Apart? A group of American urban policymakers, city planners, scholars, elected officials, arts administrators, and others convened in San Antonio in 1979 to explore "a utopian marriage of culture—of design, art, and performance—and astute city planning" (Covatta quoted in R. Porter, 1980, p. i). However, in spite of growing interest in the arts and the culture sector as catalysts in community and economic development, cultural planning remains on the periphery of city planning. Chapter 2 looks at a number of forces and ways of thinking endemic to both planning practices that have kept the two apart. This hopefully sheds light on how they might grow closer in both theory and practice.

Chapter 3—Back to the Familiar: Culture, Place, and Ways of Living Together. Finding an approach to culture that serves as a foundational element in city planning is the goal of Chapter 3. Drawing on anthropology and other social sciences, I offer ways to think about culture and an approach useful to shaping more inclusive and equitable communities in an increasingly heterogeneous and globalized world. Ways of life of people in communities and *ways of living together*, I argue, need to be central in city planning to advance a more holistic understanding of communities, those who live in them, and how people can best share places and better live and work together.

Chapter 4—A Force Awakens: Cultural Planning at 40—A Turn to Community in the Arts. A research study I undertook for this book, *Cultural Planning at 40* (Borrup, 2018), reveals that the cultural sector in the United States resisted more inclusive thinking about culture, thus perpetuating an understanding of culture as Eurocentric and institutionally driven artistic practices. Rebalancing priorities and financial resources to reflect greater population diversity, while a goal in some cultural plans, yielded minimal results. Led by arts agencies for 40 years, cultural planning has helped local institutional cultural sectors better organize themselves and begin to carve out an expanding role within some city-building efforts. This research parallels and is benchmarked with a landmark 1994 study of cultural planning in the United States so as to see what has and has not changed.

Chapter 5—Place Odysseys: Meaning, Attachment, and Belonging. A key area in which culture and municipal policy overlap is in how people feel about and take responsibility for where they live. In this chapter, I reflect on scholarship and experience related to place attachment and how the nature of places as well as behaviors of individuals are at work in forming such bonds. Recommendations advanced by the American Planning Association to divorce planning from residents' emotions related to place are examined and critiqued. Better understanding of place identity and attachments highlight one potential area of synergy between cultural and city planning.

Chapter 6—Artistic Intelligence: Creativity in Public Process. Planners are often caught off-guard, not fully understanding or having the tools to make the most of public engagement activities or to address conflict. Addressed in this chapter is *public process*, something generally required but often problematic for city planners. Achieving significant and meaningful engagement and constructive outcomes with public process remains a challenge. Some cultural planners and artists have devised strategies that add great value. The chapter offers a history, rationale, and examples for inclusion of artists as facilitators and collaborators in public engagement. They are able to get at deeper concerns often rooted in differences in cultural norms, ways of "speaking," and ways of being heard. In real and symbolic ways, artists can activate participation and learning, and engage residents in the practice of making things together.

Chapter 7—The Maps Strike Back: From Empires to Equity. Maps represent power. Mapmaking can be a process to empower communities, not to mention to discover shared values and meaning planners weren't aware of. City planners typically begin with two-dimensional maps representing the built environment, land parcels, transportation corridors, and other physical infrastructure. Without a profound understanding of differing meanings of places occupied by different people over different periods of time, can planners anticipate or avoid conflict? Where do different ways of mapping and understanding place converge? Applying participatory practices to mapping and mapmaking provides another way to engage and to foster community co-creation in city planning. This chapter reviews different ways of thinking about maps, the process of mapping, and their value across planning practices.

Chapter 8—Guardians of Democracy: The Right to Design the City. Design and aesthetic choices are important in how cities are organized and built and how people experience them and feel about them. People of different cultural backgrounds bring different ways of using and relating to space. Aesthetics and design have profound, if often unarticulated, meaning that is not the same for everyone. In this chapter I describe the concepts of aesthetic justice, aesthetic democracy, and the critical role of planners and designers in modeling and promoting grassroots democracy. The ultimate, although never-achievable, realization of aesthetic justice comes through applying principles and practices of democracy (in their most localized sense) to ongoing city planning and design processes.

Chapter 9—Downsizing: The Vernacular and the Creative Economy. Since the 1980s, the notion of creative cities and the creative class gained worldwide traction. This includes the Creative Economy, creative industries, creative or cultural districts, and development of place identity. The Creative Economy, a slice of the business and nonprofit sectors based in cultural and creative endeavors, grabbed the attention of some economists and leaders, especially in postindustrial cities desperate to leverage their assets to repopulate and grow their economies. Chapter 9 focuses attention on creative enterprises that are based in place, which emerge from endogenous natural resources and local traditions or skills. Creative Economy is sometimes a focus in cultural planning, along with highlighting the identity and unique character and skill sets of communities. I stress the importance of a vernacular focus to help people develop sustainable livelihoods based in culturally and locally rooted creative work.

Final Thoughts—Cities on the Edge of Tomorrow. Planners cannot solve all the complex challenges the world faces—certainly not alone. This book makes the case that city planners and cultural planners need to reach across practices and rethink and recommit efforts to help bring about a more just and sustainable world—one in which people from all backgrounds can better share space and live together with the planet. I assert that embracing culture, in a broader sense, can help planners achieve this work. The book offers multiple ways communities can benefit through culturally based planning practices that focus on users, on people, their ways of life, and ways of living together. Every element of city planning has a cultural dimension, which is mostly invisible to planners. Ways of understanding people, their diverse cultures, and their relationships with each other, with public space, and with the natural world impact every element.

It is not possible to address all the areas of city planning and potential overlaps with cultural planning in one book. This volume represents an effort to further such conversations. Hopefully this book contributes to the work of city planners by providing a glimpse at how some tools from cultural planning and community-based arts can help address complex challenges of the 21st century.

References

Agyeman, J., & Erickson, J. S. (2012). Culture, recognition, and the negotiation of difference: Some thoughts on cultural competency in planning education. *Journal of Planning Education and Research, 32*(3), 358–366. doi:10.1177/0739456X12441213

Baeker, G. (2002). *Beyond garrets and silos: Concepts, trends and developments in cultural planning.* Department of Canadian Heritage. Ontario Ministry of Culture, Quebec Ministry of Culture and Communications.

Baeker, G. (2010). *Rediscovering the wealth of places: A municipal cultural planning handbook for Canadian communities.* St. Thomas, ON: Municipal World.

Blokland, T. (2017). *Community as urban practice.* Cambridge: Polity Press.

Borrup, T. (2018). *Cultural planning at 40: A look at the practice and its progress.* Washington, DC: American for the Arts. Retrieved from https://www.americansforthearts.org/by-program/reports-and-data/legislation-policy/naappd/cultural-planning-at-40-a-look-at-the-practice-and-its-progress

Collins, B. (2018). Whose culture, whose neighborhood? Fostering and resisting neighborhood change in the multiethnic enclave. *Journal of Planning Education & Research,* 1–14. doi:10.1177/0739456X18755496

DiAngelo, R. (2018). *White fragility: Why it's so hard for White people to talk about racism.* Boston, MA: Beacon.

Escobar, A. (2017). *Designs for the pluriverse: Radical interdependence, autonomy, and the making of worlds.* Durham, NC: Duke University Press. doi:10.1215/9780822371816

Evans, G. (2013). Cultural planning and sustainable development. In G. Young & D. Stevenson (Eds.), *The Ashgate research companion to planning and culture* (pp. 228–238). Abingdon: Ashgate.

Forester, J. (1999). *The deliberative practitioner: Encouraging participatory planning process.* Cambridge, MA: MIT Press.

Grogan, P., & Proscio, T. (2001). *Comeback cities: A blueprint for urban neighborhood revival.* Boulder, CO: Westview Press. doi:10.5860/choice.38-6497

Hou, J. (2013). *Transcultural cities: Bordering-crossing and placemaking.* London: Routledge. doi:10.4324/9780203075777

Jung, Y. (2018, May). *Social justice: Approaches to teaching in arts administration. Paper to the annual conference of the Association of Arts Administration Educators,* Houston, TX.

Maginn, P. J. (2007). Towards more effective community participation in urban regeneration: The potential of collaborative planning and applied ethnography. *Qualitative Research, 7*(1), 25–43. doi:10.1177/1468794106068020

Mattila, H. (2002). Aesthetic justice and urban planning: Who ought to have the right to design cities? *GeoJournal, 58,* 131–138. doi:10.1023/B:GEJO.0000010832.88129.cc

Montgomery, J. (1990). Cities and the art of cultural planning. *Planning Practice & Research, 5*(3), 17–24. doi:10.1080/02697459008722772

Pader, E. J. (1993). Spatial relations and housing policy: Regulations that discriminate against Mexican-origin households. *Journal of Planning Education & Research, 13*(2), 119–135. doi:10.1177/0739456X9401300204

Porter, L. (2016). *Unlearning the colonial cultures of planning.* Abingdon: Routledge. doi:10.4324/9781315548982

Porter, R. (Ed.). (1980). *The arts and city planning.* New York, NY: American Council for the Arts.

Qadeer, M. A. (1997). Pluralistic planning for multicultural cities: The Canadian practice. *Journal of the American Planning Association, 63*(4), 481–494. doi:10.1080/01944 36970897594

Sandercock, L. (1998). *Making the invisible visible: A multicultural planning history.* Berkeley: University of California Press.

Sandercock, L. (2003). *Cosmopolis II: Mongrel Cities in the 21st Century.* London: Continuum. doi:10.5040/9781472545527

Sandercock, L. (2004). Towards a planning imagination for the 21st century, *Journal of the American Planning Association, 70*(2), 133–141. doi:10.1080/01944360408976368

Sidford, H. (2011). *Fusing arts, culture and social change: High impact strategies for philanthropy.* Washington, DC: National Committee for Responsive Philanthropy. Retrieved from http://heliconcollab.net/wp-content/uploads/2013/04/Fusing-Arts_Culture_and_Social_Change1.pdf

Sidford, H. (2017). *Not just money: Equity issues in cultural philanthropy.* New York, NY: Helicon.

Soja, E. W. (2010). *Seeking spatial justice.* Minneapolis, MN: University of Minnesota Press. doi:10.5749/minnesota/9780816666676.001.0001

Stein, S. (2019). *Capital city: Gentrification and the real estate state.* New York, NY: Verso Books.

Vazquez, L. (2009). Cultural competency: A critical skill set for the 21st century planner. *Planetizen.* Retrieved from http://www.planetizen.com/node/42164

Vazquez, L. (2012). *Creative placemaking: Integrating community, cultural and economic development.* Unpublished paper, Bloustein School of Planning and Public Policy, Rutgers University, New Brunswick, NJ.

Young, G. (2008). *Reshaping planning with culture.* London: Routledge. doi:10.4324/9781315605647

Young, G. (2013). Stealing the fire of life: A cultural paradigm for planning and governance. In G. Young & D. Stevenson (Eds.), *The Ashgate research companion to planning and culture* (pp. 393–410). Abingdon: Ashgate.

Chapter 1

Inception

Purposes, Beginnings, and Promises

> *This approach to local and regional planning, which is sensitive to the culturally distinctive assets and resources of a locality as well as its community's needs, aspirations, and perceptions of place, is essential for sustainable development.*
>
> —Janet Pillai (2013, p. 43)

To better understand cultural planning, this chapter explores the beginnings of the practice, some of its promises, and its evolution. Malaysian cultural scholar, Janet Pillai, quoted above, expresses a contemporary, holistic view of planning. She was writing based on her experience in cultural planning. Her statement describes the kind of city planning I hope to advance. Her description, however, is not descriptive of still-dominant practices in the United States. In this chapter I attempt to provide a working understanding of the evolution of cultural planning, what it endeavors to achieve, and how it differs from place to place. I draw on a variety of sources and my own experiences over the last two decades. For city planners, it is helpful to grasp this background to look for relevant overlaps and opportunities to collaborate.

It is noteworthy that the majority of academic research, as well as professional guidebooks and training on cultural planning, come from outside the United States. Over the past two decades, creative cities, the creative class, cultural districts, and creative placemaking have drawn the attention of American scholars interested in local cultural policy with little paid to cultural planning. Yet, for local governments, cultural planning remains their primary tool for comprehensive policy-setting in this arena.

Tracing the origins of any profession or practice is never in a straight line, nor are its beginnings simply attributable to any one person, organization, or event. Practitioners, advocates, scholars, observers, and others on multiple continents have contributed to the definition, directions, and ongoing evolution of cultural planning, although general agreement places its formal practice originating in the United States. One of its categorical outcomes, especially in the United States, is its effectiveness at helping arts and cultural organizations, agencies, and sometimes artists on a local level organize as a sector to act collectively on their own behalf. In some cases, cultural planning helps local cultural sectors find ways to contribute to their communities above and beyond performance and delivery of their arts and culture programs. This is often through participation in economic development, tourism, education, improvement of public spaces, and other areas.

My formal involvement in cultural planning began in the United States around 2000, motivated by broad community and social interests through arts and cultural work. In contrast, many cultural planners focus on advancing the institutional interests of the cultural sector in what I characterize as "arts promotion." What some practitioners and scholars, particularly outside the United States, point out is that the potentials of cultural planning are greater. This chapter surveys the origins, variety, and aspirations of the practice. A later chapter provides details of a 2017 study I conducted to understand specific ways the practice has evolved in the United States over its 40 years.

For various reasons, cultural planning evolved differently in the United States than in other parts of the world. Most significantly, this country's dominant market-driven and philanthropic underpinnings of the cultural sector contrast with most other countries, where the public sector has historically provided most of the resources to arts and cultural organizations. In this and other chapters I examine some of these differences, as well as variations in how the understanding and application of the term *culture* influences the trajectory of cultural planning.

Global Varieties and Purposes

Distinct from many other aspects of cultural policy governing media, philanthropy, intellectual property, and the like, cultural planning is local and primarily place-based. Identifying and celebrating the distinctive character and cultural resources of each community, along with its physical and organizational assets, activities, and stories, is a core function of cultural planning. These are also critical ingredients in building social cohesion, identity, and capacity of people in communities to work together. While public policy in general, including most cultural policy, typically relies on one-size-fits-all solutions, Montgomery (1990) argued that each place requires unique approaches and solutions "because towns and cities are unique, they will have different problems, different potentials, and different opportunities. It is important to build from what exists rather than pluck 'off-the-shelf' models from other towns and cities" (p. 23). This differentiates cultural planning as something that goes beyond policy development and that needs to be strategic and action-oriented, tailored to unique local conditions and aspirations. Of course, similar statements can be made relative to city planning.

As a strictly local endeavor, cultural planning typically involves taking stock of (AKA mapping), connecting, and leveraging different cultural resources and traditions, as well as creative activities within municipal jurisdictions. Because of its strictly local nature, Evans (2013) found that "different approaches and rationales for cultural planning have therefore emerged, rather than a single grand theory or conceptual model" (p. 223). For better or worse, lack of uniformity or even a set of core principles or methodologies make cultural planning difficult to characterize. Cultural plans fall on a spectrum from endeavoring to elevate and equitably empower diverse communities and their varied cultural practices, to applying the collective resources of formal arts and cultural sectors to address various community challenges, to perpetuating or obfuscating cultural inequities while advancing dominant institutional interests.

In spite of its variety, cultural planning is situated in the context of local sector organizing and policy development. In her 2014 book, *Cities of Culture*, Deborah Stevenson, an Australian geographer and global scholar of cultural planning, followed many iterations of the practice as it spread across continents in the 1980s. She noted that "along the way the shape and concerns of cultural planning have changed often quite considerably" (Stevenson, 2014, p. 59). Similarity in cultural plans comes more from the practices and biases of consultants hired to prepare them and from templates shared among local agencies to specify the type of plan they want to commission. Recommendations in most plans are extra-legal in that they call for voluntary actions or new collaborations among local actors. They also might recommend municipal policies related to such factors as public sector funding or agency capacity-building, public art programs, regulations pertaining to use of public spaces, and provisions for creative districts or artist live-work spaces.

In a part of the world where it is a more recent practice, Czech scholars, Katerina Vojtiskova, Marketa Polakova, and Vera Patockova (2016) examined cultural planning in two small- to mid-sized Czech towns. They described the approach as "a participative approach to city planning based on communication, cooperation, and the mapping of cultural resources" (p. 22). They reported

One of the significant benefits of cultural planning was that it contributed to more communication and the general acquaintance of people from the fields of culture, tourism, education, and sport. It encouraged thinking, and opened discussions on topics such as the role of culture in town development and tourism, introducing issues of cooperation and its barriers and opportunities, and how to gain political support and take collective action.

(p. 30)

While not as holistic or integrated into the fabric of wider local concerns as Pillai's characterization at the beginning of this chapter, the Czech authors reflected an approach similar to some contemporary American cultural plans, yet one more comprehensive than most in the United States prior to 2005.

In some countries and provinces, municipalities have been required to conduct cultural planning. In the United States, it remains a strictly local option. Thus, cultural plans typically serve a single municipality. However, just as the environment or infrastructure relative to water, transportation, electrical grids, and such can be hard-pressed to exist independently within a city's footprint, cultural interests and activities do not conform to municipal boundaries. Thus, two or more jurisdictions within an area or a county occasionally join in cultural planning. Eleonora Redaelli, an Italian cultural policy scholar teaching in the United States, asserted that whether through a cultural plan or the mapping of assets, the promotion of regional thinking is a less-recognized benefit of cultural planning. She wrote, "Cultural planning is much more than a policy framework for the arts because it links cultural resources to the localities' wide range of social and economic needs" (Radaelli, 2013, p. 31). Good cultural planning, even when focused on a single municipality, requires and facilitates engagement of leadership and stakeholders who cross jurisdictions, as well as a regional analysis of identity, populations, assets, conditions, and needs.

Purposes of Cultural Planning

Cultural planning in the United States grew primarily as a strategy of arts and cultural agencies and nonprofit arts organizations to improve their financial fortunes and capacities for carrying out their work. Local arts agencies that commissioned plans often sought to elevate their positions as leaders within their jurisdictional territory. These are not, in themselves, negative or inappropriate goals. They're simply limited and limiting. Most cultural planning in the United States continues to be spearheaded by arts agencies that are sometimes units of local government, sometimes private nonprofits, and, at other times, hybrids of the two. In most other parts of the world, cultural agencies are part of one or another form of local government and typically control a larger portion of the financial resources that support arts and cultural organizations and activities within their jurisdictions. This is a key reason why the practice has evolved differently.

In a 1994 doctoral dissertation, which is still, in my view, the most significant study on cultural planning in the United States, American cultural planner Craig Dreeszen described the practice as "a structured community-wide, public/private process that engages the members of a community in communications to identify their community's arts and cultural resources, needs, and opportunities, and to plan actions and secure resources to address priority needs" (p. vi). He evaluated 116 cultural plans from across the country and included a survey of arts agencies. Dreeszen (1994) went on to add,

> Cultural plans attempt to promote a community's arts and culture, amenities, or overall quality of life. The issues cultural planning attempts to resolve may be within the arts community (e.g. artists need access to studio space) or the plan may apply the power of arts and culture to help resolve problems within the larger community (e.g., the downtown is deteriorating).
>
> (p. 20)

He found that strategies and actions in the plans he evaluated addressed city-wide arts marketing and audience development, sector advocacy, cultural facility development, tourism promotion, the institution of public art programs, or coordinated arts education programs, among others. As such, this approach to cultural planning is akin to sector-based organizing and coordinated strategic planning.

Unlike other "industries," nonprofits may collude for the benefit of the public or even to advance their institutions. Thus, cultural planning enables nonprofits to join together to map, strategize, and advance their collective endeavors. That said, many individual organizations within cities consider themselves in competition for limited resources and audiences, thus such coordinated efforts have only come about in some cities and after some time, usually through successful or repeated cultural planning efforts.

Dreeszen (1994) also found that cultural planning increasingly included wider participation of community stakeholders outside the arts sector, and as such, some of these earlier plans began to address a wider spectrum of community concerns beyond bolstering arts and cultural resources, activities, and participation. Addressing this wider spectrum, he found, was a strategic move to garner additional resources through other sources such as community, economic or open-space development, education, health and wellbeing, etc. Describing this evolution, Stevenson (2014) wrote,

> The significant shift was to link the arts with a range of economic, social, and physical goals in an attempt to attract new sources of funding. In other words, cultural planning developed explicitly in an effort to find additional or indeed alternative sources of support for the arts at the same time as it came to be regarded as a resource to be utilized to support local economies.
>
> (p. 78)

This is not to say that such efforts to address wider community concerns were entirely mercenary. Many were genuine, and in some communities the cultural sector makes significant contributions to a spectrum of concerns.

In contrast, Americans for the Arts, the predominant service and advocacy organization for local arts agencies and nonprofit arts in the United States, characterized cultural planning as "One concrete way we infuse the arts and culture into a community is cultural planning, a community-wide process of creating a vision for cultural programming and development" (Americans for the Arts, 2015, para. 1). This outdated description reflects an outside-in or colonizing process to *infuse* a community with something considered lacking. In the Americans for the Arts approach, the external force (the "*we*" in the above characterization) determines there is a need for and place in a community for *the arts*, and thus enables its *development*. This description assumes Eurocentric institutional concepts of arts and culture in that culture is *programmed* as opposed to emergent from and reflective of unique local practices in daily life as well as traditional community events and celebrations. The purpose of cultural planning, as prescribed by Americans for the Arts, remains the advancement of arts agencies and nonprofits. While this represents the foundational mission of the advocacy group, it is out of sync with its own recent work emphasizing that the cultural sector should embrace community concerns and advance cultural equity and social justice.

Relative to most other parts of the world, the United States has an arts and culture sector that relies on a complex mix of mostly private and some public financial resources. While support for major institutions, outside the Smithsonian and a few government-sponsored institutions, is predominantly private, some cities or counties provide significant resources in the form of cash, operational support, personnel, and/or facilities. Smaller organizations scramble for competitive private foundation grants, small public sector grants (in some communities), and a lot of contributions of volunteer time.

In a survey of tax-exempt nonprofit arts and cultural organizations in Silicon Valley that my associates and I conducted during the writing of this book, just over 1,000 such organizations were found to be active in that region. Of those, 65% reported expenditures of less than $10,000, and just under half reported no financial activity. As a follow-up to a similar study 10 years earlier (Borrup, 2011), this showed a cultural sector teeming with mostly off-the-radar, voluntary activity.

Cultural planning in the United States thus grew differently than in most other countries. While some cultural plans addressed broader community issues, the dominant practice has largely declined to lift its sights beyond institutional interests. The evolution of the practice in the United States has remained focused on resource provision. As a result, its counterparts in other parts of the world got a head start on developing other dimensions of cultural planning.

Describing its wider purposes in a Canadian context, Baeker (2010) wrote,

> Cultural planning is about harnessing the assets of a community; celebrating the unique resources, such as heritage properties, natural assets, and community spirit; revitalizing downtown cores that too often have deteriorated; honouring and respecting the unique contributions of our artists and artisans; creating diverse and safe neighborhoods; raising the bar for urban design; protecting our green spaces and becoming better stewards of our environment; and the many other elements that make up a community moving forward confidently in the 21st century.
>
> (p. vi)

In his study of cultural plans in Ontario, Canadian geographer Jason Kovacs (2011) asked whether cultural planning is "anything more than a fairly traditional arts policy with a different name … that usually fail to address more than arts sector concerns" (p. 321). He found that was not the case there.

With the exponential growth of the formal arts sector in the United States beginning in the 1950s, public sector support remained scarce. Arts advocates looked to other Western democracies where governments provided all or a majority of financial support to cultural institutions and sought ways to leverage greater subsidies from all levels of government. Cultural planning in the United States thus took more of an advocacy role in attempts to garner financial support. Dreeszen (1994) observed that new or increased financial resources for the arts tended to follow the completion of a cultural plan. This propelled arts agencies to see the primary purpose of planning as leveraging new or increased funding. Reflecting a more recent shift, research presented in Chapter 4 indicates that cultural plans in the United States have begun to move towards addressing broader community concerns.

Roots of Cultural Planning

Both Dreeszen (1994, 1998) and Lia Ghilardi (2001), a planner and scholar working in Europe, traced the roots of cultural planning to the late 19th century City Beautiful Movement, the 1930s WPA (Works Progress Administration) in the United States, and the community arts movement of the 1940s. American community arts activist Maryo Gard Ewell (2000) pointed to the beginning of the Village Improvement movement in Massachusetts in 1853 for its efforts to plant trees, pave streets and sidewalks, and secure recreational facilities and other amenities. American city-planning scholar Jacqueline Leavitt (1980) likewise detailed civic improvement groups in various cities in the United States led by women in the late 19th century that addressed issues including parks and playgrounds, street lighting, tree planting, establishing libraries, and funding sidewalks, as well as advancing civic pride. Dreeszen pointed out ways cultural planning shares antecedents and methods with city-planning practices formalized during the mid-20th century such as participatory neighborhood-level planning that address local amenities, opportunities for youth, local economic growth, and organizing for collective action, among other local concerns (see Rohe, 2009).

Ewell described the social reform movements that began in the late 19th century, and how, in particular, the Junior League was formed to support Settlement Houses in New York City, at which cultural practices of immigrants were frequently celebrated. The Junior League, was, in turn, instrumental in helping form many of the early local arts agencies in the late 1940s and 1950s. She continued,

> Perhaps you didn't know that the Junior league had a Senior Vice President for Community Arts, Virginia Lee Comer. In 1943, she was invited by the Winston-Salem Junior League to inventory the community and its cultural assets including such things as union halls and radio stations. She had devised a process called "the Arts and Our Town," which was, in effect, a cultural planning template. Many of the early local arts agencies that she helped form used this exercise. (personal communication, February 27, 2020)

Ewell also related that in 1975 she worked for the Arts Council of Greater New Haven where "we did a cultural plan and called it that. I think that this may have been one of the very first plans of the 1970s Renaissance of cultural planning" (personal communication, February 27, 2020). The plan was conducted with economist, Frank Penna, and included an inventory of New Haven and its cultural assets. However, like most of the early cultural plans, she affirmed "it was first and foremost an arts plan that asked: 'How can arts organizations and individual artists work together to both protect our sector, secure new venues, and collectively attract more audiences, money and stature?'" (personal communication, February 27, 2020). At the same time, however, the Arts Council was working with the city redevelopment agency and planning departments to attract arts groups and housing developers to a formerly blighted area of the city, which is now the Audubon Whitney Arts District.

There surely are many theoretical threads as well as local innovations in the trajectory of cultural planning. Baeker (2010) cited Canadian administrator, educator, and consultant Donna Cardinal, who claims to have found evidence of cultural planning in city documents in that country from as early as the 1950s. According to Baeker, Cardinal argued that Vancouver, Calgary, Edmonton, Toronto, and Kitchener explicitly addressed culture through citizen participation, diversity, and pluralism, and used the term "*community cultural development* [emphasis original] as the integrating framework for linking arts, heritage and cultural industry to broader civic concerns" (p. 30). These elements were written into those city plans, rather than in stand-alone cultural plans, the form that remains prevalent in the United States.

As another contributing element, Ghilardi (2001) cited the "tradition of radical planning and humanistic management of cities championed in the early 1960s, chiefly by Jane Jacobs and the idea of the city as a living system" (p. 125). An American urban design critic and community organizer, Jacobs and her seminal book *Death and Life of Great American Cities* (1961/1965), are among the most-cited inspirations for contemporary city planners (Planetizen, 2017). Mercer (2006), as well as Baeker (2010), claimed that the essence of cultural planning appears in the work of Patrick Geddes, as well as that of mid-20th-century historian and sociologist Lewis Mumford, whose impacts on city planning have been profound.

Planning and Community Amenities

As a defined practice, cultural planning is widely considered to have emerged in the late 1970s and through the 1980s in the United States. American planning and community development scholar Bernie Jones (1993), British creative cities consultant and author Charles Landry (2000), and Ghilardi (2001), as well as Stevenson (2014) have all credited American Robert McNulty for advocating for new thinking about cultural policy and planning beginning in the mid-1970s. Founder of Partners for Livable Places (later Partners for Livable Communities), a Washington, DC, advocacy, research and publishing nonprofit, McNulty expanded on the standard intrinsic value proposition (that art is simply good for you) advanced by most arts institutions and advocates. His writing, activism, and international speaking was influential in Australia and the United Kingdom as well. According to Ghilardi (2001), McNulty "placed the arts and culture in the broader context of community development, building on their economic role, and expanding that role to include other social and community concerns" (p. 127).

McNulty built on the concept of community livability, championing what he called *amenities* as critical and transformational assets. These included parks, performing arts centers, museums, libraries, recreational facilities, craft centers, festivals, and cultural and creative activities of all kinds. He called for more work to promote "greater understanding of how the cultural, social, natural, and built environments affect the quality and prosperity of communities" (Partners for Livable Places, 1983, p. 18). This set the stage for more holistic thinking about the role of arts and culture in urban regeneration (Baeker, 2010; Borrup, 2006). In full disclosure, I had opportunity to work with McNulty between 2003 and 2009 as a consultant on a Ford Foundation project and had his assistance in writing my 2006 book, *The Creative Community Builders Handbook*.

In an early 1980s report, McNulty described that many cities involved in his organization since 1975 "identified some aspect of cultural planning as a focus for their local projects" (1983, p. 55). In the same report, he recounts a 1976 conference when he was employed by the National Endowment for the Arts (NEA) and subsequent conversations with Los Angeles-based city planner and professor Harvey Perloff about examining cultural amenities in Los Angeles. A 1978 NEA grant to a group led by Perloff helped fund this cultural plan. Perloff's (1979) resulting treatise on how the City of Los Angeles should address the arts may not constitute the origins of the practice, but the 1979 plan has been recognized by various scholars and practitioners as the first *cultural plan*.

During that same year, a group of American policymakers, city planners, scholars, arts administrators, and others convened in San Antonio, Texas, to explore what Annette Covatta, documenting the meeting, called "a utopian marriage of culture—of design, art, and performance—and astute city planning" (as quoted in Porter, 1980, p. i). Proceedings, published as *The Arts and City Planning* by the American Council for the Arts (forerunner of Americans for the Arts), set the stage and a bar still challenging to both city and cultural planners. The marriage or combination ordained at the 1979 meeting was never consummated.

As Dean of the School of Planning at the University of California Los Angeles, Perloff applied the label of *cultural plan* to his report (Dreeszen, 1998; Kunzmann, 2004) called "Arts in the Economic Life of the City." This plan established a framework for communities to identify and apply their cultural resources to community improvement, particularly economic development. Perloff offered a blueprint for arts and culture in Los Angeles—a plan that was largely activated within a decade. The plan made recommendations in four broad areas along with establishment of a "cultural element" in city and county general plans to enhance the arts in city development. Its four major provisions were to:

1. provide more information about arts activities;
2. make broader and more flexible use of public and private facilities for arts;
3. probe for ways the arts can be tied into public services so as to enlarge the scope of arts-related employment, and
4. make plans for the fuller use of the arts in urban development and redevelopment.

Perhaps because Perloff was a highly-regarded city planner, this early cultural plan was more outwardly focused than the New Haven plan described above by Ewell, as well as most plans over the subsequent 20 years, and it was explicitly embedded into formal city and county plans. In the 1980s, cultural plans in the United States narrowed to become more internally focused, conducted by, for, and about the institutional arts sector. While Perloff prescribed a relatively broad role for the arts, his plan did not invoke a broad definition of culture as did later planners, particularly in Australia and Canada (Baeker, 2010; Dowling, 1997; Mercer, 2006; Stevenson, 2014). This focus on arts (versus culture) perhaps set the stage for the planning process to divert attention to the needs of the formal arts sector rather than advocate ways the sector can serve cities and their diverse populations and cultures.

Funding increases experienced by communities that had conducted cultural plans stood in contrast to national trends in the mid-1990s as arts funding came under political attacks (Dreeszen, 1994). Seeing pots of gold at the end of planning rainbows, the practice was promoted by the NEA as well as state and local arts agencies and Americans for the Arts. A variety of monographs and practical handbooks were published by entities promoting the arts in the 1980s and 1990s. These provided arts agencies with tools to support cultural planning. Authors included Louise K. Stevens and Craig Dreeszen in the United States; David Grogan and Colin Mercer in Australia; and Gord Hume and Greg Baeker in Canada.

Promises and Realities: Putting Community in Cultural Planning

Through his efforts in the 1970s and 1980s, McNulty was largely articulating work artists and community activists had been doing for some time. However, he framed it in ways attractive to mayors and other municipal policymakers. As mayors comprised the bulk of McNulty's membership for Partners for Livable Communities—and in the 1980s and 1990s, physical and economic revitalization were at the top of their agenda—McNulty focused on how cultural amenities could be leveraged for economic impact.

Arts agencies in the United States at the time had not adopted such outward-facing community practices. One exception was the Arts Council of Winston-Salem, North Carolina. Its director, Milton Rhodes, described long-range planning his agency undertook in 1971 when the organization decided "We were not in the business of serving only the arts institutions in our community. We were in the business of serving the whole community on behalf of the arts" (as cited in Porter, 1980). Decades later, this philosophy has spread but is still hardly the norm.

As a parallel or precursor to the formal practice of cultural planning, McNulty's *amenity development strategies* included taking stock of local assets such as public spaces, design quality, cultural resources, natural and scenic resources, tourism and community image, distinctive neighborhoods, and marketing plans. He did not, however, articulate a formal cultural asset-mapping practice (the subject of Chapter 7).

In the United Kingdom, Charles Landry, an early creative city proponent, formed the consulting practice Comedia in 1978 to bridge thinking about city life, creativity, and postindustrial revitalization. Landry helped put arts and culture to work in urban transformation across Europe, Australia, and elsewhere. His work and writing (e.g., Landry, 2000) as well as that of his collaborators made significant impacts on cultural planning and how culture and creative solutions are applied across many areas of municipal policy and city development. According to Baeker (2010), "Many consider the Cultural Plan for Glasgow developed by Comedia in 1990, to be the first integrated cultural plan in which cultural resources were used as a catalyst for urban regeneration" (p. 25).

"Airport Cultural Planning"

In some regions of Australia and provinces of Canada, and during some periods in the United Kingdom, municipal governments were required to produce cultural plans so as to best coordinate and maximize public-sector spending and the contributions of local cultural assets to their communities. According to Stevenson (2005), all major cities in Australia had cultural plans by the early 1990s. In New South Wales, all local governments were required to have them by 2004. In the rush to produce them, Stevenson (2014) saw "striking similarities between the discourses, assumptions and approaches" (p. 75) in cultural plans in Australia and the United Kingdom. A handful of consultants flew between the two countries, generating plans in what she called "an 'airport cultural planning' approach whereby a steady flow of consultants and advisors 'sell' generic cultural plans to local governments" (p. 55).

Such approaches have also been characterized as "homogenizing" through the use of what Young (2013) called "copy-paste planning templates" (p. 12). City leaders in the United States, who tend to be risk-averse, find such planning templates comforting. They often want to know what has worked elsewhere so they can transplant "proven" solutions into their city. Simultaneously, this enables sponsoring arts agencies to get quicker, less-expensive plans while consultants earn fees with less effort. These plans rarely address local needs well. In the United States, rather than maximizing the contributions of local cultural assets to their communities, the focus of many plans, at least through much of the 1990s, was to maximize contributions from communities to local arts institutions (Dreeszen, 1994).

Seeing More from Cultural Planning

In a retrospective on the broad impacts of the practice in Australia, cultural geographer Robyn Dowling (1997) observed that "The theory of cultural planning begins with a fluid and broad definition of culture" (p. 23). Such an approach was advocated by fellow Australian, Colin Mercer (2006), among others. In practice, however, most cultural planning still focuses narrowly using a material and Western European definition of culture. Some early practitioners and observers, including Bianchini (2004) and Montgomery (1990), along with Mercer and the group convening in San Antonio in 1979, felt it could be more.

Australian geographer Deborah Mills (2003) asserted that cultural planning should not be

> an argument for justifying why arts and culture should receive public support. Nor is it an argument for the arts as a tool for achieving government economic, environmental, and social objectives. Rather, it is a way of making visible what has until now remained invisible to planners, the cultural concepts which

underpin, often implicitly, many public planning policies. If we can acknowledge these concepts and recognize them as living, breathing parts of individual
and community life, then we can give new meaning and force to efforts to
achieve sustainable economic, social and environmental development.

(p. 9)

The above writers argued that cultural planning holds the promise of being
a novel approach to municipal policy and planning, or, what Kovacs (2011)
described as "an ethical corrective to physical planning" (p. 322). Putting this a
different way, Ghilardi (2001) wrote, "cultural planning is not the 'planning of
culture', but a cultural (anthropological) approach to urban planning and policy" (p. 125). Whether ethnical corrective or an anthropological approach, cultural planning practices have the potential to bring more value to city planning.
They can provide a humanistic lens to give city planners a way of balancing
solutions that are often overly technocratic.

As an early practitioner and leading thinker, Mercer (2006) saw cultural planning as part of a larger strategy. He argued that "it has to make connections with
physical and town planning, with economic and industrial development objectives, with social justice initiatives, with recreational planning, with housing and
public works" (p. 6). To make an impact, cultural planning cannot come after
the fact of other municipal planning. For cultural plans to be seen as decorative,
or as a follow-up meant to program or activate spaces already designed or built,
marginalizes culture (as in the ways of life of people) and disadvantages city
planning by leaving it without a full understanding of culture (as in people and
how they live together).

A more anthropological definition of culture fosters a way-of-life approach
to cultural planning, described by Montgomery (1990) as "having a vision for
the future (as well as respect for the past), setting goals, and building up a bank
of initiatives to get us from where we are to where we want to be" (p. 23).
Adopting such an approach, forces planners to look at cities in a new way,
Montgomery argues, "from the standpoint of *users* rather than *uses* [emphasis
added], and with an awareness of quality. The result is to root planning in a cultural sense of place" (p. 23).

The Evolving Purpose

Just a year prior to Dreeszen's (1994) study, University of Colorado planning professor Bernie Jones (1993) surveyed 52 American communities that
had completed cultural plans; he reviewed 32 plan documents. Similar to and

building on the structure of the Perloff (1979) plan for Los Angeles, Jones summarized their typical goals as follows:

1. enhancing community image and promoting economic development;
2. promoting cooperation among cultural organizations;
3. calling for development of cultural facilities;
4. identifying financial resource needs and improving organizational management;
5. enhancing arts marketing and promotion;
6. increasing quantity, quality, and diversity of arts programs;
7. advocating arts education; and
8. supporting individual artists.

These represent a more internal-sector focus than the Perloff plan. Well into the twenty-first century, they remained common elements in cultural plans that focus on the formal, nonprofit cultural sector's needs and aspirations.

As cultural planning has evolved in the United States, however, more plans have begun to serve wider community-centered purposes, as described in Chapter 4. While what follows is not a linear or consistent progression, nor mutually exclusive, I see plans falling on this spectrum of purposes:

1. Sustain or increase funding and favorable policies for formal arts activities and organizations.
2. Enhance the capacity of arts and cultural organizations to act collectively to advance their individual and common missions.
3. Adopt municipal codes and regulations to accommodate more formal and informal cultural practices in public and other regulated spaces.
4. Identify and build on distinct cultural assets and community identity, typically for tourism marketing and product branding.
5. Animate public spaces and/or civic processes through creative and culturally attuned design, activities, and public art.
6. Expand the range of people and cultural practices included in the identity of a community and/or resource and space allocations.
7. Employ cultural assets to address economic and/or neighborhood development or other social or educational challenges.
8. Determine complex community-wide challenges and devise strategies that bring cultural resources to bear to advance a community vision and/or to address challenges.

9. Analyze and strategically leverage unique and diverse cultural characteristics, resources, and activities of both people and places to inform and serve an array of municipal issues and policies such as transit, housing, recreation, health, and education.

Summary

While cultural plans that serve as strategic plans for the nonprofit cultural sector continue to have merit, cultural planning by and for the cultural sector has only begun to evolve into a more inclusive process that makes visible and addresses diverse needs of people, their many cultures, ways of living together, and collective well-being. At the same time, with more nuanced knowledge of the people in a community, the cultural dimensions of policy options across a spectrum of municipal concerns become more meaningful and can move communities forward in more just and inclusive ways.

Ghilardi (2001) argued, "Cultural planning can be instrumental in creating opportunities for a variety of social and cultural constituencies" (p. 5). She went on to say, "[it] can help urban governments to identify the *distinctive* cultural resources of a city or locality and to apply them in a strategic way to achieve key objectives in areas such as community development, place marketing or economic development" (p. 5).

In addition to these instrumental roles for culture and creative practices in local development and problem-solving, this book explores ways cultural and creative practitioners can contribute more to city planning. Greater understanding of culture, ways of living together in communities, and creative methods can help the city-planning profession advance a spectrum of municipal goals in ways that are more inclusive, just, and sustainable.

In the next chapter, I look more deeply into the nature of cultural planning and of city planning and discuss critical ways in which they are different. This is in an effort to find how they may grow closer and bring greater balance between places and people to better connect the physical and human dimensions of communities.

References

Americans for the Arts (2015). *Culture & communities: Strengthening and enriching communities through the arts.* Retrieved from https://www.americansforthearts.org/by-topic/culture-and-communities

Baeker, G. (2010). *Rediscovering the wealth of places: A municipal cultural planning handbook for Canadian communities.* St. Thomas, ON: Municipal World.

Bianchini, F. (2004, February). *A crisis in urban creativity? Reflections on the cultural impacts of globalisation, and on the potential of urban cultural policies.* Paper presented at the International Symposium: The Age of the City – The Challenges for Creative Cites, Osaka, Japan. Retrieved from http://www.artfactories.net/IMG/pdf/crisis_urban_creatvity.pdf

Borrup, T. (2006). *The creative community builder's handbook: How to transform communities using local assets, arts, and culture.* St. Paul, MN: Fieldstone Alliance.

Borrup, T. (2011). The emergence of a new cultural infrastructure: Lessons from Silicon Valley. *Journal of Urban Culture Research, 2,* 16–29.

Dowling, R. (1997). Planning for culture in urban Australia. *Australian Geographical Studies, 35*(1), 23–31. doi:10.1111/1467-8470.00004

Dreeszen, C. (1998). *Community cultural planning: A guidebook for community leaders.* Washington, DC: Americans for the Arts.

Dreeszen, C. A. (1994). *Reimagining community: Community arts and cultural planning in America* [Doctoral dissertation]. Retrieved from ProQuest Dissertations and Theses Database. (UMI 9510463).

Evans, G. (2013). Cultural planning and sustainable development. In G. Young & D. Stevenson (Eds.), *The Ashgate research companion to planning and culture* (pp. 228–238). Abingdon: Ashgate.

Ewell, M. G. (2000). Community arts councils: Historical perspective. *Culture Work: A Periodic Broadside for Arts and Culture Workers, 5*(1). Eugene: Institute for Community Arts Studies, Arts and Administration Program, University of Oregon. Retrieved from https://scholarsbank.uoregon.edu/xmlui/bitstream/handle/1794/346/CultureWork_Vol5_No1.pdf?sequence=1&isAllowed=y

Ghilardi, L. (2001). Cultural planning and cultural diversity. In T. Bennett (Ed.), *Differing Diversities: Transversal study on the theme of cultural policy and cultural diversity* (pp. 123–134). Strasbourg: Council of Europe.

Jacobs, J. (1965). *The death and life of great American cities.* Harmondsworth: Pelican. (Original work published 1961)

Jones, B. (1993). Current directions in cultural planning. *Landscape & Urban Planning, 26*(1–4), 89–97. doi:10.1016/0169-2046(93)90009-3

Kovacs, J. F. (2011). Cultural planning in Ontario, Canada: Arts policy or more? *International Journal of Cultural Policy, 17*(3), 321–340. doi:10.1080/10286632.2010.487152

Kunzmann, K. R. (2004). Culture, creativity and spatial planning. *Town Planning Review, 75*(4), 383–404.

Landry, C. (2000). *The creative city: A toolkit for urban innovators.* Oxford: Earthscan.

Leavitt, J. (1980). *Planning and women, women in planning* [Doctoral dissertation]. Retrieved from ProQuest Dissertations and Theses Database. (ProQuest document ID 303025754)

Mercer, C. (2006). *Cultural planning for urban development and creative cities.* Retrieved from http://www.kulturplan-oresund.dk/pdf/Shanghai_cultural_planning_paper.pdf

Mills, D. (2003, May). Cultural planning—Policy task, not tool. *Artwork Magazine, 55,* 7–11.

Montgomery, J. (1990). Cities and the art of cultural planning. *Planning Practice & Research, 5*(3), 17–24. doi:10.1080/02697459008722772

Partners for Livable Places. (1983). *Toward livable communities: A Report on partners for livable places, 1975–1982.* Washington, DC: Partners for Livable Places.

Perloff, H. S. (1979, December). Using the arts to improve life in the city. *Journal of Cultural Economics, 3*(2), 1–21. https://doi.org/10.1007/BF02427550

Pillai, J. (2013). *Cultural mapping: A guide to understanding place, community and continuity.* Kuala Lumpur: Strategic Information and Research Development Centre.

Planetizen. (2017, October 9). *The 100 most influential urbanists.* Retrieved from https://www.planetizen.com/features/95189-100-most-influential-urbanists

Porter. R. (Ed.). (1980). *The arts and city planning.* New York, NY: American Council for the Arts.

Redaelli, E. (2013). Assessing a place in cultural planning: A framework for American local governments. *Cultural Trends, 22*(1), 30–44. doi:10.1080/09548963.2013.757893

Rohe, W. M. (2009). From local to global: One hundred years of neighborhood planning. *Journal of the American Planning Association, 75*(2), 209–230. doi:10.1080/01944360902751077

Stevenson, D. (2005). Cultural planning in Australia: Texts and contexts. *Journal of Arts Management, Law, and Society, 35*(1), 36–48.

Stevenson, D. (2014). *Cities of culture: A global perspective.* London: Routledge.

Vojtiskova, K., Polakova, M., & Patockova, V. (2016). Cultural planning: New inspiration for local governments in the Czech context. *Journal of Arts, Management, Law, and Society, 46*(1), 22–33.

Young, G. (2013). Introduction: Culture and planning in a grain of sand. In G. Young & D. Stevenson (Eds.), *The Ashgate research companion to planning and culture* (pp. 1–20). Abingdon: Ashgate.

Chapter 2

Close Encounters
What Keeps City and Cultural Planning Apart?

The power of Western scientific discourse to separate the natural and cultural, and to reify the cultural as Other, is not easily undone.

—Libby Porter (2016, p. 137)

A central point of this book is that city planning and cultural planning, while cousins, don't speak to each other much. I argue that by bringing together the best of their abilities, they can produce greater outcomes. Both practices strive for a better quality of life for their communities. They share some ancestors and use many of the same tools in doing their jobs. They sometimes work for the same boss. They see things differently, but rarely, if ever, do they quarrel. So, why don't they get along better?

As the previous chapter reveals, some early advocates of cultural planning saw the two practices as working hand-in-hand, or even married. As is known from planning practices in other parts of the world, and from some examples in the United States, city planning and cultural planning can be far more complementary. As the history of cultural planning suggests, their interests grew apart before they had opportunity to get to know one another. This chapter explores a number of reasons I believe their predicted marriage has not come to be.

Libby Porter, in the quote at the beginning of this chapter, touches on one of the deepest divisions—the Cartesian separation of the body from the mind, the built environment from the social, the rational from the emotional. While a more holistic vision of communities will not come about through technocratic thinking, I hope it is possible to bring these practices closer together. The analysis that follows is intended to open a path—or at least push a conversation—for the two practices to find ways to produce greater synergy.

Keeping Their Distance

In Dreeszen's (1994) survey on cultural planning, 49% of the respondents indicated their cultural plan was adopted in some formal way by their local municipality. Numerous field leaders and scholars, including Dreeszen, advocated that cultural plans should be more integral to city comprehensive or master plans. However, the same question in a survey I conducted in 2017 revealed that only 51% said their cultural plan was formally adopted. This reflects no meaningful change over those 23 years (Borrup, 2018).

In her book *Connecting Arts and Place*, Redaelli (2019) affirmed this disconnect. She examined city comprehensive plans as well as cultural plans from 18 cities in the United States that have all made significant commitments to their arts and culture sector. While not addressing the question of why city and cultural planning have remained largely separate, she found nuanced relationships between city plans and cultural plans. Some cities, Redaelli wrote, "extensively integrate arts into their comprehensive plan but have not engaged in a cultural plan" (p. 33). She went on to observe that "other cities have robust cultural plans, but their comprehensive plans do not mention the arts" (p. 33).

In recent decades, creative cities, arts-based economic development, creative placemaking, and the like have captured increasing interest among city planners and policymakers as well as leaders within the cultural sector. Rank and file city planners for at least the past half-century have responded to occasional opportunities to develop cultural districts or flagship cultural facilities ranging from Lincoln Center in New York to smaller cultural compounds in cities across the country and around the world (Ashley, 2015; Kong, 2009). Widespread interest in arts and culture as a revitalizing agent for postindustrial cities began to take root beginning in the 1980s and have been widely written about and championed.

While many of these arts- or culture-based development efforts enabled new forays or potential bridges between city planning and the cultural sector, *culture in its wider sense*—a way of understanding ethnic groups, social traditions, and activities, aesthetic, or design choices, and variations in human behaviors—has not been part of the equation.

Circling the Wagons

The cultural-planning practice grew over its first few decades but is not as ubiquitous as early advocates anticipated. Especially in the United States, cultural planning emerged more as a circle-the-wagons strategy to defend the institutional cultural sector against those who would attack, censor, or eliminate the arts from public sector budgets. As research later in this book points out, those wagons also served to keep out cultural groups and practices outside of Western Eurocentric arts (see Chapter 4). Meanwhile, city planning, as practiced widely by towns and cities of all sizes, tends to ignore a deep understanding of dimensions of human culture that impact patterns of behavior, livelihood, settlement, socializing, recreation, and other things central to everyday ways of life.

Jones (1993) characterized cultural planning as emerging at the intersections of city planning and the arts and called for greater involvement of city planners in cultural planning to help improve and grow the practice. City planners, he wrote,

> bring to the table more thorough models of planning and tougher-minded methods. They can help build into plans more of the features that enhance the chances for plans being implemented. Finally, planners could greatly facilitate the integration of cultural plans with comprehensive plans, thus blending the arts more fully into the community.
>
> (p. 97)

In spite of such calls, cultural planning remains largely on one corner of that intersection, usually with cup in hand seeking spare change. The disconnect between the two planning practices has stifled the progress of both fields. Evans (2001) argued that

> land-use and culture are fundamental natural and human phenomena, but the combined notion and practice of culture and planning conjure up a tension between not only tradition, resistance and change; heritage and contemporary expression, but also the ideals of cultural rights, equity and amenity.
>
> (p. 1)

Western concepts of land ownership and the willful subjugation of land to human needs represent a culturally based concept that provokes tensions, particularly with Indigenous peoples and others who strive to live harmoniously with the natural world. City planners may also be guilty of circling their wagons around the primacy of dividing land based on function and the prime directive of highest and best use.

Among the reasons for the two practices maintaining their distance, in what follows I first describe generic resistance to change that impacts virtually every practice or institution. In addition, I cite four specific dynamics I believe these practices must confront.

Confronting Change

First, it's helpful to explore one of the common barriers to change that afflicts any profession, industry, or organization—what has been called "immunity to change" (Kegan & Lahey, 2009, p. 7). Local cultural agencies that generally commission cultural plans and city planning departments are made up of individuals burdened by such immunities. American organizational change theorists Robert Kegan and Lisa Lahey described immunity to change as counterposing competing commitments. Individuals, organizations, and, by extension, communities discover their stated goals are subconsciously sabotaged by other commitments or beliefs they hold that are often embedded in policies and established practices. In most cases, people inside those systems can't easily see the direct tension between new goals and their ways of working.

For instance, an arts agency may say one of its top priorities is to become more inclusive of diverse ethnic or immigrant groups through their programs and/or grantmaking. At the same time, they stand behind their established standards of "artistic quality" grounded in Eurocentric values and methods of producing, distributing, and experiencing art. They also expect cultural organizations to produce and/or deliver art through nonprofit structures grounded in hierarchical, industrial-era models of production and distribution (Borrup, 2011). At the same time, the agency can't figure out why they are unable to gain traction with their diversity goals. They are waiting for and sometimes "helping" artists and communities of color to fit their cultural practices within the Eurocentric, aesthetically based criteria and adopt organizational structures that conform to agency expectations. The agency hasn't confronted that they need to overhaul their criteria and embrace other models for making and sharing culture. Thus, they are unable to make meaningful progress towards their goals.

Another example might be a city planning department called on to support an economic development goal to increase pedestrian traffic in a commercial or downtown area. At the same time, they subscribe to street widths, turning radii, and vehicle speeds favored by traffic engineers that enable the efficient flow of automobiles. Until pedestrians lose their fear of death or planners find ways to alter their commitment to the primacy of cars, they cannot help achieve this goal. To be fair, meaningful change is being seen in this way in some cities.

As Kegan and Lahey (2009) pointed out, individuals often find it difficult to recognize such deeply seated competing commitments, even if those seem simple to the outside observer. And, while individuals may be prepared to change, long-standing professional practices are more resistant. The same is true with organizations and cities whose institutional cultures, entrenched policies, procedures, and belief systems are complex and difficult to see from the inside.

Barrier 1: Cultural Understanding as Gravity

In the first of the four specific barriers I postulate, limited use and understanding of culture is central. While not using the term *gravitational pull*, Mercer (2006), Mills (2003), Stevenson (2005), and Landry (2008) all implicitly describe the phenomenon in their arguments for how the promise of cultural planning has been sidetracked. Gravity within the nonprofit cultural sector originates with a default definition of culture promoted by formal arts institutions and agencies who endeavor to keep cultural planning within their orbit.

As a cultural planner, when introducing a planning process to an assembly of community leaders, I offer the short definition of culture as *ways of living together* (see Chapter 3). This broad starting point allows each community to subsequently focus on what they think that statement includes, and it opens an important conversation. In further elaboration, I describe that this might include things people make—usually by hand—and events they celebrate together; qualities of places in which people feel pride; music, dance, art, poetry, and foods people enjoy; how people communicate, learn, and exchange goods; special places people gather and recreate; and, activities that bring both joy and new ways of thinking to life that expand people's understanding of each other and the world. My goal is not to define culture but to plant the idea that a community can conduct conversations about what they think it should include and that they have the responsibility to choose the operative parameters for their cultural plan.

However, I find this broader way of understanding and describing culture often goes in one ear and out the other. I have encountered wonderful exceptions where this more inclusive notion was the right thing at the right time, where activities in the natural environment, seasonal celebrations, urban design, safety for the vulnerable, or layered historical narratives speak to community values, uniqueness, and other ways of living together. Typically, however, people in the room are community stalwarts—municipal, business, and arts leaders and volunteers—who are engaged and heavily invested in local institutions and other formal civic endeavors.

For decades or even generations, these stalwarts have painstakingly built and maintained local institutions, championed cultural practices and creative activities—the very cultural and creative experiences that brought meaning and/or joy to their lives. No doubt they want new generations and newcomers to have similar experiences with these tried-and-true practices and organizations. Yet new generations and new arrivals might have different ideas. Describing cultural planning as inclusive of these new ideas and a multitude of dimensions of community life is something not everyone is ready to hear. Admittedly, such an expansive approach represents an ambitious agenda for cultural planning. It's a stretch in thinking for most communities. However, stretching ways of thinking seems an appropriate role for any planner.

Often outsiders to communities, cultural planning consultants can only stretch people so far. It is appropriate to facilitate community conversation and decision-making and to respect local choices. Community leaders of all stripes tend to default to "opera-house culture" (see Chapter 3), the standard cluster of Eurocentric activities, organizations, and aesthetic values that comprise formal arts institutions and practices. Surprisingly, individuals from ethnic communities who have been excluded from the local cultural equation sometimes do the same thing. They also describe culture as what they have understood and/or how they think they should describe it—which might leave out their own cultural traditions and practices!

I call this the *gravitational pull*. Of course, in a community context, gravitating back to the familiar is an understandable phenomenon. People can only begin with what they know and then potentially move a step or two to expand on the familiar, what American futurist Steven Johnson (2010) called the "adjacent possible" (p. 23). Moving the collective thinking of a town or city is slow, and sometimes individuals and institutions purposefully work to pull the conversation back to what is familiar so as to further the missions of existing institutions and community programs.

In her analysis of cultural plans in Australia, Stevenson (2014) found a similar phenomenon. Some plans laid out a broad approach to culture, then reverted to an arts context. She described this slippage as "between the conceptualization of culture as a process and everyday life that is espoused in the framing sections of the document, and the explicit focus on galleries, artists, museums and other forms of 'art' featured elsewhere" (p. 63). In Europe, wrote Ghilardi (2001), "where aesthetic definitions of culture tend to prevail and policies for the arts are rarely coordinated with other policies, cultural planning has had, so far, little application [in broader aspects of city planning]" (p. 126). European traditions, also found in the United States, separate the arts from other aspects of life, and this is indeed one of the obstacles.

Expecting a standardization or uniform understanding of culture across the geographies such as states or countries would not only be unreasonable but frightening. Culture is neither uniform nor static. Describing culture requires regular dialogue. Moreover, smaller cities in particular have distinct aesthetic character grounded in their geography or history that offers the promise to focus civic spirit and foster economic development. In these cases, a frequent challenge for cultural planners, in my experience, is to help communities believe that their unique qualities have merit.

Cultural planning in most cases, including outside the United States, is commissioned or overseen by arts or cultural agencies. In a Canadian context, Kovacs (2011) wrote, "the placement of cultural planning in an arts-centered department only reinforces the narrow understandings of what culture and cultural planning are all about" (p. 332). Organized arts communities have developed a sense of ownership of cultural planning that Stevenson (2005) concluded has "privileged art over culture" (p. 40). Describing such cultural plans, German planning scholar Klaus Kunzmann (2004) called them "unhelpful and tiresome culture-related shopping lists" (p. 399). Cultural planning, argued Mercer (2006), "cannot be generated from the self-satisfied and enclosed position which holds that art is good for people and the community" (p. 6).

These authors reinforce that cultural planning drifts towards serving limited interests in communities, using the art-is-good-for-you rationale, even in places where the people and the cultural mix have changed—sometimes significantly. In other words, privileging art over culture in planning denies communities the opportunity to experience more of their cultural richness and to apply a culturally informed lens across the elements of city planning and policy. The sway over cultural planning and its outcomes held by local arts agencies serves to secure resources and elevate their capacities to produce and deliver artistic and cultural experiences with which they're familiar. While this is not an unworthy undertaking, it discounts a wider range of cultural needs and potentials within a community. As Kovacs (2011) wrote, "this discriminating and extremely powerful concept blinds us to the existence of other cultural systems" (p. 323). Keeping the definition of culture locked in a Eurocentric arts silo denies social systems and civic infrastructure the benefits of a deeper understanding of their own cultural biases and of new and more culturally attuned pathways to solve complex problems.

Barrier 2: Professional Silos

The second factor, and a fairly obvious one, in the disconnect between cultural and city planning is based in professional silos. On the one hand, most cultural planners have limited preparation for their work. Bianchini (1999) described the experience of many cultural planners. Narrow training in arts administration, he wrote, is

> inadequate for cultural planners, who also need to know about political economy and urban sociology, about how cities work (as societies, economies, polities, and eco-systems, as well as cultural milieux) and of course about physical planning itself, otherwise they cannot influence it.
>
> (p. 200)

Bianchini's comments, while two decades old at the time of this writing, remain pertinent, at least in the United States, where there continues to be limited opportunities in the academic arena for preparing cultural planners and little change among agencies hiring planning consultants.

Research for this book revealed that only 41% of the consultants employed to assist cities in cultural planning consider it to be their primary area of expertise. The next largest group of cultural planning consultants, at 23%, specialize in nonprofit arts management or strategic planning. Others bring skills in marketing or economic development. Fewer than a handful of university-level courses in cultural planning are offered in the United States. Most cultural planners are self-taught and self-defined. Some bring long associations with large institutions, others with community-based creative practices. Some bring a narrow approach to culture, others a more expansive one.

According to some observers, including Montgomery (1990), Kunzmann (2004), Young (2008), and Stevenson (2014), cultural planning has been marginalized by a city planning profession unable to see beyond quantitative or technocratic thinking and the seeming imperative of land-use allocation. Academic training helped build these silos, even rigidify them. City planners have greater opportunities—and requirements—for their training, but it too has limits and biases.

The walls of the academy were already quite thick when formal city and regional planning education took root. Planning programs sprouted from different origins within institutions. Some arose from civil engineering and architecture and maintain a technical formalism or design focus; some came from public policy schools that emphasize sociological data; and others were from geography and bring spatial analysis. City-planning programs became ubiquitous among universities in the last half of the 20th century, and degrees became a common expectation among the estimated 39,100 planners working in the United States in 2018 (U.S. Bureau of Labor Statistics, n.d.).

City planners bring or develop a variety of biases. Some graduate from planning schools that are politically progressive while others come from conservative programs. City planners work under the direction of risk-averse city managers, mayors, councils, or commissions that can change upon retirements or election cycles, sometimes dramatically. City planners have personal interests and political leanings. Some align with large developers and real-estate interests, while others orient towards grassroots community organizers and nonprofits. Some favor low-density, car-oriented development patterns; others work to enhance mass transit or pedestrian environments, and so on.

The formal field and practice of city planning has been unsure how to welcome or accommodate cultural planning or even to see its relevance outside the occasional creative district, arts facility, or tourism initiative. Bianchini (1999) framed the planning profession in the context of the historical development of cities:

> Every period ... seems to need its own forms of creativity. Urban planners this century [the 20th] have been especially influenced by the creativity of engineers and scientists ... responding to problems of overcrowding, mobility, and public health generated by the Industrial Revolution.
>
> (p. 195)

Looking towards the 21st century, Bianchini argued that there is a growing awareness that "physical and scientific approaches can only be part of the solution" (p. 195). Creativity, facilitation, and cultural competency are core skills now needed by city planners. Based partly in their training and partly in the systems within which planners work, these have been slow to be embraced.

Applicable to planners and designers across the professional spectrum, Escobar (2018) advocated that "conventional discipline-based design education cannot contribute to substantial change unless students are inducted into understanding theories of power, social structure and social change, and the like" (p. 49). Such fundamentals are not often given much attention in a field where there is so much technocratic knowledge to be learned. "In short what urban planners also need today," wrote Bianchini (1999), "is the creativity of artists, more specifically of artists working in social contexts" (pp. 195–196).

Some city-planning critics lament the scientifically driven focus on land-use and data-driven analysis that dominates the profession (Kunzmann, 2004; Landry, 2008; Sandercock, 2003). Mercer (2006) argued that city planning provides a "professional specialization in developing a two-dimensional relationship to the urban environment without a feel for what is actually going on in those coloured rectangles and between those model buildings" (p. 5).

Part of what city planners are rarely trained to appreciate are symbolic elements of place and even the symbolism embedded in their own methods and actions. Bianchini (1999) asserted that planners "have to learn something from the process of thinking used by people working in the field of cultural production— i.e., the production of meanings, images, narratives, and ideas" (p. 199). Meanings of place often fit more into the silo of landscape architecture but are less often foregrounded in city planning. Mercer (2006) maintained that "planning is not a physical science but a human science" (p. 5), echoing Geddes, who said planners need to be "anthropologists, economists, and geographers, not just draftsmen … They need to know how people live, work, play, and relate to their environment" (as cited in Mercer, p. 5). The latter are attributes that cultural planners bring from which city planners can benefit.

In his sharp critique of city planning, Kunzmann (2004) wrote, "creativity has become a topical theme, though still only with a very small audience" (p. 391). He went on to call for bridging the arts and city planning in profound ways, and he makes a blunt assessment of planning education, suggesting "their creative skills development is neglected, sacrificed on the altar of science" (p. 400). Almost three decades ago, and still highly relevant, Jones (1993) made similar observations: "Many people, both in planning and in the arts, still have a hard time reconciling the left-brain activity of planning with the right-brain one of artistic expression" (p. 89). Understanding the depth and significance of culture, creativity, and city planning, of course, requires both hemispheres.

Barrier 3: Outsiders and Insiders

The third reason I assert city and cultural planning practices experience difficulty finding synergy stems from a distinct difference in their origins. Cultural planning grew as a self-interest-based organizing effort among arts nonprofits and arts advocacy groups. With the growth of the cultural sector from the 1960s, most within it, with the exception of some major institutions, felt socially marginalized. Like any industry or professional sector that feels on the outside, banding together proved more effective in order to influence government policy, the media, and private-sector powerbrokers, including philanthropies. Cultural plans pressed for more favorable public policies and funding related to events, celebrations, art in public spaces, live-work spaces, and matters related to zoning or other city regulations. Cultural plans typically include a multitude of goals that the arts and cultural sector understands are best achieved through collective action. This required the proverbial "herding cats," as arts organizations and artists sometimes don't get along, as they feel in competition with one another for limited charitable support and for audiences.

Cultural planning and policy can be contentious in matters between the cultural sector and municipal administrations as well as within the sector itself. In most communities, different groups have disparate ideas of what constitutes arts and culture and, of course, who is getting funding and who is not. Successful cultural plans find ways to build consensus, devise goals that are widely shared, and forge stronger working relationships among players within the cultural community as well as with other key community leaders. To its credit, within a few decades cultural planning helped many once-fractured arts and cultural communities learn to work better together. In the survey on cultural planning detailed in Chapter 4, among the highest expectations and reported outcomes was organizing for sector advocacy.

In essence, cultural planning represents bottom-up work incorporating strategies of community organizing. Feelings of "outsider-ness" experienced by players within local arts and culture sectors through the 1970s, 1980s, and 1990s propelled them to pull together to formulate shared visions and to convince local powers-that-be that they have value, are deserving of support, and, more recently, that they should be included in strategic thinking related to broader community concerns.

The origins or DNA of cultural planning are steeped in this sense of marginalization and the need to organize. Those who are truly marginalized socially, politically, and economically would have little sympathy and consider these mostly Eurocentric arts agencies, nonprofits, and artists part of a privileged mainstream. In the eyes of city planners, an organized cultural sector represents another potentially loud, cranky, and occasionally helpful voice at the table—another interest group to placate or navigate, similar to business associations, neighborhood alliances, environmental activists, or other groups planners reckon with.

City planning has a different origin story. Since 1900, it has addressed public health, infrastructure development, and environmental concerns. However, the practice still carries baggage from settler colonialism, whereby patriarchal institutions that represent power impose expert-driven solutions. City planners may be made to feel less than powerful by some city leaders, well-heeled developers, or business interests, yet the practice has established "insider" status in city halls. City planners are generally included in formal decision-making processes. For those outside the practice, city planners are typically seen as part of the "top-down" force that precipitates, steers, or sometimes hampers development, change, and major public and private investments. Critiquing the origins and development of planning from a feminist perspective, Leavitt (1980) observed, "Planning in search of legitimacy, has allied itself with mainstream ideology and enhancing the status quo" (Abstract, para. 5).

Imposition of city plans has been cited among the tools of the trade of Roman and Spanish conquerors who used predetermined templates for building or rebuilding cities (see Chapter 3). Expert-drafted city plans dispatched by an emperor or king reinforced power both symbolically and practically. Such plans and ways of building cities remain ancestors of the practice—with a few more consultative steps now involved in the process!

Escobar (2018) described planning and design as rooted in Western patriarchal domination of the natural environment with "Cartesian license" (p. 81) that not only placed "man" (sic) on the highest rung of the ladder of being, but "led science to investigate reality by separating mind and matter, body and soul, and life and nonlife" (p. 81). In this way, Escobar asserted, humans exercised the right to alter the natural world in what was "a kind of forgery that imagined a dead cosmos of inanimate matter" (p. 81). The planning mantra of *highest and best use*, Escobar argued, represents the taking of the natural world as well as erasure or diminishment of Indigenous people.

Colonial practices, usually understood as invasions and forceful taking of others' lands, may seem like ancient history to those in the contemporary city-planning profession. However, the DNA of settler colonialism carries into the present practice. Porter (2016), in her important book, *Unlearning the Colonial Cultures of Planning*, found that within planning practice, "the *cultural* traits of colonialism endure as 'a variety' of colonial representations and encounters [that] both precede and succeed periods of actual possession and rule" (p. 16). She examined how planning practices, including the concept of highest and best use, impacted Indigenous communities in New Zealand. Planners justified dispossession of lands because "Indigenous peoples were not recognizably 'improving' their territory and therefore could not be recognized as sovereign rulers of that territory (or indeed as owners of property)" (p. 26). Contemporary planning, asserted Porter, is fully steeped in a process of imposition or an outside-in process with roots in "the violent hierarchy of imperial power" (p. 36).

While it is a stretch for city planners today to see themselves as part of a violent hierarchy of imperial power, people dispossessed of their homes and/or communities through planning, development, and/or market forces still feel this legacy. The patriarchal man-over-nature origins and power hierarchies Escobar and Porter described remain part of the practice and are tough to overcome. Porter (2016) and Young (2008) both called these *cultures of planning.* This, I argue, contributes to the disconnect between the two planning practices. A top-down, masculine-oriented city-planning practice has a hard time finding common ground with bottom-up cultural sector organizing, except to the degree that the latter may amuse and decorate.

Barrier 4: Housework or *Real* Work?

Finally, the two practices have, in their DNA and outward identities, gender differences. Two planning scholars from Australia who now teach in North America, Leonie Sandercock and Ann Forsyth, observed, "The paradigms on which planning and theorizing about it have been based are informed by characteristics traditionally associated with the masculine in our society" (Sandercock & Forsyth, 1992, p. 55).

The city planning profession was largely a men's club for the majority of its first 100 years of formal practice. Women were not employed in any meaningful numbers until feminists drew attention to this employment record beginning in the 1970s. In 1970, it was estimated women held just over 10% of the professional positions in city planning. By 1980, that had risen to about 15% of an estimated 25,500 professional planners at that time in the United States (Leavitt, 1980). By the second decade of the 2000s, the field boasts near gender parity with women holding 47% of professional positions (https://datausa.io/profile/soc/urban-regional-planners#demographics), although men still hold most of the senior and more highly paid positions.

Leavitt's (1980) dissertation at Columbia University took an in-depth look at women in city planning, impacts women had on the practice, and the practice's lack of attention to women's needs. Unfortunately, it was never published. She described how between 1930 and 1970, not only were there few women who fulfilled the same planning roles as men, they were not even a consideration in the work of planning. Tensions evolved within the field that she described as based partly on "the reluctance of the profession to address questions about women as beneficiaries of planning" (Leavitt, 1980, Abstract, para. 5). She didn't use the term *culture* to describe planning practices in the same way as Porter or

Young, but Leavitt distinguished between the individuals who practice planning and the *way* planning is practiced.

American economist Ann Markusen, who later in her career actively bridged the realms of planning, economics, and the arts, wrote in her article, "City Spatial Structures, Women's Household Work, and National Urban Policy,"

> The fundamental separation between "work" spheres and home correspond roughly to the division of primary responsibility between adult men and women for household production and wage labor, at least historically. Since patriarchy is the organizing principle of the former sphere, urban spatial structure must be as much a product of patriarchy as it is of capitalism. Patriarchy may thus contribute to and condition urban problems.
>
> (as cited in Leavitt, 1980, p. 328)

Such paradigms are slow to change, Sandercock and Forsyth (1992) pointed out:

> With more women entering the planning profession, gender inequity is not merely an issue for the numerical dominance of men. Rather it is male dominance in the theories, standards, and ideologies to guide planning work that is, in the internal culture of planners.
>
> (p. 54)

Escobar (2018) explained these profound differences in terms of patriarchy,

> [which] goes well beyond the exploitation of women; it explains the systemic destruction of nature. Conversely, matriarchy is not defined by the predominance of women over men, but by an entirely different conception of life, based not on domination and hierarchies, and respectful of the relational fabric of all life.
>
> (p. 10)

Employing more women and people of color may represent change in the planning profession, but decolonizing and feminizing the practice itself will require a far more profound overhaul of assumptions and ways of working.

Leavitt (1980) also traced significant impacts women made in planning during the late 19th century, even before it became a recognized profession. In fact, she argues, women helped to shape the practice. She wrote, "Women's role in civic improvement committees paralleled and, in some cases, paved the way for early planning efforts" (p. 188). Nonetheless, Leavitt asserted, most of the work achieved by a multitude of middle-class, voluntary women's clubs was characterized by city fathers as extensions of housework: "Whereas men had license to address any element of planning, women's roles were more narrowly determined" (p. 191). Given the origins of cultural planning come significantly from women's efforts (see Chapter 1), is it any wonder it has remained marginalized within city planning?

Groundbreaking scholars in the field like Jane Jacobs, Patsy Healey, Leonie Sandercock, Hanna Mattila, Dolores Hayden, Jacqueline Leavitt, Libby Porter, Emily Talen, Ann Markusen, Ann Forsyth, Lia Ghilardi, Liz Plater-Zyberk, and many more not only represent fresh thinking in city planning but urgently needed new leadership.

In contrast, the arts and cultural sector is dominated by women, except in the most senior institutional positions. According to "The White House Project Report: Benchmarking Women's Leadership," 73% of employees in the overall nonprofit sector are women (The White House Project, 2009). More specifically in arts and culture, a study by Americans for the Arts (2018) affirmed what is widely known: White women dominate the field, with 78% of the staff of public and private arts agencies identifying as cisgender female, and 82% are White or Caucasian. For this and other reasons, the sector is not taken seriously in city planning except when it provides architects opportunities to design buildings or serves to add beauty to urban landscapes that are often aesthetically dreadful.

Moreover, the practice of art is considered a feminine pursuit born of leisure and frivolity, providing little more than diversion from important business and civic matters. Creative practices produce decorative features to embellish the substance of built infrastructure, public spaces, and the interiors of homes—the traditional domain of women. Artmaking involves working with available materials, ranging from words on the page, to the human body and voice, to scraps of cloth, clay, paint, wood, metal, glass, and the like. These are often available as waste from another industry or earlier use. Imagination and skill fashion these "materials" into something with new meaning, value, and beauty. Creative practices and behaviors, if not frivolous and ignorable, are otherwise considered disruptive. Artists have a reputation as troublemakers, best appreciated in the safety of museums that reflect on their contributions after they're dead.

Gender-based differences between the two fields of practice are profound. Would this make a "marriage" of the two fields more plausible? Perhaps it would if the historic or "traditional" power dynamic was maintained in which the female is in service to the male. However, these power differentials, and lack of ability of the professions to open their silo walls and move beyond the paradigms in which they've operated, have made a true and more equitable partnership a difficult thing to achieve.

Summary

I join many voices over the past three decades to call for a shift in how both city planners and cultural planners approach their work. Language and resistance, or immunity to change, have kept the two professions and practices apart, yet they both have much to contribute and learn from one another. Culture, conflated with elitist notions of art that perceive it as either frivolous or dangerous, leave critical understanding of human cultures (ways of life) and human diversity off the table.

The grounding of city-planning practice in Western science, as well as in settler colonialism and patriarchy, separate it from a more profound understanding and appreciation of the ways of life of people. At the same time, dominant cultural institutions—and by extension, many cultural planners—all too willingly remain focused on Eurocentric concepts of culture within which are also embedded White supremacy and colonialist approaches to advancing values, practices, and hierarchies. Cultural planning has gravitated to planning by and for these institutions and their artistic practices and not towards a process to understand and improve how people live together in communities. With the lack of such understanding, city planners are unable to see the cultural dimensions and implications of plans and policies across a spectrum of municipal concerns. This results in policy choices and physical development patterns that privilege some while denying others equitable access to resources and to spaces that respect and accommodate different ways of life.

If cities and communities of all sizes are going to become more just and equitable, and to welcome and accommodate new people seeking safe ground, city planners must gain a deeper understanding of their own cultural biases and of those embedded in their practice, as well as those of the different people that make up their cities. If city planners continue to fixate on spatial and physical uses without giving deeper consideration to users, they can't effectively resolve deeper challenges across domains of city planning, from transportation and recreation to health and housing.

Likewise, if the arts and culture sector continue to see cultural planning as defensive posturing with a primary purpose to leverage resources for the ongoing operations of established institutions, they restrict the potential of cultural planning and, instead, become a force for stagnation and furtherance of inequity.

As a result, cultural divisions and xenophobia will continue to grow, and cities will be ill-equipped to address human needs and major challenges as effectively or equitably as they could and must.

The next chapter addresses ways of understanding and talking about culture and looks more deeply into ways of life and of living together.

References

Americans for the Arts. (2018). *Local arts agency salaries 2018: A report about salaries and compensation in the local arts agency field.* Retrieved from https://www.americansforthearts.org/by-program/networks-and-councils/local-arts-network/facts-and-figures/local-arts-agency-salaries-2018

Ashley, A. J. (2015). Beyond the aesthetic: The historical pursuit of local arts economic development. *Journal of Planning History, 14*(1), 38–61. doi:10.1177/1538513214541616

Bianchini, F. (1999). Cultural planning and time planning: The relationship between culture and urban planning. In C. Greed (Ed.), *Social town planning* (pp. 195–202). London: Routledge.

Borrup, T. (2011). The emergence of a new cultural infrastructure: Lessons from Silicon Valley. *Journal of Urban Culture Research, 2* (January–June), 16–29. doi:10.14456/jucr.2011.1

Borrup, T. (2018). *Cultural planning at 40: A look at the practice and its progress.* Washington, DC, Americans for the Arts. Retrieved from https://www.americansforthearts.org/by-program/reports-and-data/legislation-policy/naappd/cultural-planning-at-40-a-look-at-the-practice-and-its-progress

Dreeszen, C. A. (1994). *Reimagining community: Community arts and cultural planning in America* [Doctoral dissertation]. Retrieved from ProQuest Dissertations and Theses Database. (UMI 9510463)

Escobar, A. (2018). *Designs for the pluriverse: Radical interdependence, autonomy, and the making of worlds.* Durham, NC: Duke University Press.

Evans, G. (2001). *Cultural planning: An urban renaissance?* London: Routledge.

Ghilardi, L. (2001). Cultural planning and cultural diversity. In T. Bennett (Ed.), *Differing Diversities: Transversal study on the theme of cultural policy and cultural diversity* (pp. 123–134). Strasbourg: Council of Europe.

Johnson, S. (2010). *Where good ideas come from: The natural history of innovation.* New York, NY: Riverhead Books.

Jones, B. (1993). Current directions in cultural planning. *Landscape & Urban Planning, 26*(1–4), 89–97. doi:10.1016/0169-2046(93)90009-3

Kegan, R., & Lahey, L. L. (2009). *Immunity to change: How to overcome it and unlock the potential in yourself and your organization.* Boston, MA: Harvard Business Press.

Kong, L. (2009). Beyond networks and relations: Towards rethinking creative cluster theory. In L. Kong & J. O'Connor (Eds.), *Creative economies, creative cities* (pp. 61–75). Dordrecht: Springer.

Kovacs, J. F. (2011). Cultural planning in Ontario, Canada: Arts policy or more? *International Journal of Cultural Policy, 17*(3), 321–340. doi:10.1080/10286632.2010.4 87152

Kunzmann, K. R. (2004). Culture, creativity and spatial planning. *Town Planning Review, 75*(4), 383–404. doi:10.3828/tpr.75.4.2

Landry, C. (2008). *The creative city: A toolkit for urban innovators* (Rev. ed.). Oxford: Earthscan.

Leavitt, J. (1980). *Planning and women, women in planning* [Doctoral dissertation]. Retrieved from ProQuest Dissertations and Theses Database. (ProQuest document ID 303025754)

Mercer, C. (2006). *Cultural planning for urban development and creative cities.* Retrieved from http://www.kulturplan-oresund.dk/pdf/Shanghai_cultural_planning_paper.pdf

Mills, D. (2003, May). Cultural planning—Policy task, not tool. *Artwork Magazine, 55,* 7–11.

Montgomery, J. (1990). Cities and the art of cultural planning. *Planning Practice & Research, 5*(3), 17–24. doi:10.1080/02697459008722772

Porter, L. (2016). *Unlearning the colonial cultures of planning.* Abingdon: Routledge. doi:10.4324/9781315548982

Redaelli, E. (2019). *Connecting arts and place: Cultural policy and American cities.* London: Palgrave Macmillan.

Sandercock, L. (2003). *Cosmopolis II: Mongrel cities in the 21st century.* London: Continuum. doi:10.5040/9781472545527

Sandercock, L., & Forsyth, A. (1992). A gender agenda: New directions for planning theory. *Journal of the American Planning Association, 58*(1), 49–59. doi:10.1080/01944369208975534

Stevenson, D. (2005). Cultural planning in Australia: Texts and contexts. *Journal of Arts Management, Law, and Society, 35*(1), 36–48.

Stevenson, D. (2014). *Cities of culture: A global perspective.* London: Routledge.

The White House Project. (2009). *The White House Project report: Benchmarking women's leadership.* Washington, DC: Author. Retrieved from https://www.in.gov/icw/files/benchmark_wom_leadership.pdf

U.S. Bureau of Labor Statistics (n.d.). *Occupational outlook handbook: Arts and design occupations.* Retrieved from https://www.bls.gov/ooh/arts-and-design/home.htm

Young, G. (2008). *Reshaping planning with culture.* London: Routledge. doi:10.4324/9781315605647

Chapter 3

Back to the Familiar

Culture, Place, and Ways of Living Together

Culture is subtle and complex in nature, its concepts are fluid and abstract, and there is a lack of understanding of suitable techniques and approaches for accessing and incorporating detailed and qualitative cultural knowledge in planning.

— Greg Young (2008, p. 5)

Culture is indeed complex, fluid, and abstract. It's a difficult concept to wrap one's head around. The simple word *culture* is used to describe a variety of social phenomena. Its meaning is easily and frequently misused and misinterpreted. Agreeing on what culture means in any context is a tough task, let alone within a field as multilayered as city planning. How then do city planners formulate plans and policies to address culture and to appreciate its implications?

Debates in scholarly literature about culture go back at least a century and a half. At the same time, culture and city planning have a largely unspoken history well before the formalization of the practice. The challenge here is to land on workable approaches to culture relevant to city planners and to identify ways to incorporate an understanding that is applicable within a profession that is by necessity practical.

In earlier chapters, I looked at planning itself as a cultural practice, one that has a culture of its own and baggage that it brings. In this chapter, I hope to illuminate constructive ways for city planners to talk about culture and to identify approaches to learn about the cultures of their communities. This will be useful for planners' efforts to better understand residents, how they relate to place and place identity, how they interact and communicate differently, and ways that spatial organization and design impact how different people feel and work together. This chapter reviews some different descriptions anthropologists and others have of culture and ways that culture is a force in different settings. It concludes with a series of framing questions planners can employ to better understand the dynamics of the multiple cultures within their communities and the overall culture of their community.

Cultures are infinite. They sometimes change rapidly, sometimes refuse to budge. As the culture, or more appropriately, cultures in every community are unique, it is especially incumbent on cultural planners to take time up front in their process to address culture as I described in the previous chapter. In so doing, they can facilitate discussions about culture among community members—not to fix a definition, but to set the stage for understanding that culture is expansive and dynamic and to introduce ways to see it and talk about it. Oddly, cultural planners rarely articulate or describe the very thing they put at the center of their work, yet they have tools and opportunity to do just that.

Finding Culture in Planning and Development

As a dynamic phenomenon, culture evolves as a result of everyday life and in ways that are propelled by a variety of forces, not the least of these are increasing global mobility, mass media, and social media. Yet professionals within the cultural sector rarely have explicit conversations about culture, what it means, how it changes, and, importantly, whose cultures they include or exclude in their work. To add to the confusion, the terms *culture, art,* and *creativity* are often used interchangeably. As Stevenson (2014) observed, "There is no developed language within cultural planning for uncoupling these definitions or for tracing their parameters, interconnections, and political implications" (p. 13).

Like culture, art is a long-debated and contentious word and concept. Nonetheless, I will explain an understanding and usage of the term applicable in the context of planning. Simply put, *art,* when used as a noun, typically refers to objects or performative experiences, like a painting, sculpture, or dance by a skilled practitioner. As most commonly used, art includes various forms or formal practices from music to dance, cinema, literature, visual art, theatre, and so on. Art describes the product but is also used to describe the process of applying creativity to the making of a product or experience. When used as a verb, art refers to the *way* of achieving something, as in doing something *artfully*. Not all art objects, activities, or techniques are new or unique. A traditional practice, whether a song or a prepared food, may replicate one made before, but is still art and can be done artfully.

Art is most often akin to *creativity*, a word that is typically used to describe the essential energy and wherewithal used in making an art object or experience. However, creativity does not exist exclusively within formal structures or disciplines of artmaking. Creativity is practiced in daily life across professions and industries by everyone to solve simple and grand problems, to make things from a meal to a symphony to an airplane. Creativity is also employed in the daily practice of everything from conducting a conversation to driving a car to packing a grocery bag.

Culture, on the other hand, represents much more. Some describe it as the operating system or DNA of human behaviors, thought processes, and ways of communicating—how meaning is made, experienced, understood, and shared. A culture, or a shared way of life, may, in fact, encourage or discourage creativity or the making or experiencing of some forms of art. I like to think of culture as the primordial soup (as well as governing principles of physics and chemistry), creativity as the spark, and art as the wonderous as well as very practical outcomes.

Municipal decision-makers and city planners find themselves regularly and often unwittingly making choices and setting actionable policies based on their own cultural point of view and impacting the culture and cultures of their communities but with little to no awareness of its meaning or positive or negative implications or potentials. According to Qadeer (1997), as described in the Introduction in relation to tree-trimming policies, city plans and policies impact the culture of their communities in profound ways, both symbolic and real, yet, how they do this is rarely visible, let alone explicitly considered. Such choices affect virtually every planning arena including, but certainly not limited to, recreation, transportation, housing, urban design, and the formal arts and culture sector.

Contemporary city planning, at its best, finds win-win solutions, better ways to connect people and places, and a better and more sustainable quality of life for everyone. This same practice may also reinforce a status quo that may be out of balance with the daily realities of residents and their well-being. In so doing, city planning increases material and cultural inequities. Planning involves assessing situations, formulating and weighing options, and setting the stage for making optimal choices. Australian social scientist Glen Searle (2013) observed that "planning can be seen as an essentially political activity that involves contestation of outcomes" (p. 135). Both space and culture are common issues in such contests, although city planners may only see the former and not how the two may be related.

Describing a Moving Target

Widely cited Welsh cultural critic and theorist Raymond Williams (1976) said, "culture is one of the two or three most complicated words in the English language" (p. 76). He went on to settle on the use of a rather simple three-word phrase, the *way of life* of a people. In this, he included material, intellectual, and spiritual aspects of civilizations. Other scholars of cultural planning cite Williams and this broad definition as an appropriate starting point in understanding and planning for the cultural life and, in fact, for all aspects of life in a community. Most city planners, cultural planners, policymakers, and community development professionals often limit the idea of culture by seeing it inside the frame of *high culture*, as in elitist Western European art forms. Even those outside the arts professions, who have positive personal experiences with artistic or creative practices, may think arts and culture are "nice" but find little relevance for them in serious civic matters. Others, especially those more left-leaning, react negatively to the very word *culture* because it carries this social class association.

Cultural planners, who presumably have more sophistication relative to the subject, largely come from professional backgrounds in the arts. They also tend to default to the narrower and more exclusive understanding. Their clients are generally arts agencies that aspire to have a cultural plan that advances their institutional missions. Cities that commission cultural plans or comprehensive city plans, as Stein (2019) described, are motivated to seek higher property and sales tax revenues that typically come with higher-income residents and businesses attracted by these more exclusive art forms and institutions.

Some Cultures Change Slowly

In his 1871 work, *Primitive Culture,* British anthropologist Edward Tylor offered a definition of culture that long served as a standard, although at least 165 distinct definitions had been offered by 1952 (Noman & Gurr, 2020). Tylor described culture as "that complex whole which includes knowledge, belief, art, morals, law, custom, and any other capabilities and habits acquired by man [sic] as a member of society" (as cited in Young, 2013b, p. 397). In this definition, Tylor identified society as a whole, and its individual members, as distinct entities in a kind of dialogue with each other. One hundred years later, 20th-century American anthropologist Clifford Geertz (1973) described culture as "a system of inherited conceptions expressed in symbolic forms by means of which men [sic] communicate, perpetuate, and develop their knowledge about and attitudes towards life" (p. 89).

A century apart, Tylor and Geertz both reference *men* in their definitions of culture, an indication of how slowly change comes to language used within the academic culture to which they belonged. Geertz placed importance on the transferability of culture passed through generations as well as person-to-person via communication and learning. Of special relevance in his view was that culture is a system of concepts that are translated into symbolic forms of expression that, in turn, help develop knowledge. His ideas situated culture as malleable and subject to continuous evolution. This was in comparison to many anthropological, frozen-in-time ideas of a way of life. Reflecting on such changes in the field of anthropology, Blokland (2017) wrote, "Anthropologists have urged us to move away from rather fixed, ethnocentric, and primordial understanding of culture" (p. 54). Itself more fluid, culture includes and goes beyond place and historical ethnicity. It is understood as a governing agent in social dynamics—in essence, a kind of evolving social DNA. It both fosters and restricts change. It is itself both a vehicle for powering change and a result of change.

Opera-House Culture

American anthropologist Roy Wagner (1975) connected the concept of culture to what he called its "contemporary opera-house sense" (p. 21). He traced the word to the Latin verb *colere*, to cultivate, as associated with the tilling of the soil. Wagner also cited the Middle English meaning of "a plowed field" (p. 21) and described how culture then took on a more specific meaning, "indicating a process of progressive refinement and breeding in the domestication of some particular crop, or even the result or increment of such a process" (p. 21). Like Tylor and Geertz, Wagner also used only the male gender, writing,

> The contemporary "opera-house" sense of the word arises from an elaborate metaphor, which draws upon the terminology of crop breeding and improvement to create an image of man's control, refinement, and "domestication" of himself. So, in the drawing rooms of the eighteenth and nineteenth centuries, one spoke of a "cultivated" person as someone who "had culture," who had developed his interests and accomplishments along approved lines, training and "breeding" the personality as a natural strain might be "cultured."
>
> (p. 21)

Wagner layered on Darwinian evolution, which, he said, "added a historical dimension to this notion of man's breeding and tempering of himself, resulting in the optimistic concept of 'progress'" (p. 21). The idea of being "cultured" and its association with progress, cemented the use of the word and concept of culture in the 20th century, lodging the cultural sector within a narrow silo in which only the most privileged or "well-bred" belong. This legacy continues to dominate the understanding of the word "culture." The idea of "opera-house culture" unfortunately persists as the most widely assumed meaning.

The Right to Culture

People often define themselves through the culture they hold and express that is most commonly in relation to a place where they feel most attached, as in a place of birth or place with family or ethnic history. In contemporary cities, this attachment increasingly comes with choices people make, as in relocating to be part of a community, whether professional, ethnic, or some other affinity. Some associate or even judge themselves and others relative to an assumed hierarchy of cultures as the basis for assessing and assigning human value. In a critical way, people of color might describe their own relative privilege and power in White-dominated society coming as a result of "proximity to Whiteness," or the degree of perceived conformity to White normativity in appearance, speech, education, values, foodways, cultural practices, and the like. Invisibility and dismissal come in shades of grey the further one is situated from these White norms. This spills into city planning, as the institution and practice are steeped in such norms that cause planners to be tone-deaf to or even dismissive of cultures and everyday practices unfamiliar to them.

The 1948 Universal Declaration of Human Rights identified cultural rights among the defining rights of humanity. Elaborating further, the 1982 UNESCO Mexico City Declaration on Cultural Policies offered this understanding of culture:

> [I]n its widest sense, culture may now be said to be the whole complex of distinctive spiritual, material, intellectual and emotional features that characterize a society or social group. It includes not only the arts and letters, but also modes of life, the fundamental rights of the human being, value systems, traditions and beliefs.
>
> (UNESCO, 1982, p. 41)

When analyzing a distinctive tribal society or "past" civilization, anthropologists learn about and piece together a group's way of life. This includes such things as diet, language, relationships to the natural environment, forms of social organization, dress, artmaking, forms and styles of habitat, patterns of settlement, and trade practices. Anthropologists might ask if it is a war-like, domineering culture or a peace-loving, compassionate culture. These elements and others add up to an approximation and description of the culture or way of life of a people in a given place in a given period.

Notwithstanding connections between culture, identity, and place, the simple phrase suggested by R. Williams (1976), *the way of life of a group of people*, serves city planning only in a two-dimensional sense. As the geographic footprints planners address are increasingly multicultural and multiethnic in their populations, this definition is not adequate. Williams's definition implies stasis in addition to providing a lens restricted to a singular culture; these are ideas clearly not optimal for contemporary city planning. In this context, Young (2008) suggested planners use R. Williams's phrase in the plural, as in *ways of life*. I argue, however, this is still not adequate.

More recently, American anthropologist Bruce Knauft (1996) described culture as "not as an integrated entity, tied to a fixed group of people, but as a shifting and contested process of constructing collective identity" (p. 44). One might consider this contested process much like robust city planning: messy, protracted, and creative with many participants and results that rarely satisfy everyone. It is critical to acknowledge that the outcome of a shifting and contested process is not a new mongrel or hybrid culture but a space accommodating multiple cultures. There needs to be room for the bottomless well of cultures of the world.

Scarcity Versus Abundance

An important way to understand culture is through the lens of scarcity and abundance. Is culture a bottomless well of traditions? And, is creativity found in every corner of daily life to be continually explored, enjoyed, and fostered? Or is culture a finite cache of aesthetic treasures, and is creativity a set of high-powered practices closely held by elite institutions and highly trained artists to be guarded and judiciously disseminated? Young (2008) asserted that it is important for culture "to be found and explored everywhere and not viewed as a scarce commodity" (p. 71).

Seeing culture as scarce or abundant is essential in understanding the difference between colonial and exploitive capacities of culture versus its ability to empower and enable. In thinking about where culture resides, what creativity means, and who engages in traditional and creative practices, it is critical to consider scarcity versus abundance. These are fundamentally different theories and approaches embedded in concepts of culture and planners' relationships with communities.

A scarcity mindset is part of a colonialist or missionary concept of bringing the benefits of culture or enlightenment to the "uncultured" masses. Abundance acknowledges and celebrates culture as ubiquitous and present in the lives and identities of all people. How many times has someone said that a part of a city, a suburb, a rural place, or even people, are "devoid of culture"? I have heard people say that about themselves! Of course, this is not even possible and represents an expression of denial, disapproval, or disdain for the culture or cultures that are most certainly present. Such a remark also reveals a lack of tools and empathy to see and appreciate the endless manifestations of culture and the values in diversity.

When planners acknowledge the abundance of cultures in their community and strategize ways to appreciate and constructively respond to them, goodwill can be generated along with productive relationship-building. An unintended consequence that is currently seen in the political realm is that by leveling the playing field, a previously or still-dominant cultural or ethnic group may feel something has been taken from them. This plagues culture and politics in the 21st century, breeding fear of immigrants, sociopolitical polarization, xenophobia, and the rise of nationalism and White supremacist groups—all social dynamics planners find themselves confronting in various forms. Might planning sometimes unintentionally feed such dynamics, or can planners help build culturally sensitive cross-cultural relationships?

Whether implicitly or explicitly practiced, the scarcity mindset creates a hierarchy that stratifies cultural forms and practices, valuing or devaluing one over another and thus sets up or reinforces power-based relationships. South African planning professor Vanessa Watson (2013) called culture "dynamic, socially produced and shaped by power. It can be strategically mobilized often in relation to processes of marginalization or domination" (p. 122). Not only is culture shaped by power, but it can represent and wield power. Playing out on the simplest level, Blokland (2017) described how "people create their own values and meanings, while some may also suppress the meanings and values of others, so that culture cannot be thought of as being independent of power" (p. 55).

Culture, Planning, Politics, and Power

Culture, in all its forms, is highly political. While the term "culture wars" became a standard part of the political vocabulary in the United States in the 1990s (e.g., Gates, 1993; Hunter, 1992), this conflict over public funding of controversial art represented the tip of the iceberg given the intensity of culturally based discord in 2020. Conflicts throughout history, as well as most current global tensions, are in large part cultural. In both cultural and city planning, culture is inherently political. Any action or policy that recognizes or privileges one cultural or creative form, practice, group, or organization over another is a political act, just as a policy that might privilege one parcel of land or roadway over another is an exercise of power and thus a political act.

Cultural as well as physical, political, and economic domination have been tools of conquest and empire-building across history. Some point out that city-planning practitioners have been complicit, active partners in the exercise and abuse of power for centuries. Young (2008) described how "Roman generals carried city plans with them on wars of conquest through the empire, spreading the visible culture of a square, gridded city on a cruciform layout" (p. 33). Spanish conquistadors in the Americas employed the same practice, carrying the *New Laws of the Indies* from the King of Spain (Stevens, 1893). These included city plans that situated institutions of power (government and church) in equally prominent locations surrounding a central zocalo or plaza with a street grid extending outward. Such forms were designed to reflect power, order, and subordination.

These are part of what American social scientists Herbert Gans (1991), Watson (2013), and others called *spatial determinism*. The organization of spaces enables or disenables movement, activities, and ways in which relationships are formed. Spatial design, as I describe further in Chapters 5 and 8, is also culturally based and represents an enormous and often under-recognized force in individual and social life.

Young (2013a) called this the "darker role" of city planning that emanates from centuries of European colonial practice with a "'civilizing mission' that led to usurpation of indigenous cultures in the process of implanting foreign governance and urbanism and an extractive development infrastructure" (p. 6). Writing about neighborhood transitions in contemporary Los Angeles, Collins (2018) used the apt term "invasion and succession" (p. 2), which describes a concept from Burgess's zonal models (as cited in Quinn, 1940).

British planning scholar Stephen Ward (2013) also suggested that planning can have an insidious agenda to camouflage colonialist intentions. He wrote, "At a symbolic level, planning also helped promote the notion of imperialism as a benevolent force. This widely-accepted progressive self-image of planning could help portray imperialism as an enlightened project of modernization" (p. 44). While Ward was describing city planning, most cultural planning could be similarly portrayed as an enlightened project of modernization or progress and a practice that, perhaps unwittingly, finds itself in service to White supremacy and imperialism (cultural *and* economic), replacing working class and recent immigrant ways of life with more "cultivated" or "higher" forms of culture, art, and lifestyles.

Making no apologies for imperialism or ravaging the natural world, Wagner (1975) described this triumph:

> Our collective Culture is a vast accumulation of material and spiritual achievements and resources stemming from the conquest of nature and necessary to the continuance of this effort. It includes the substantial foundations of our cities and economic life, the massive banks of "information" and "knowledge" that fill our libraries and computers, the triumphs of art and science, and the arcane and ubiquitous labyrinths of technology. These are our heritage, our property, our life and our work, and our means of carrying forth our ideals and commitments.
>
> (p. 140)

Reflecting a healthy dose of pride in this collective "achievement," Wagner's version of "our" culture is clearly a form of power, an instrument of imperialism and domination of the natural environment—and by extension, other people.

City planners need to explicitly recognize the power of culture that plays out across so many dimensions of their work. In this sense, culture, like planning, is a practice. Its power can produce destructive behaviors and social dynamics or help bring about new bridging relationships, empowerment, and enhanced sensitivities to the needs of others and the natural world.

Culture and Place

British sociologists Michael Benson and Emma Jackson (2012) described how "places are made through repeated everyday interactions and interventions that work both on the neighborhood and the individual" (p. 794). They echo French social philosopher Henri Lefebvre (1974/1991), who constructed a three-part process he called the "production of space" (his book title). In the first part, which Lefebvre called the *perceived*, he includes multiple aspects and dimensions of the natural and built environments. Into the second, that he wrote of as the *conceived*, he folds the economic, political, legal, and other abstract enabling and governing processes. The third, and perhaps most overlooked of Lefebvre's dimensions, he called *everyday lived experience*, an idea very much in tune with *ways of life* and the city planning approach of recognizing *local knowledge* (Corburn, 2003; Geertz, 1973; Healey, 1998). Through this third dimension, people inhabit and use spaces that exist; they create and tell stories about these spaces; they make these spaces part of their ways of life and, in turn, impact how these spaces are shaped and reshaped.

Some might consider this part of *placemaking*—a term I earlier expressed reservations about. British-born design scholar living in Australia, Paul Carter (2015), described this process as "places made after their stories" (his book title). As such, the production of space is ongoing and dynamic, driven by a variety of interdependent forces. Israeli geographers Yuval Karplus and Avinoam Meir (2013) described space as "emotionally and poetically infused with symbolism and meaning derived from the lived experience of everyday life" (p. 25). The symbolism and meaning and the ways people interact with and "perform" their ways of life in public, Blokland (2017) asserted, is what defines and creates community; a sense of belonging and connectedness with others.

In spite of how cultural planning and city planning have been practiced in parallel over the past 40 years, there is no separating spatial planning from cultural planning. In other words, all three of Lefebvre's dimensions in the production of space are necessary and present in both, whether acknowledged or not. Winston Churchill, British Prime Minister during World War II, famously said, "We shape our buildings and afterwards our buildings shape us" (House of Commons, 1943, para. 1). In recognition of this complex interrelationship between culture, aesthetics, and physical space and how they act on one another, Stevenson (2014) wrote, "the multidimensional nature of culture and the extent to which culture and cultural practices are embedded in, and shaped by, cities and their spaces" (p. 154). This is to say that culturally based aesthetics, as well as hierarchical ordering, get baked into cities, their basic plan, design concepts, physical structures, and even their green or so-called "natural" spaces.

While some physical infrastructure and other elements of the built environment may be considered permanent, building cities and communities is a continuous and iterative process of meaning-making and place-shaping. In addition to, or sometimes despite, the grand schemes of city planners, designers, and architects, cities are shaped by those inhabiting them and by the everyday lived experiences—and patterns of use—of their inhabitants. In this light, American urban design and planning scholars Emily Talen and Cliff Ellis (2004) beautifully described cities as "collective works of art unfolding through time" (p. 28). Architectural historians and others attuned to the aesthetic qualities of the sequentially built environment can "read" the layers and the sociocultural dynamics shaping each piece over time (Childs, 2008).

Reflecting on how space interactively shapes the individual and creates a sense of community, Knauft (1996), like Churchill, described this reciprocal dynamic in this way:

> On the one hand individual practices are seen as constrained and orchestrated by collective structures of cultural logic or organization. But individuals are also seen as agents who reinforce or resist the large structures that encompass them. Socio-cultural life is thus both a product of societal structure and individual agency.
>
> (p. 106)

In fact, many critics of city planning and design place considerable blame on physical structures as well as socioeconomic systems of cities and suburbs for inequities and the disintegration of community life, or the ability of cultural groups to build and retain a sense of cohesion and connection to place. Such places can take many forms in daily life, including places where people live, shop, recreate, and work. Each has a cultural sensibility baked into its form and aesthetic qualities (see Chapter 6).

Culture in Smaller "Places"

Over the past few decades, it has become commonplace to discuss corporate or organizational cultures and their significance relative to success or failure of enterprises of all sizes in the for-profit, nonprofit, and public sectors. This can include organizations from two to hundreds of thousands of people. Concepts and language used to describe corporate and organizational cultures emerged in the 1960s and became widely used by the 1980s. Consultants, managers, and academics work diligently to describe and understand the culture of a company and behaviors of people within it. Those same consultants, managers, and academics may then apply concerted efforts to try to alter those cultures.

Shared or generalized beliefs, values, and behaviors often grow organically or unintentionally. Founders, charismatic leaders, and employee responses to those personalities and their policies also drive organizational cultures. Culture both enables and is enabled by management and its strategies. These include ways of communicating with and treating employees, customers, clients, and suppliers. Culture holds sway over the work environment and informs everything from appropriate dress, diversity, gender privilege, and communication protocols to risk-taking or risk aversion.

American corporate strategy guru Peter Drucker is famously supposed to have said, "culture eats strategy for breakfast" (though others lay claim to the aphorism—see "Culture Eats," 2017). Organizations and leaders have found that smart strategies, strong capitalization, strong brand identity, and other such ingredients do not constitute a recipe for success in the face of a dysfunctional culture.

In the wake of globalization and increased international workforces and customers, many global companies and even some smaller ones operating within diverse communities have learned the value of and need to create positive cross-cultural experiences and facilitate more cohesive and productive internal cultures. They invest in training to improve openness and creativity, and intentionally construct work teams with diverse members.

It has also become clear that while a corporate culture is partly attributable to founders, leaders, and employees, it is also influenced by local, regional, or national cultures and traditions of places in which the enterprise is set and where its employees reside. Inversely, corporate cultures can have a significant impact on those local cultures. The latter is particularly evident in smaller cities with a long-dominant industry, large company, and/or a powerful tycoon who set a tone for how people are treated and expectations around civic responsibilities—or lack thereof. Corporate and community cultures are thus symbiotic.

AnnaLee Saxenian, an American political economist, in her book *Regional Advantage* (1994), explored reasons for Silicon Valley's successes with the concurrent decline of Boston's high-tech corridor during the 1980s. She found that very different cultures embedded in these regions and in these companies were responsible for their success and failure. She wrote,

> It is helpful to think of a region's industrial system as having three dimensions: local institutions and culture, industrial structure, and corporate organization. ... The institutions shape and are shaped by the local culture, the shared understandings and practices that unify a community and define everything from labor market behavior to attitudes towards risk-taking.
>
> (p. 7)

Saxenian's broad sense of a region's cultural environment—its shared understandings and practices—is key to understanding how corporate and regional culture prepares some companies for contemporary global challenges and new thinking while ushering others to the scrap heap. Corporate culture, and that of the communities in which they originate and operate, may not only share characteristics, but require clear and explicit attention. "A region's culture is not static, but rather is continually reconstructed through social interaction," Saxenian wrote (1994, p. 7).

While perhaps harder to see and often more complicated than the culture of a company or institution, distinctive cultures also develop in cities, towns, and regions. Similarly, the health of that culture is critical in their success or failure. Academics, consultants, and organizational managers may be hard at work to create more healthy cultures in their efforts to ensure success of business enterprises. But who—if anyone—is addressing the cultures of cities? And, how do such complex systems change? Who, in fact, has the "right" to change the culture—*the way of life* or *ways of life*—of a community? Or, does each and every person knowingly or unknowingly contribute to these ever-changing cultures? It could be argued that city planners and designers by the very nature of their work are routinely and significantly meddling with the cultures of their communities. How aware, or intentional, are they of making such impacts?

Change Happens

In all its complexity, culture is something that changes and can itself be a force in the process of change—or in resisting change. Cultural change is constant and considered positive or negative depending on the vantage point of and the impacts on the individual, subgroup, or larger cultural entity. How cultures change is the focus of considerable debate. German anthropologist Gisela Welz (2003) argued,

> Agents of cultural change may well remain unaware of what it is they are doing because, as often as not, cultural transformation is the inconspicuous and unintended side effect of social life as it is lived, with small-scale diversions and experiments coalescing into bigger cultural trends that may eventually envelop entire societies.
>
> (p. 260)

Many artists, cultural workers, and cultural planners—let alone corporate culture consultants—might agree that they engage in small-scale diversions and experiments. They might dispute, however, that their efforts to impact the culture are unintended or meant to be inconspicuous. For many city planners and designers, it is surely unintended. Geertz (1973) suggested that the conceptions expressed in symbolic forms leave openings—evolutionary or revolutionary—in the process of communicating, perpetuating, and developing knowledge and attitudes. Similarly, Blokland (2017) recognized the evolution of cultures through daily life. Culture, she wrote, is "produced, reproduced, challenged or changed; it is in constant interaction with other cultures" (p. 44).

Forces of change and stagnation can be well-intentioned but are always present and often in opposition. Welz (2003) described how agents of change, as well as agents of the status quo—or what Wagner called opposing forces of invention and convention—interact and both draw from and pull at one another. Welz wrote,

> Cultural entities can only survive over long stretches of time by immuniz-
> ing themselves against change, but at the same time cultures are threatened
> to deteriorate into mere fossils unless they manage to transcend what they
> are and transform themselves into something new.
>
> (p. 259)

She went on to cite Wagner (1975), who wrote, "Invention changes things, and convention resolves those changes into a recognizable world" (Wagner, 1975, p. 52). This dialectical process keeps change in check while, at the same time, allows small steps to produce a brief "new normal."

Paradigm shifts are tough and their impacts not often fully evident while they're in process. The question remains, can planning embrace a broader understanding of culture, see how planning both impacts and is impacted by cultures, and foster new ways to practice planning in service to equity and the well-being of communities?

Situating Culture in Planning

What tools do city planners possess to access, understand, and navigate both with and through the multiple ways of life of people who make up cities, towns, and regions? How can they find ways to improve the condition and vibrancy of those multiple cultures and how they coexist? Can they understand and navigate power dynamics through privileging or finding equity and balance among the abundant ways of living in a given place?

In its constructive forms, culture can be a means to bring about social cohesion and peace, according to UNESCO's *Thematic Indicators for Culture* (2019). UNESCO also works to advance "the role of intangible cultural heritage as a driver and guarantor of sustainable development and how to fully integrate the safeguarding of living heritage into their development plans, policies and programmes" (p. 14). In this sense, UNESCO recognized how culture "contributes to development both as a sector of activity and transversally across other sectors" (p. 10). As such, culture is a means or vehicle for development, while it also adds value in other development areas such as health, environmental sustainability, governance, and education. Cultural approaches to development increase the relevance, sustainability, impact, and efficacy of interventions by responding to local values, traditions, practices, and beliefs. As UNESCO recognized, especially in urban centers, communities are made up of multiple cultures representing different ways of life and possessing differing dynamic trajectories or ways of maintaining and changing.

City-planning practices seem to assume that a community is either culturally homogeneous or that by ignoring cultural differences, successful planning will make it so—as if cultural homogeneity is the desired state or ultimate outcome. This way of thinking, argued Blokland (2017), "does not quite fit the contemporary world of mobilities and diversity" (p. 7). To the degree a city or community is not homogeneous, land-use planning draws boundaries and divides people, activities, and services based on limited understanding of their cultural, economic, functional, or social characteristics and ways of life.

City planners may deny that such boundaries are based on racial or cultural differences. In any event, such separations have contributed to new, more sophisticated modes of ethnic and economic segregation. American economic geographer Richard Florida (2017) provided evidence that racial and economic segregation in the United States is greater in the second decade of the 21st century than it was 60 years earlier. Legal changes had the intent of desegregating communities, but centuries of racist practices baked into institutions, systems, and the built landscape perpetuate and even further segregation and inequity.

Ways of Living Together

To address increasing diversity and a heightened role of culture in economics, politics, and other aspects of life, Young (2008) advocated for the culturalization of city planning. He cited Williams' concept of culture as a way of life, and wrote, "I pluralise his terminology to emphasize 'ways of life' and introduce it as a component in a broad synthesis of culture in my proposed planning system" (p. 19). Acknowledging multiple ways of life or cultures within a community of any size is a beginning. However, no planner can pretend to deeply understand many cultures, especially within complex urban spaces. And, while it remains important to "map" and acquire awareness and appreciation of diverse cultures and creative practices (see Chapter 7), a different approach is required to conduct effective planning that can contribute to more highly functional communities.

I advocate that planners work to understand and find ways to make an impact on *ways of living together*. "Culture expresses the connective in life," wrote Young (2008, p. 42). It is around this connective, I believe, that both cultural and city planners can most effectively focus to begin to bridge differences and formulate plans for more just, equitable, and sustainable communities.

Citing the source of the phrase *ways of living together* as a 1996 UNESCO paper by Javier Perez de Cuellar, Canadian scholars Dick Stanley and Sharon Jeannotte (2002) elaborated, saying this phrase "suggests that culture is a set of tools to help us make sense of the world and relate to each other, and to define us to each other" (p. 134). Stanley and Jeannotte saw commonality among all forms of culture, from Wagner's opera-house culture to the wider anthropological concept. They wrote,

> All "ways of living together" require and involve a degree of creativity and artistic expression ("high" and otherwise) and all our appreciations of 'the arts' inform us of what our ways of living together are. There is therefore no contradiction between these various definitions.
>
> (p. 134)

Embracing all forms of creative expression, as they suggest, fosters more welcoming and equitable communities. Privileging some forms excessively—which is the norm in the cultural sector in American cities—fosters the opposite.

From Theory to Practice

I hope theory and sociological analysis provide valuable insights for city planners. The demands of their work, however, require they get concrete. Turkish scholar Tüzin Baycan and Italian scholar Luigi Fusco Girard (2013) offered a list of cultural resources or assets relevant in a planning context, resources that can be subject to policy frameworks or initiatives. They provided one framework for mapping the culture of a community that included,

1. history
2. heritage including archeology, gastronomy, local dialects, and rituals
3. diversity of local people: the cultures of youth, ethnic minorities, and communities of interest
4. diversity and quality of leisure, cultural, eating, drinking and entertainment facilities and activities

5. arts and media activities and institutions
6. natural and built environment including public and open spaces
7. the repertoire of local products and skills in crafts, manufacturing and services, including local food products, gastronomic and design traditions
8. local milieu and institutions for intellectual and scientific innovation, including universities and private sector research centres.

(p. 274)

Most of Baycan and Girard's cultural assets are material or tangible. While a good beginning, these are limited, and do not include the many intangibles—those based in identity, proximity, the intellectual, or the spiritual. They provide a good framework for assets mapped by some progressive cultural planners; in Chapter 7, I expand on the discussion of cultural assets and approaches to mapping them. However, only a few of the resources in the list above are typically included on maps generated by most city planners.

Interestingly, Baycan and Girard's (2013) cultural resource list includes food in at least three of their eight categories. In my 2017 survey of the cultural resources included in cultural plans in the United States, described in Chapter 4, it is curious that local food and culinary arts ranked the lowest among cultural resources. While useful in looking at material elements of communities, Baycan and Girard's list provides a limited framework. It does little to expose meanings and relationships—what Young (2008) called the *connective*. I offer a framework below to help planners explore the *connective*.

Exploring Ways of Living Together

American sociologist Robert Putnam (2000) used the metaphor *bowling alone* in his illuminating work around social capital—both the bonding and bridging varieties—and how he found connective social capital decline in America in the second half of the 20th century. Formal and informal associations, such as amateur sports leagues and community theatres, are productive places to look to grasp the functionality of the less visible ways of living together. Additional areas, outlined below, map these bridging resources or the connective in communities. I present these as a set of questions or process of discovery to reveal how well communities are prepared to be more inclusive and connected. They also serve to identify assets that can be built on or deficits needing remediation.

Planners can ask questions such as the following:

- *Common values*—What things (places, organizations, events, community traits) do different people value in common? What brings people together across cultures? How do they gather and where? What kinds of spaces serve as cross-cultural gathering places? Is there an abundance of social clubs or sporting or recreational activities, and are they ethnically mixed or serving distinct groups?
- *Languages and information*—Are multiple languages present and how do people best navigate that? How do people communicate or conduct exchanges across language or ethnic groups? Where do they get information about local social, cultural, and civic affairs?
- *Civility and openness*—On a social level, how civil is the environment? Will newcomers tell you they feel welcome? Is compassion evident in public policy, daily behaviors, or in local media? Are there active efforts to bridge divides and build relationships across cultural, ethnic, and economic groups?
- *Decision-making*—How are decisions made—among small groups or across more formal governance structures? How is public debate and controversy handled—in the open or behind closed doors? Is the power structure transparent or difficult to penetrate? Does this vary for some people based on their ethnicity, gender, or sexuality? Is volunteerism valued? Is it limited to certain insider/old-timer groups? Are there many activist groups organized around a variety of local, national, and/or international issues?
- *Conscious design*—Is there evidence the community values thoughtful design of public spaces and prominent private structures? Do the designs of those spaces reflect the cultures of people present, and do structures express openness, fear, or exclusion?
- *Regulations*—Are municipal agencies and departments known as restrictive or enabling? Are they overly regulatory in terms of activities in public spaces, or are they permissive and help individuals and groups find solutions to conduct social, cultural, and commercial activities?
- *Transport and security*—How do people move about the community? Do they walk, drive, use public transit, and ride bicycles or scooters, and how do they interact with one another in public spaces? Is the community rife with gated subdivisions and/or is there evidence in the architecture of heavy security concerns? Or does it feel welcoming and open?
- *Education and youth*—Are education and youth enrichment valued? Are there spaces and varied activities for young people? Are the elderly present, visible, active, respected, and cared for?
- *Valuing the natural environment*—Is there concern for the natural environment, clean waterways, recycling programs? How well are parks, green

spaces, and recreational facilities funded? Are they well used and cared for by users? Do activist groups make up for inadequate public funding by raising private dollars for youth, parks, libraries, or schools?

- *Appreciating history*—Is the local history and the histories of some subgroups recognized by institutions and in the public realm, and are others not? Whose histories are acknowledged, celebrated, contested? Is there a sense of pride or shame in that history; if so, around what events or personalities?
- *Food*—Is locally sourced food valued? Are there active farmers' markets and restaurants that boast farm-to-table menus? Are small businesses and entrepreneurs supported? Is there a wide mix of ethnic restaurants and groceries? Are they patronized across cultural groups?
- *Arts and artists*—Is there a vibrant community of artists and arts and cultural organizations? Do they represent and include people of many ethnicities? Are there a variety of organizations that include professional, voluntary, grassroots, or those of long- or once-dominant cultural groups?

Some of these questions are more or less complicated depending on a community's size and character. The real value of Putnam's phrase *bridging social capital* is in the individual's or community's *capacity* to bridge. Capacity is ultimately a more important measure than the number of bridges. Capacity is surely harder to see but becomes evident when answers to the above questions show patterns of active bridging or exclusion. Together, this portrait or map of a community provides excellent data on whether a community can be successful and has capacity to foster productive ways of living together.

Summary

A core question for both cultural planners and city planners is how culture is described and how ways of understanding culture privilege some ways of life—cultural practices, use of public space, access to resources and services, and other aspects of community life—over others. Masking the profound importance of culture by conflating it with narrowly delineated creative practices, institutions, and art forms, exacerbates inequities and denies full inclusion and empowerment across all dimensions of concern to city planners and policymakers.

The myriad areas of concern city planners face cannot be fully understood or addressed unless culture and its implications are made part of the explicit process of discovery and conversation. Lack of understanding of the various cultures and ways of life within a community and how they coexist and best function together results in policy choices and physical development patterns that institutionalize privilege for some while denying others access to resources and to fully exercise their ways of life. In the face of such a lack of understanding, the entire community remains constrained in its ability to include new people and to function as a diverse, inclusive, and multicultured community. Like a dysfunctional corporate environment, a dysfunctional community signals decline.

Can city planners, as well as cultural planners, come together around such a shift in ways of understanding and including culture in their work? Can they help their communities be more open and highly functional? Rather than beginning with deep dives into land use, can city planners start by mapping and appreciating many ways of living together among residents, workers, newcomers, and visitors? Can city and cultural planning practices refocus on understanding and improving life and ways of living together? Or will the two planning practices continue to confine themselves within a narrow understanding or even obliviousness to culture in ways that, in fact, feed dysfunction and perform a disservice to their communities?

The next chapter focuses on cultural planning in the United States, how it has evolved, and in what ways it has both held back and contributed to the ability of communities to welcome and include more ways of life and ways of living together.

References

Baycan, T., & Girard, L. F. (2013). Case study window – Culture in international sustainability practices and perspectives: The experience of 'slow city movement – Cittaslow'. In G. Young & D. Stevenson (Eds.), *The Ashgate research companion to planning and culture* (pp. 273–292). Abingdon: Ashgate.

Benson, M., & Jackson, E. (2012). Place-making and place maintenance: Performativity, place and belonging among the middle classes. *Sociology, 47*(4), 793–809. doi:10.1177/0038038512454350

Blokland, T. (2017). *Community as urban practice*, Cambridge: Polity Press.

Carter, P. (2015). *Places made after their stories: Design and the art of choreotopography*. Crawley: UWA Publishing.

Childs, M. C. (2008). Storytelling and urban design. *Journal of Urbanism, 1*(2), 173–186. doi:10.1080/17549170802221526

Collins, B. (2018). Whose culture, whose neighborhood? Fostering and resisting neighborhood change in the multiethnic enclave. *Journal of Planning Education and Research*, 1–14. doi:10.1177/0739456X18755496

Corburn, J. (2003). Bringing local knowledge into environmental decision making: Improving urban planning for communities at risk. *Journal of Planning Education and Research, 22*(4), 420–433. doi:10.1177/0739456X03022004008

Drucker, P. (2017). Culture eats strategy for breakfast. *Quote Investigator*. Retrieved from https://quoteinvestigator.com/2017/05/23/culture-eats/

Florida, R. (2017). *The new urban crisis: How our cities are increasing inequality, deepening segregation, and failing the middle class – And what we can do about it.* New York, NY: Basic Books.

Gans, H. J. (1991). *People, plans, and policies: Essays on poverty, racism, and other national urban problems.* New York, NY: Columbia University Press.

Gates, H. L. (1993). *Loose canons: Notes on the culture wars.* Oxford: Oxford University Press.

Geertz, C. (1973). *The interpretation of cultures.* New York, NY: Basic Books.

Healey, P. (1998). Building institutional capacity through collaborative approaches to urban planning. *Environment and Planning A, 30,* 1531–1546.

House of Commons. (1943, October 28). *House of Commons rebuilding.* Retrieved from https://api.parliament.uk/historic-hansard/commons/1943/oct/28/house-of-commons-rebuilding

Hunter, J. D. (1992). *Culture wars: The struggle to control the family, art, education, law, and politics in America.* New York, NY: Basic Books.

Karplus, Y., & Meir, A. (2013). The production of space: A neglected perspective in pastoral research. *Environment and Planning D: Society and Space, 31*(1), 23–42. doi:10.1068/d13111

Knauft, B. M. (1996). *Genealogies for the present in cultural anthropology.* New York, NY: Routledge.

Lefebvre, H. (1991). *The production of space* (D. Nicholson-Smith, Trans). Oxford: Blackwell. (Original work published in 1974)

Noman, M., & Gurr, D. (2020). Contextual leadership and culture in education. In G. W. Noblit (Ed.), *Oxford research encyclopedia of education.* New York, NY: Oxford University Press. doi:10.1093/acreforce/9780190264093.013.595

Putnam, R. D. (2000). *Bowling alone: The collapse and revival of American community.* New York, NY: Simon & Schuster.

Qadeer, M. A. (1997). Pluralistic planning for multicultural cities: The Canadian practice. *Journal of the American Planning Association, 63*(4), 481–494. doi:10.1080/0194436970897594

Quinn, J. A. (1940). The Burgess zonal hypothesis and its critics. *American Sociological Review, 5*(2), 210–218. doi:10.2307/2083636

Saxenian, A. (1994). *Regional advantage: Culture and competition in Silicon Valley and Route 128.* Cambridge, MA: Harvard University Press.

Searle, G. (2013). Case study window – Discourse, doctrine and habitus: Redevelopment contestation on Sydney's harbor-edge. In G. Young & D. Stevenson (Eds.), *The Ashgate research companion to planning and culture* (pp. 135–152). Abingdon: Ashgate.

Stanley, D., & Jeannotte, M. S. (2002). How will we live together?. *Canadian Journal of Communication, 27*(2/3), 133–139.

Stein, S. (2019). *Capital city: Gentrification and the real estate state.* New York, NY: Verso Books.

Stevens, H. (1893). *The new laws of the Indies for the good treatment and preservation of the Indians promulgated by the Emperor Charles the Fifth 1542–1543* (Facsimile reprint of the original Spanish edition). London: Chiswick Press. Retrieved from https://books.google.ca/books?hl=en&lr=&id=tuQ1AQAAMAAJ&oi=fnd&pg=PA1&dq

=New+Laws+of+the+Indies+&ots=P5CqKNZPfl&sig=W_
L0Wi38xqwsKncU2AAly-lOli0#v=onepage&q=New%20Laws%20of%20the%20
Indies&f=false

Stevenson, D. (2014). *Cities of culture: A global perspective*. London: Routledge.

Talen, E., & Ellis, C. (2004). Cities as art: Exploring the possibility of an aesthetic dimension in planning. *Planning Theory & Practice, 5*(1), 11–32. doi:10.1080/1464935042000185044

UNESCO. (1982). *World conference on cultural policies, Mexico City, July 26–August 6, 1982.* Paris: UNESCO. Retrieved from https://unesdoc.unesco.org/ark:/48223/pf0000052505/PDF/052505engo.pdf.multi

UNESCO. (2019). *Thematic indicators for culture in the 2030 Agenda*. Retrieved from https://unesdoc.unesco.org/ark:/48223/pf0000371562?posInSet=24&queryId=dd28b7d8-d0de-4630-b2ba-edff805e3af4

Wagner, R. (1975). *The invention of culture*. Chicago, IL: University of Chicago Press.

Ward, S. (2013). A cultural history of modern urban planning. In G. Young & D. Stevenson (Eds.), *The Ashgate research companion to planning and culture* (pp. 37–52). Abingdon: Ashgate.

Watson, V. (2013). Planning theory and practice in a global context. In G. Young & D. Stevenson (Eds.), *The Ashgate research companion to planning and culture* (pp. 121–134). Abingdon: Ashgate.

Welz, G. (2003). The cultural swirl: Anthropological perspectives on innovation. *Global Networks, 3*(3), 255–270. doi:10.1111/1471-0374.00061

Williams, R. (1976). *Keywords: A vocabulary of culture and society*. New York, NY: Oxford University Press.

Young, G. (2008). *Reshaping planning with culture*. London: Routledge. doi:10.4324/9781315605647

Young, G. (2013a). Introduction: Culture and planning in a grain of sand. In G. Young & D. Stevenson (Eds.), *The Ashgate research companion to planning and culture* (pp. 1–20). Abingdon: Ashgate.

Young, G. (2013b). Stealing the fire of life: A cultural paradigm for planning and governance. In G. Young & D. Stevenson (Eds.), *The Ashgate research companion to planning and culture* (pp. 393–410). Abingdon: Ashgate.

Chapter 4

A Force Awakens
Cultural Planning at 40—A Turn to Community in the Arts

> *Since late in the twentieth century, the relationship between art-making and commu-*
> *nity-making has been transformed by a surge of new or renewed interest in the idea*
> *of community across all art forms.*
> —Wyatt, MacDowall, and Mulligan (2013, p. 82)

Is such a turn-to-community that Wyatt et al. observed affirmed through the practice and outcomes of cultural planning? Are more arts and culture agencies and local cultural sectors turning part of their focus outward to impact their communities in multiple ways? Understanding more about the directions and outcomes of cultural planning may help city planners better see how cultural sector aspirations and impacts are addressed through cultural planning and where their work may intersect. Data and cases in this chapter explore whether cultural planning has shown itself catalytic in local policy-setting and organizing the sector to apply its capacities to address a range of community needs.

My recent study, *Cultural Planning at 40* (Borrup, 2018), found that cultural planning continues to produce a turn to community, earlier observed by Dreeszen (1994):

> The larger-than-the-arts community involvement in cultural planning accelerates what would otherwise be a gradual shift in emphasis from arts development to also embrace community development. Planning sometimes

helps achieve a better balance between these dual objectives. It may be during cultural planning that the potential for reciprocity may be understood and the arts and larger communities appreciate what each may do for the other.

(p. 91)

While this is not the case in all communities, and not without shortcomings, research presented in this chapter affirms that cultural plans—like most plans—are aspirational and do make an impact even when short of achieving all their goals. Findings reviewed here look at cultural planning in the United States as of 2017 with many direct comparisons to Dreeszen's research 23 years earlier.

Citing plans in four cities as outliers that he felt addressed wider community involvement of their local arts and cultural sector, Dreeszen (1994) found they were "not typical of cultural planning documented in this study," and he went on to speculate that they may "represent the next generation of the practice" (p. 244). In exploring this next generation of cultural plans, this chapter includes a survey of 50 cities and describes three such next-generation plans produced in recent years.

With arts agencies that he saw exemplifying this next generation, Dreeszen (1994) wrote that they "find themselves as facilitators, conveners, partnership brokers, problem-solvers, information centers, and advocates of the community and the arts" (p. 239). This, however, was in contrast to his finding that most cultural plans focused on advocating that communities should contribute more to the arts, rather than identifying how the arts can contribute more to their communities—a pattern that shows some change in the 2017 data.

In *Cultural Planning at 40*, I explored these questions: Have cities embraced cultural planning as integral to their comprehensive planning as Dreeszen advocated? Have cultural planners stepped up to more sophisticated research and planning techniques? Has cultural planning contributed to a community turn, and in what ways? In the study, I surveyed arts and culture agencies in the United States that commissioned cultural plans within the most recent decade. Data were collected through an online survey I designed in consultation with Dreeszen as well as Randy Cohen and Graciella Kahn at Americans for the Arts. A total of 50 surveys from cities of a variety of sizes were completed. The survey included many of the same questions asked by Dreeszen (1994) so as to compare trends in the cultural planning process, characteristics of plans, their intentions, and subsequent community outcomes as reported by the entities leading or sponsoring cultural plans.

Cultural planning practice and plans produced in communities across the United States demonstrate changes in approaches and topical concerns in some areas, while in others there has been surprisingly little change. My study detected some progress in the levels of planning professionalism and in the breadth of community concerns addressed. Interesting comparisons were revealed in areas where the two studies (Dreeszen's and mine), over two decades apart, asked the same questions. The scope of issues addressed, and expectations community leaders had for planning versus outcomes they experienced, illustrate some of the most significant changes. However, progress in the impacts of cultural planning fell short in two significant areas: integration of cultural planning with city planning, and expanding inclusion of and resources for "underrepresented communities"—meaning communities of color and immigrant communities, populations that actually represent majorities in many cities.

Equity in Cultural Planning

As described earlier, variations in cultural planning from place to place and over time put its purposes on a spectrum that ranges from reinforcing dominant institutional cultural practices to identifying and equitably weaving the capacities and cultural assets of communities into a broad complement of civic concerns. Most cultural planning in the United States falls closer to the former, old-school side of this spectrum. More recently, however, a trend towards widening approaches to culture and to the cultural sector serving broader community goals has emerged.

There are haves and have-nots in every community when it comes to the financial resources, facilities, and policies pertaining to cultural practices, the things cultural planning typically addresses. In so doing, planning generally favors one or more groups of people (or cultures) over others. Cultural planning, however, has not done a good job at arriving at a more equitable balance. Findings show that many who sponsor cultural plans express a goal to achieve a more inclusive and equitable distribution of resources across diverse ethnic culture groups, but outcomes fall far short of these intentions.

Landing on a more inclusive understanding of culture, or—more appropriately—an approach to addressing it within a local context, as described in earlier chapters, could help clarify the value and unique local purpose of cultural planning. The *process* of arriving at a local understanding in itself may be of greatest value as a way of opening the discussion in each given place and time.

Recent Cultural Plans: Framing Culture

Dreeszen (1994) found that during the first dozen years of formal cultural planning in the United States, practitioners did not articulate what they meant by culture, yet plans expressed a narrow approach. He observed that "neither art nor culture is defined in plans or in the literature on cultural planning" (p. 20), and that,

> With some notable exceptions, most cultural planning centers upon the interests of arts organizations, arts audiences, and artists. Some plans focus on the arts and assert no pretensions to transform communities. Others purport to plan for the entire community but are concerned with that community mostly for its potential support of the arts.
>
> (p. 243)

Dreeszen drew his assessment of how culture was defined from an analysis of the text of over 100 plan documents. *Cultural Planning at 40* did not replicate his text analysis but asked a series of questions of local arts and cultural agencies related to elements of culture included or cultural resources addressed in their planning process. Similar to Dreeszen's findings, my more recent survey found that few cultural plans explicitly describe a meaning of culture. He acknowledged the challenge of determining "widely shared aesthetic values" in cultural plans (Dreeszen, 1994, p. 237) and observed that "cultural plans are usually concerned with nonprofit visual and performing arts, artists, arts audiences, arts education, public art, arts facilities and systems of funding support" (p. 20), thus suggesting a limited concept.

In the 2017 survey, the top cluster of cultural resources included in plans, as indicated by more than three-quarters of surveyed plans, were as follows:

- The nonprofit arts sector—94%
- Art fairs and festivals—86%
- Independent artists—80%
- Cultural organizations including history and heritage—78%
- Youth service organizations with creative or cultural activities—78%

Rounding out the top third were the following:

- Organizations serving ethnic communities—74%

- Neighborhood- or city-wide festivals celebrating other aspects of history, culture, or ideologies—74%
- Educational entities—66%

The above are commonly, although clearly not consistently, assumed among the typical players and venues in a contemporary arts community. Among a less commonly identified mix of activities and entities, as indicated by between 50% and 60%, were the following:

- Activities promoting civic engagement—60%
- Public celebrations recognizing outstanding people or ideas—58%
- Neighborhood-based or social service organizations with creative or cultural activities—56%
- For-profit creative businesses that sell, display, or present unique or locally designed products or services—54%
- For-profit creative businesses that design or produce unique local products or services—52%
- Recreational, outdoor, or environmental organizations and activities—50%

The cluster between 50% and 60% includes resources outside what are typically considered arts entities and activities; none of them were named in Dreeszen's (1994) study. These included for-profit enterprises in the creative sector along with recreational and environmental activities. However, the fact that only 56% included the creative or cultural activities within neighborhood-based or social service organizations is sad. On the other hand, that likely represents a significant change from 1994.

Among activities selected by fewer than 50%, there was a precipitous drop to below one-third:

- For-profit creative businesses that present or exhibit products imported into the community—32%
- Local food growing or producing entities—24%
- Culinary arts—22%

From Vermont to Louisiana, among other regions of the United States, culinary arts and local food products are core to their sense of identity and creative endeavors—not to mention local economies—yet those resources scored lowest of all cultural resources.

Recent Cultural Plans: Inequity in Resource Distribution

One area of my inquiry (Borrup, 2018) was the impact of cultural planning on underrepresented communities—known also as communities of color and/or immigrant communities. Among 17 outcome categories tracked for cultural plans, allocation of more resources for underrepresented communities ranked the lowest. While 70% said they entered the planning process hoping to see more resources allocated to underrepresented communities, only 30% reported this an outcome and a mere 4% reported allocating "much more" with 26% reporting "somewhat more." This represents the largest divide between expectations and outcomes. The fact that 58% reported allocations were the same as before planning represents the highest rating of "no change" out of all outcome categories. Only 2% indicated that less was allocated to underrepresented groups following cultural planning, and 10% said they didn't know (Figure 4.1).

In other responses, under half (48%) said their plan included specific actions to address issues of diversity, equity, and inclusion in the cultural life of the community. This leaves a majority who said it did not, a shocking finding for the cultural sector in the United States in a 21st-century context. In a related question about the removal of barriers to create more cultural participation, 82% entered cultural planning expecting this outcome with 52% reporting progress subsequent to planning. The spread of 30% between expectation and outcome

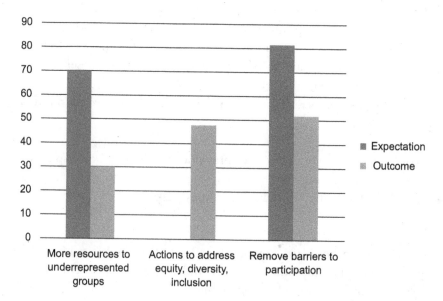

Figure 4.1 Expectations versus outcomes relative to cultural equity and inclusion in cultural plans (Borrup, 2018).

is nearly double the average variation between expectations and outcomes in all areas surveyed, indicating a high level of disappointment with progress or inability to achieve progress in this area.

Overall, the 2017 study showed cultural planning to be aspirational—as it should be—and that the cultural sector increasingly works to address a growing range of civic concerns. However, as the data above indicates, efforts related to diversity, equity, and inclusion showed the lowest results.

Recent Cultural Plans: Types and Planning Process

Most cultural planners do not conform to consistent or strictly-adhered-to typologies or methodologies. Dreeszen outlined a menu of nine types of plans in a 1998 workbook published by Americans for the Arts used by many cities across the United States for over two decades. The 2017 survey revealed more plans were considered *Comprehensive Community Cultural Plans* versus those with a focus on specific issues—such as facility planning—or cultural district or community arts plans. Respondents were also asked to choose from a variety of descriptions that characterize the process of planning ("process" was defined in the question as *the way the planning was conducted to involve the public, artists, organizations, and municipal agencies.*) Respondents could select as many choices as they liked, and the average number of choices per respondent was 2.5 (Figure 4.2).

The most common descriptor, *robust and engaging*, was selected by 64%. The second, at 58%, was *well worth the time and resources.* While these represent a positive experience, it may be discouraging that 36% and 42% respectively did not feel the process was robust and engaging or well worth the time and resources. The characteristic of *creative*, selected by 38%, presumably contrasts with the 12% who said it seemed *academic or research-based*, or the 28% who characterized it as *standard municipal planning*. Only 22% said it was *efficient*, with only 12% saying it was *abbreviated* and 8% describing it as *too long*. In the aggregate, this suggests a majority felt the time spent was appropriate and planning was engaging and worthwhile.

Quality planning processes appear to have an impact on the outcomes. Using the same definition of planning process as above, 80% responded that the process itself made a positive difference, indicating that well-constructed planning was appreciated by a strong majority. This also indicated that cultural planners have developed techniques to strengthen community involvement. In some cases, these planning processes have spawned tangential or unexpected positive outcomes, as many open-ended comments described.

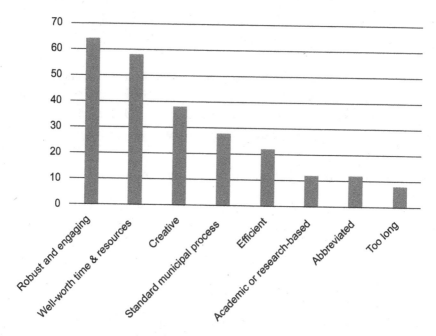

Figure 4.2 Character of the planning process (Borrup, 2018).

Professionalization of Cultural Planning

Between 1994 and 2017, average time for planning grew a little shorter (Figure 4.3) while costs of planning increased about 10%, adjusted for inflation (Figure 4.4). There was an increase in the number of plans that were led by consultants, and data collection methods became more sophisticated. Together, these suggest an increasing professionalization of the practice.

During the decade of cultural planning studied by Dreeszen, between 66% and 70% of plans involved a consultant. Of respondents to the 2017 survey, 80% reported the use of consultants. This indicates an increase in the use of professionals in the field and/or a sense among local agencies that the process had grown more complicated and required assistance from experienced or qualified planners. Of consultants employed, the 2017 survey found that a majority were considered national consultants and just under one-third were from the local area or region. Teams that mixed local and national consultants were used in 17.5% of plans, and a small number of consultants were considered international. Dreeszen did not seek similar data to characterize consultants.

However, the 2017 survey found that only 41% of consultants engaged to conduct or facilitate cultural planning were understood to have cultural planning as their primary area of expertise (Figure 4.5), and 17% of respondents

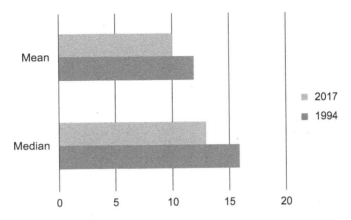

Figure 4.3 Duration for completion of cultural plans (Borrup, 2018).

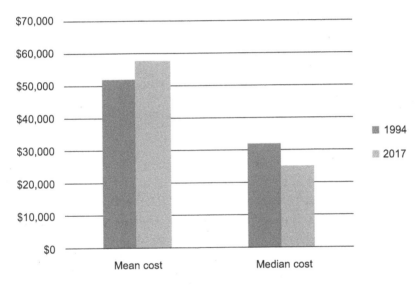

Figure 4.4 Mean and median cost of cultural plans adjusted to 2016 dollars (Borrup, 2018).

said they didn't know the primary expertise of consultants their community engaged. Others brought expertise in economic development, arts management and marketing, and other specialties.

Because early cultural planning in the United States grew as a vehicle to address the interests of arts organizations, Dreeszen (1994) found it borrowed methods from strategic planning and marketing research. He wrote, "the tendency of cultural plans to rely upon the simplest planning methods suggests that some training into more sophisticated techniques would be helpful" (p. 234). In the same light, Dreeszen asserted that "local arts agencies and [cultural]

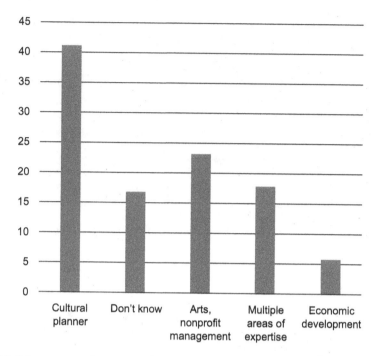

Figure 4.5 Primary areas of expertise of cultural planning consultants in 2017 (Borrup, 2018).

planning consultants could learn more about the political nature of community planning" (p. 234).

In the United States, there is no organized *field* of cultural planning and no recognition of the profession of cultural planner. There is a *marketplace* in which municipal or cultural agency *buyers* issue requests-for-proposals or for qualifications to which independent consultants or firms respond with a variety of skills to compete for contracts. In a few cases, cultural agency staff produce plans as a service to their municipal or institutional constituencies. The mix of professional backgrounds of those conducting cultural plans reflects the dearth of professional training and development in the practice, as well as a lack of understanding of the practice and/or a mix of expectations by commissioning entities.

As described in Chapter 2, different cultural planners bring different orientations and processes. There is no formal accreditation, training, professional associations, or publications for cultural planners. People who call themselves cultural planners range from former executives at nonprofit arts organizations or local arts agencies, to community arts activists, to city planners or strategic planners with an interest in the arts. During the Great Recession of 2007–2009, some desperate-for-work architecture firms competed, sometimes successfully, for cultural planning contracts, bringing a built-environment emphasis. There are no standards of practice or formally recognized methods.

Cultural Planning Methods

Data gathering does appear to have become more sophisticated since 1994, as Dreeszen (1994) recommended. Respondents to the 2017 survey indicated they used more sources of data and tools for engaging their communities. In his 1994 research, Dreeszen found the top five methods employed were:

1. focus groups
2. interviews with opinion leaders
3. surveys of arts and cultural organizations
4. public/town hall meetings
5. random sample public surveys

He reported only two other techniques: economic impact research of the cultural sector and audience/demographic research.

The 2017 survey of data-gathering methodologies (Figure 4.6) offered more choices in response to a proliferation of known data-gathering and community engagement methods, and there appeared to be growing use of such techniques.

The top three remained the same as in 1994 but not in the same order. The top five in 2017 were:

1. interviews with opinion leaders
2. community focus groups
3. surveys of arts and cultural organizations
4. audience or demographic research
5. economic impact of the cultural sector

Also employed in more than half the plans and at the same rate in both surveys were public/town hall meetings. Public or town hall-style meetings are a formal requirement for most city planning processes in the United States. Thus, it seems surprising that it was used by fewer than 60% of cultural planning projects.

Perhaps most interestingly, several techniques reported in the 2017 survey were not found in the Dreeszen study: cultural asset mapping, used by 42%;

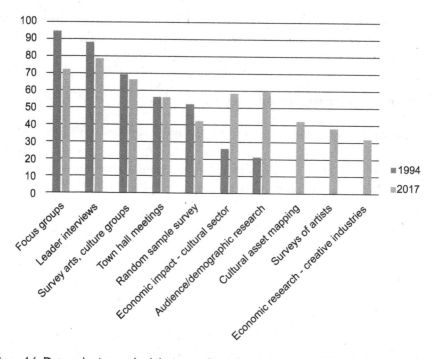

Figure 4.6 Data gathering methodologies used in cultural planning in 2017 (Borrup, 2018).

surveys of artists, used by 38%; and economic research on the creative industries, used by 32%. While cultural asset mapping is widely accepted in other parts of the world as the first step in cultural planning, at least in the United States, it was not recognized as a planning method until the early to mid-2000s. And, given that fewer than half those surveyed in 2017 used asset mapping, it still cannot be considered standard practice.

In descending order, additional methods not reflected in Figure 4.6 used by between 20% and 30% were:

- branding/identity research
- artist–led creative processes
- interactive web/social media
- partnerships with municipal agencies
- partnerships with community groups
- partnerships with academic institutions

This wider mix of methods suggest greater sophistication and presumably inclusion of more people, organizations, and data sources.

Relationship to City Comprehensive Plans

Dreeszen (1994) asked a singular question related to the relationship of cultural plans to municipal planning and found 49% of plans had been adopted formally as part of their respective city comprehensive plan. As described in an earlier chapter, my 2017 survey (Borrup, 2018) found insignificant change since the early 1990s, with 52% reporting their plan had been adopted into the city comprehensive plan. While Dreeszen (1994) advocated that cultural planning "needs to be integrated with other forms of community-wide planning" (p. 234), the lack of progress in the percentage of cultural plans adopted into city comprehensive plans was another disappointing finding.

Expectations Versus Outcomes

Reasons for entering into cultural planning were the subject of a series of questions in the early part of the 2017 survey. Parallel questions towards the end of the survey related to outcomes or changes respondents observed. In most cases, expectations for planning were greater than outcomes reported. In all but one of 22 questions, expectations exceeded subsequent outcomes by an average of 18 points. More importantly, in comparison with data from 1994, the types of expectations and outcomes changed significantly.

Planning to Advance Cultural Sector Needs

The highest positive outcome reported in 2017 was in building connections among the cultural activities in the community. Eighty-eight percent hoped to achieve this result, in contrast to 84% who rated this as a positive outcome, also one the highest expectation-to-outcome showings (Figure 4.7).

The greatest variation between expectation and outcome in the 2017 survey was in finding new financial resources for the arts and cultural work, where 90% rated this an important goal against 46% who reported it as an actual outcome. This leaves 44% who were disappointed in this regard. Were expectations inordinately raised about the power of cultural planning to produce new resources, or had cultural planning taken on more expanded meaning?

In other outcomes, 80% in the 2017 survey indicated they entered planning hoping to better organize the cultural community to advocate on its own behalf, and 72% reported they achieved more capacity for advocacy after planning. In 1994, Dreeszen found that 59% entered planning with this expectation compared with only 19% who indicated favorable outcomes in capacity for

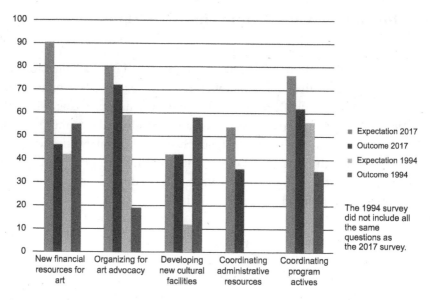

Figure 4.7 **Expectations versus outcomes relative to concerns within the cultural sector** (Borrup, 2018).

collective advocacy. This suggests cultural planning, after a couple subsequent decades of work, has emerged as an efficient vehicle for sector organizing.

An area with one of the lower expectations was assessing the need and viability of new cultural facilities, with 42% expecting progress in that area and the same percentage indicating affirmative results. Dreeszen reported only 12% in the 1994 survey entered planning with that expectation but 58% indicated new facilities as an outcome. This was one of two areas in the Dreeszen report where outcomes rated higher than expectations. The other, mentioned above, was in finding new financial resources. These suggest that cultural planning from the 1980s was, as Dreeszen concluded, centered more on the interests of arts organizations and arts audiences.

Planning to Advance Community Needs

The top reason cited for conducting a cultural plan in the 2017 survey, at 94%, was to enable the cultural sector to make greater community impact. The kind of impact was not specified, but this indicates a desire to contribute outwardly to the community rather than an inward focus on benefits planning could bring to the sector. Considerably fewer—76%—reported greater community impact resulted from their plan, and 18% reported impact had not changed (Figure 4.8).

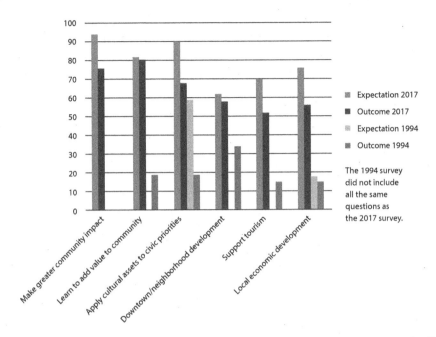

Figure 4.8 Expectations versus outcomes relative to community-wide concerns (Borrup, 2018).

The second-highest positive outcome was in learning new ways arts and culture can bring value to the community, with 80% reporting gains in this area against 82% hoping for this result, the most consistent expectation-to-outcome. In the 1994 study, only 19% reported learning new ways to bring value to the community as an outcome, a dramatic change in the nature of expectations between the two time periods.

In the 2017 data, tied for second-highest expectation with finding new financial resources was identifying strategies to apply cultural resources to civic priorities. In this case, 90% anticipated this from planning while 68% indicated improvement in applying cultural resources to civic concerns. This compares with only 19% who indicated it as an outcome in 1994.

Involvement in downtown or neighborhood development as well as economic and tourism development are all areas that showed consistently higher outcomes in 2017. These are areas that seem to have more contemporary relevance as the cultural sector began to see itself taking a role in local economic development since the 1990s. Organizing arts and culture for downtown or neighborhood development was an expectation among 62% in 2017, with 58% reporting greater impact on development. In 1994, 34% indicated downtown or neighborhood development as a result. Mobilizing the cultural sector to pro-mote tourism was an expectation among 70% in 2017, with 52% experiencing positive outcomes. Only 15% of respondents in the Dreeszen study indicated favorable outcomes related to tourism.

The contrast in outcomes between the 1994 and 2017 surveys reflect con-siderably different priorities. The most significant single outcome reported in 1994 was that new financial resources were generated for the arts. The second most significant was bolstering education and youth development followed closely by new cultural facilities. In 2017, these were among the lowest out-come areas. Instead, building connections within the cultural sector, learning new ways to add value to communities, better organizing the cultural commu-nity for greater community impact, and better organizing for advocacy were the top outcomes. This indicates both changing conditions and expectations in the arts sector and a shift in the purpose of cultural planning. It provides evidence of a community turn.

Another Generation of Cultural Plans

As a cultural planner in various communities, I have the opportunity to open discussions of how culture should be considered through the planning pro-cess and how to include personal, family, or subgroup traditions and various cultural and creative practices. In some northern cities, I have found winter sports enthusiasts readily adopt the idea that their favorite outdoors pursuits should be considered central to the community's cultural life. Youth and ama-teur sports are often a big part of the community ethos. Also, I have found cyclists and pedestrians working to change attitudes and behaviors towards nonmotorized modes of transportation to be happy to consider their work as addressing the culture of their community. Local beer, wine, or craft food producers enthusiastically embrace their products as emblematic of the local culture and sense of identity, not to mention a center of social activity. Some individuals from communities of color and immigrant groups are pleased to come to planning tables although skeptical that the latest invitation will bring about actual change, as previous invitations have not. In some places, traditions, celebrations, and ways of life of underrepresented communities have inched into institutional recognition.

At least during blue-sky planning activities, I find thinking among some lead-ers expanding, as described above. However, when it comes time to codify the work into municipal policy and resource distribution, the gravitational pull of the arts, described in Chapter 2, often brings them back to the familiar. However, opening space for public conversations about the meanings and parameters of culture in cultural planning remains an important and underdeveloped purpose.

Next-Generation Plans: Three Case Studies

The following are three cases that represent a generation of cultural plans where broader community concerns drove the planning process. Rather than beginning with propelling the growth and development of the cultural sector, in these cases, the community took stock of its cultural and creative resources and capacities and looked for ways to build partnerships across community actors to address broader community concerns.

Des Moines, Iowa

In 2016, forward-thinking and civically minded leadership in Des Moines launched a project to broaden the impact of the cultural sector in a rapidly growing and diversifying metropolitan area. The effort was led by the President of Drake University, a prominent private institution with wide-ranging interests in the future of the area and wide-ranging expertise to call upon and facilitated by a team I co-led. Bravo Greater Des Moines was the sponsoring agency, a nonprofit formed to aggregate and distribute regional arts, culture, and heritage funding generated by lodging taxes from 17 adjoining municipalities. A select group of community leaders assembled to guide the effort to "identify opportunities to leverage arts and culture as essential drivers of quality of life and economic development in Central Iowa" (Bravo Greater Des Moines, n.d., para.1).

Seeking to ground the efforts in well-researched and broadly vetted community concerns, the project chose a recent plan by Capital Crossroads, a broad-based initiative to rally key players around a vision and problem-solving strategies in the Central Iowa region. Capital Crossroads' plan included 10 "catalyst priorities" (Bravo Greater Des Moines, n.d., para. 4) ranging from vibrant downtowns and workforce development to transportation, educational opportunities, water and soil quality, inclusivity, and housing. These served as touchstones for the cultural assessment and guideposts for strategy development. Surveys, focus groups, steering committee meetings, and a town hall meeting were conducted. Explicit community-based sessions were coconvened and cohosted by leaders from African American, Latinx, Asian American, youth services, education, and other important communities. Mapping included identifying existing ways that cultural programs, organizations, and individual artists addressed the 10 Capital Crossroads priorities. Steering committee members subsequently prioritized the following areas based on these criteria:

- current traction and relationships
- affinity, passion, and interest
- overall viability to make a difference
- existence of multiple avenues to approach the concern
- potential broad, formal, and informal community participation

They arrived at four strategic initiatives:

- advance more active and vibrant neighborhoods and community hubs;
- build the local economy by developing the talents and skills of creative entrepreneurs;
- expand community diversity, inclusiveness, and equity by recognizing and supporting more diverse arts, cultures, and heritages; and
- ensure that all young people have access to education and recreation infused with creative and cultural experiences

This effort represented a turning point in thinking about how the cultural sector can bring unique value to key areas of civic concern rather than approaching it as an exercise in broadening support for the arts. From a process point of view, the planning effort began not with the needs and concerns of the cultural sector but with the needs and concerns of the larger community. It then explored ways the cultural sector does and can make contributions to community-wide priorities.

Lawrence, Kansas

In a 2015 cultural planning project commissioned by the City of Lawrence, our team found a progressive and highly engaged cultural community that quickly focused on social, economic, physical, and educational concerns of the larger community (Borrup & Harris, 2015). While not unconcerned with the infrastructure and support of the cultural sector itself, larger community concerns were palpable and foremost. Artists and cultural leaders wanted to find ways to address homelessness and mental health, safety of children walking to school, healthy and sustainable food systems, and other matters.

When we arrived, the community was embroiled in a controversy where an aggressive downtown visual arts center had launched a well-funded creative placemaking effort. The nonprofit was sandwiched between a historically Black working-class neighborhood and the downtown. In an unusual situation, artists and neighbors organized to block efforts of the art center. The strong-willed director pushed the project that included "big-name" British artists who would redesign public spaces and walkways through the neighborhood. The art center director was seen by some to be in league with developers, hotel operators, and other business interests and not considerate to the needs and interests of neighborhood residents. Local artists felt undervalued, and neighbors felt an aesthetic incursion and a long-term threat to affordability of their homes. This was not part of our planning charge but was very much "in the air" at the time and had to be addressed on a symbolic and policy level with people having the opportunity to speak out.

Local pride, a high level of community activism, and progressive thinking propelled the Lawrence plan to arrive at a set of seven key values:

- diverse and inclusive citizen engagement
- collaboration and transparency
- respect for history and heritage
- authenticity
- health and fitness
- relationship building
- making a difference in community life

The plan resulted in five priority areas:

- support creative and entrepreneurial people across all sectors;
- broad-based collaboration to build a more equitable and healthier community;
- participatory neighborhood-based planning and community building;
- cultural and creative products and activities to build a Lawrence brand; and
- opportunities for learning in cultural and creative expression and appreciation for people of all ages.

These represented a refocusing from typical cultural planning, similar to that in Des Moines—a vehicle for focusing knowledge, skills, and resources of the creative and cultural sector to address community concerns and to organize around progressive values often held by artists and nonprofit leaders.

Worcester, Massachusetts

A 19th century powerhouse of manufacturing, innovation, and immigrant inclusion, Worcester commissioned a cultural plan in 2018, inviting me to lead the process (City of Worcester, Greater Worcester Community Foundation, & Worcester Cultural Coalition, 2019). While the formal cultural sector was well organized and planful in their work, they hadn't conducted community-wide cultural planning for over a decade. The financially strapped city itself had not produced a master plan since 1987. A private foundation supported the effort in partnership with the city. With 185,000 people and while undergoing a modest revival, this postindustrial city had a thin planning staff pulled in many directions and a culture of planning that was reactive and top-down. The city, residents, businesses, and 11 colleges and universities within Worcester's borders shared virtually no experience with comprehensive planning. Typically, they jumped into localized planning and development issues when their interests were threatened, thus, in an oppositional manner.

A hunger for deliberation over shared values, goals, and places, along with a void in collective experience in planning process, necessitated the cultural plan set precedents. Those steering the plan quickly identified concerns related to

- community design
- maintenance and management of parks and green spaces
- festivals and events touching every population group and neighborhood
- transportation equity impacting youth and poorer communities
- education and family involvement in diverse cultural activities and civic life

Public process served to build on networks among various interest groups, most significantly those concerned with urban design, a topic that brought together advocates of historic preservation, artists, bicycle and walkability activists, downtown and neighborhood development interests, city planners and policymakers, and others—many for the first time. While I was warned in advance that there was "planning fatigue" and little appetite for public process, I found the opposite to be the case. Several participants in the design group, in particular, asked at the conclusion of their focus group, "When can we meet again?" A larger public forum left many with similar sentiments and, in fact, dozens volunteered to carry on more detailed topical task-force work, which they did with astonishing results. These plan implementation details, which concluded after the consultant engagement ended, were impressive. For Worcester, the cultural plan, and process of producing it, brought together many disparate interests and groups into new working relationships, and it brought the city experience with creative, rewarding, and enjoyable public process to replicate in their upcoming comprehensive plan.

Summary

Plans are aspirational by nature; findings from *Cultural Planning at 40* (Borrup, 2018) suggest cultural planning can propel a community turn (Wyatt et al., 2013), having the effect, Dreeszen (1994) suggested, of accelerating "a gradual shift in emphasis for arts development to also embrace community development" (p. 91). Changes in the practice of cultural planning are evident from a comparison of the 1994 and 2017 data. The aspirations and outcomes expressed by cultural agencies that responded can be reasonably extended to their local cultural sectors, as players in those sectors tend to be significantly invested in cultural planning processes.

However, a significant gap exists in movement towards cultural equity, building relationships with the city-planning practice, and providing professional development for those involved in the practice itself. While thinking around what comprises culture within a community has progressed somewhat in cultural planning, the sector has grown most in adopting instrumental applications of arts and culture in other dimensions of community life, such as economic and place-based development.

Perhaps most significantly, the expectations and outcomes of cultural planning have shifted since data was collected in 1994. Aspirations of cultural planning have moved from an emphasis on serving the internal needs of the nonprofit cultural sector to better understanding how the sector can address or contribute to other concerns of their communities. As such, cultural planning does appear to fulfill a leadership role in fostering a community turn in the arts. The practice brings together the cultural sector on a local level and helps it express and codify its optimistic intentions. It constructs strategies to help local arts agencies and cultural sectors find ways to take a more central role in key civic issues in their communities. However, it has fallen short in advancing cultural and social equity in most communities.

Beginning with the next chapter, the book explores five areas in which cultural planning has developed capacities I believe can be of great value to city planners and that can advance equity in planning. These begin with better understanding culturally based meanings of and attachments to place. I then move to ways artists and creative practices can enhance community engagement, then to approaches to identifying cultural assets through mapping, to connecting design and aesthetics with democratic practices to build community connections, and finally to focusing economic development efforts on local, renewable resources.

References

Borrup, T. (2018). *Cultural planning at 40: A look at the practice and its progress.* Washington, DC: Americans for the Arts. Retrieved from https://www.americansforthearts.org/by-program/reports-and-data/legislation-policy/naappd/cultural-planning-at-40-a-look-at-the-practice-and-its-progress

Borrup, T., & Harris, C. (2015, August 18). *Building on Lawrence's creative capital: A city-wide cultural plan.* Lawrence, KS. Retrieved from https://lawrenceks.org/cmo/cultural-plan/

Bravo Greater Des Moines. (n.d.). *Regional cultural assessment.* Retrieved from https://bravogreaterdesmoines.org/regional-cultural-assessment/

City of Worcester, Greater Worcester Community Foundation, & Worcester Cultural Coalition. (2019). *Becoming Worcester: The evolution of a creative city—A cultural plan for Worcester, Massachusetts.* Retrieved from https://worcesterculture.org/wp-content/uploads/2019/07/Cultural-Plan-Final.pdf

Dreeszen, C. A. (1994). *Reimagining community: Community arts and cultural planning in America* [Doctoral dissertation]. Retrieved from ProQuest Dissertations and Theses Database. (UMI 9510463)

Wyatt, D., MacDowall, L., & Mulligan, M. (2013). Critical introduction: The turn to community in the arts. *Journal of Arts & Communities, 5*(2/3), 81–91. doi:10.1386/jaac.5.2-3.81_1

Chapter 5

Place Odysseys
Meaning, Attachment, and Belonging

Meanings that places carry, and the feelings people develop for them, are complex. These meanings and the sense of identity people develop are often intertwined, as city planners know. This can be true in communities with diverse and mobile populations as well as those with multi-generational residents. Planners, designers, and placemakers in both direct and indirect ways make enormous impacts on these feelings and how people develop affinity, antipathy, or indifference towards places. Decades ago, American environmental psychologist Harold Proshansky and his colleagues pointed out challenges for city planners and designers that are considerable. They wrote:

> If indeed varying social groups of individuals in an urban setting identify strongly with that setting but in different ways, then this finding itself implies that many practical issues with respect to the design, construction, and use of spaces and places would have to be considered in the light of this plurality of urban dwellers.
>
> (Proshansky, Fabian, & Kaminoff, 1983, p. 81)

Planners can build on the meaning and identity of place, work to strategically change them, or dismiss them. In spite of the power of the feelings people hold for their places, city planning practice grounded in scientific approaches tends to stress detachment from such "irrational" or emotional connections people develop, especially when planners recommend changes.

Historic and current global affairs, along with bodies of academic research, affirm the significant power that comes with feelings and attachments related to place and the behaviors those feelings motivate. On a positive side, strong place attachment can translate to a greater sense of belonging, social cohesion, civic engagement, and stewardship of place. At the same time, in addition to age-old fighting over territory, there can be other negative responses stemming from historical or personal trauma. New arrivals mixed with long-term populations can cause disruption in people's sense of place. This can restrict new arrivals from developing positive feelings for places or provoke hostility towards new arrivals or—in the alternative—detachment among long-term residents.

Whether grounded in what Chinese American geographer Yi-Fu Tuan (1974) described as *topophilia*—love of place—feelings about place represent a force that city planners regularly confront. Yet, based on current city-planning practices, those in the profession are ill-prepared to comprehend and mitigate such issues when they arise. Assessing meaning, identity, and sense of attachment and belonging (or lack thereof) is not central to city planning, a practice grounded in land-use, development, rational policies, infrastructure, and statistics. "Irrational" dimensions, such as meaning, identity, attachment, and belonging are, however, a focus in cultural planning.

This chapter explores whether places, their meanings, and how people use them are better understood through scientific analysis or subjective, even artist-led, processes. Or, do both approaches offer complementary outcomes? I explore concepts of place attachment through research, theory, and experience as well as ways cultural planning techniques can contribute to understanding and promoting positive place attachment. I assert that by developing a comfort level and deeper understanding of place attachment, city planners can remove it from their list of incomprehensible annoyances. Further, by promoting the positive elements, they can leverage deeper engagement and more constructive behaviors through planning and placemaking practices.

Feelings about places and ways of understanding and using them by an increasingly diverse mix of residents cannot be resolved through the use of planning formulas, standard templates, or homogenization. Those don't work for everyone or every place, yet such cookie-cutter solutions and designs have become common practice. And, while planning and design choices will not satisfy all cultural aesthetics and use patterns, engagement in the process of finding commonly agreed-upon designs and uses brings people closer. This process is explored further in Chapter 8.

Place branding, typically related to tourism that follows the articulation of positive place identities, is sometimes an outcome of cultural planning but is not addressed in this book. Considerable literature exists on that topic. This chapter addresses the gap in how planners and communities come to see and appreciate a positive self-image based on resident experience and understanding of their community. Cultural planning can help planners and residents speak a similar language and to acknowledge and work *with* feelings rather than denying their value or purpose. I argue that some of the tools of cultural planning can contribute to better understanding and navigating diversity in communities and to finding ways of making optimal spatial and design choices for more and different people to live together better. The next chapter on public process also addresses this topic.

The Meanings of Place

Places themselves, and the feelings and attachments people form, are complicated and multilayered. "Place is one of the trickiest words in the English language, a suitcase so overfilled one can never shut the lid," wrote American architectural historian, Dolores Hayden (1995, p. 15). The word *place* is used to describe many things and has symbolic meaning that goes well beyond the professional training of most city planners. Hayden wrote about "a woman's place," illustrating how both social and physical structures profoundly impact people's lives.

When have you heard someone say, "I feel out of place"? Or, "I didn't feel it was my place to say something"? Or, when someone references a scolding by which a person was "put in their place"? Places are more than physical ground depicted by city planning maps. American sociologist Thomas Gieryn (2000) observed,

> Places are doubly constructed: most are built or in some way physically carved. They are also interpreted, narrated, perceived, felt, understood, and imagined ... the meaning of the same place is labile—flexible in the hands of different people or cultures, malleable over time, and inevitably contested.
>
> (p. 465)

Multiple meanings of place and conflicts over both places and spaces leave city planners and placemakers in a complicated position.

City planning, design, and placemaking practitioners need to fully appreciate the multiple ways of conceptualizing, constructing, and being in a place. Places are social, cultural, economic, and physical—often irrational. People have learned their position in such place hierarchies, even if they are rarely articulated. Places involve relationships and understandings grounded in power and privilege. As such, they are frequently contested—and appropriately so, in many cases. Whether intentionally or not, the work of city planning and place-making reinforces or redefines all these kinds of places. Most city planners don't have to be reminded that any and every place or space is likely to be contested for some reason. Harder to understand are the reasons why.

Historically rooted social and cultural places, such as those described by Hayden, are more difficult to change or to "make" than physical landscapes and structures. Planners, designers, and placemakers focus on building or freshening the physical elements of place, and sometimes address the economic elements; or they may activate social spaces, but they often do so without addressing inherent social and cultural hierarchies that physical spaces reflect and reinforce. This inseparability of the physical, economic, and cultural dimensions of place is critical for city planners and designers to appreciate and address if they want their plans to have impacts that are equitable and sustainable. Ignoring these relationships may reinforce or even deepen inequitable power relationships baked into the built and social environments. Power hierarchies and social places have been outside what is understood as the purview of city planners, designers, and placemakers. Some may reject that their work involves the meanings, identities, or hierarchies of place, or especially the social or power structures. Yet it does.

In the context of dynamic relationships between place and identity, Winston Churchill's declaration that, "We shape our buildings and afterwards our buildings shape us" (House of Commons, 1943, para. 1) takes on even greater significance. For many cultural planners, the meanings of place and multitude of ways people interact within those places—whether a city, district, neighborhood, or even region—is a central concern in their planning process and resulting plans. Like landscape architects, cultural planners delve into the historical and contemporary meaning of places from as many vantage points as possible and try to understand what people value, the stories they tell of their community, and how they feel about and relate to each other and to that place. Cultural planners ask: What are the aesthetic qualities people value? What unique or special things do they make or do in this place? What cultural practices and celebrations are important? How do people use spaces for different individual and group activities? What contributes to a positive sense of attachment to that place?

In cultural planning, place identity and the expression of meaning is often articulated through the identification of distinctive foods or other creative products, natural features, historical narratives, architecture and design, perceived social dynamics, special events, or other tangible and intangible cultural assets. These assets are sometimes employed through a focus on tourism, local economic development, festival production, job creation, basic community self-esteem development, and other means. However, most importantly, a sense of place identity brings value in its capacity to build residents' sense of attachment to place and in turn their investment in and/or stewardship of that place. Chapter 9 describes the use of those assets in local economic development. Unfortunately, city planners sometimes purposefully seek to diminish the significance of place identity among residents so they present less resistance to changes planners believe are needed.

Place Attachment

In *Place Attachment: Advances in Theory, Methods and Applications*, Lynne C. Manzo and Patrick Devine-Wright (2014) provided an ambitious job description for the phenomenon of place attachment: "Place attachments have bearing on such diverse issues as rootedness and belonging, placemaking and displacement, mobility and migration, intergroup conflict, civic engagement, social housing and urban redevelopment, natural resource management and global climate change" (p. i).

American architecture professor David Seamon (2014) described how "feelings for place can range from disinterest and minimal cognitive awareness to superficial fondness, stronger devotion, or attachment so powerful that people are willing to defend and even sacrifice their lives for a place" (para. 2). Of course, planners sometimes confront feelings that seem irrational and challenging based on what might be considered excessive topophilia (Tuan, 1974). Place attachments are quite real and powerful, and they are not going away. Can city planners welcome such feelings **and** work to achieve a healthy, functional balance? For planners, designers, and placemakers, these phenomena are important to understand, deliberately address, and work with rather than to battle. One approach advocated by a leading professional organization might not be so constructive.

Place Character, American Planning Association-Style

The American Planning Association (APA) periodically publishes helpful tips or "QuickNotes" for planners on its website. One of these, entitled *Measuring Community Character* by David Morley (2018), proposed a strategy for measuring the character of community. It defines character as "the distinct identity of a place … the collective impression a neighborhood or town makes on residents and visitors" (para. 1).

According to the APA, this bulletin was designed to "provide planners, local officials, and community members with a common language to understand the physical and social characteristics they value" (Morley, 2018, para. 2). It described how urban design experts evaluate a community's character based on its physical elements, and landscape architects evaluate it based on natural features. The third major player cited, were "average citizens" who, APA asserted, understand community on an intuitive level. The stated goal of the APA bulletin was to "refocus conversations on concrete characteristics of the community, rather than emotional pleas based on intuition" (Morley, 2018, para. 2). As such, APA suggested that planners diminish or devalue resident input that is not based on scientific reason.

The bulletin advocated the use of quantifiable measures to assess urban form, natural features, and demographics. In urban form, it recommended key measures such as "the heights and widths of buildings, the distances between the fronts of buildings and the edges of streets" (Morley, 2018, para. 7) among other formal relationships. In regard to natural features, APA recommended considering "the slopes and heights of hills, the heights and widths of trees, the distances between trees, the percentage of land covered by vegetation or water," and so on. In terms of demographics, measures should include, "the size of daytime and nighttime populations, population distribution by age, sex, race, and ethnicity, average household size, median household income" (Morley, 2018, para. 13) and others. All of these so-called objective measures must, of course, be interpreted and evaluated based on values the bulletin does not delineate, such as the tree maintenance policies described earlier in this book by Qadeer (1997). So-called average citizens have little basis on which to select one street width over another or to prefer one distribution of daytime population over another. Trying to divert attention from emotional responses to measurable characteristics does little to connect with or satisfy residents and does not build positive place attachment, not to mention good rapport between planners and residents.

The bulletin, *Measuring Community Character*, went on: "The risk of relying solely on intuition is that our observations, interactions, and media consumption can create highly distorted impressions of the community as a whole" (Morley, 2018, para. 12). By using objective measures, "planners, local officials, and community members establish goals and priorities for community growth and change without resorting to indefinite appeals to protect the established character" (Morley, 2018, para. 16). In so doing, this APA-recommended approach encourages city planners to diminish or negate affective or emotional bonds people may have for their community or neighborhood. Should "established character" be relegated to the scrap heap? Should city planners try to divert attachment, traditions, and historical meaning of place from consideration of the future? How can individuals' "irrational" topophilia, everyday lived experience, or attachment to place receive recognition in the conversation?

According to Italian social psychologist Maria Vittoria Giuliani (2003), the academic discipline of human geography "exerted a strong influence on environmental psychology both by encouraging alternative approaches to the quantitative method and by focusing attention on individual experience" (p. 147). Human geographers may have influenced environmental psychologists but apparently had little influence on city planning. Similarly, feminist theory seems to have had little influence. Nearly three decades earlier, Leonie Sandercock and Ann Forsyth (1992) wrote, "Feminists are increasingly critical of the traditional dualism that pits reason against passion and rationality against politics, as if reason excludes passion, as if politics, by definition, were irrational" (p. 51).

Arguing for the value of emotion in research (and by extension, planning), feminist scholars Geraldine Pratt and Victoria Rosner (2012), describe the common understanding of emotion as "the shifty and loose cousin of reason" (p. 5). Researchers, like many city planners, present themselves as objective or disinterested observers. However, feminism demonstrated to the academic world decades ago that everyone brings their experience and feelings to their work. Attempting to remove intuition and emotion from planning conversations, as advocated by the APA Bulletin, serves to exclude authentic voices of a community—perhaps especially feminist voices.

Instead, the APA prescription derives planning solutions from routine formulas and mathematical equations. Feminist insights, asserted Sandercock and Forsyth (1992), "would expand the planners perspective beyond scientific and technical knowledge to other ways of knowing" (p. 52). Pratt and Rosner (2012) similarly argued that scholars need "to understand feelings as important not just for psychologists but for fields of study as widely ranging as geography, political science, literature, anthropology, and economics" (p. 5). Feminism, and, more recently, queer studies, have sliced through the idea of unbiased academic research or discourse. Is the planning profession that far behind?

Individual and Place Identity

Similar to the ways we shape our buildings and they shape us, person and place identity can be intertwined. The term *place identity* is frequently attributed to Harold Proshansky, from his 1978 article on the city and self-identity. In it he argued that "for each of the role-related identities of an individual, there are physical dimensions and characteristics that help to define and are subsumed by that identity" (Proshansky, 1978, p. 155). Proshansky et al. (1983) further suggested

At the core of such physical environment-related cognitions is the "environmental past" of the person; a past consisting of places, spaces and their properties which have served instrumentally in the satisfaction of the person's biological, psychological, social, and cultural needs.

(p. 77)

The field of environmental psychology, wrote American scholars Jen Jack Gieseking and William Mangold (2014b), "proposes that identities form in relation to environments" (p. 73). Their assertion is that the individual does not fully form a personal identity outside of their relationship to place. This postulates a kind of chicken-or-egg conundrum or, perhaps, a dialectical relationship between the formation of the identities of self and of place, explaining part of the phenomenon of place attachment. American geographers Helen Couclelis and Reginald Golledge argued for consideration of the practice of behavioral geography: "The picture that emerges is one in which mind and world are in constant dynamic interaction" (Couclelis & Golledge, 1983, p. 333).

Many scholars, beginning with those in psychology, link the self and the physical environment as a dynamic system of identity development. As early researchers studying place attachment, Proshansky et al. (1983) explored place identity and the socialization of the self. They were responding to what they found as "an almost complete neglect of the role of places and spaces in this aspect of human psychological development" (p. 77). Psychologists have long examined the formation of attachment among individuals to objects, then to places.

Proshansky (1978) explored the "dimensions of self that define the individual's personal identity in relation to the physical environment by means of a complex pattern of conscious and unconscious ideas, feelings, values, goals, preferences, skills, and behavioral tendencies relevant to a specific environment" (p. 155). His groundbreaking work helped to propel an area of research that is now clearly more layered as people and groups are increasingly mobile and relationships with place are understood to be more complicated. Since Proshansky's early work, researchers have asserted that identity formation is more complex and that some people form attachments to more than one place (Gustafson, 2014).

Beyond physical space and identity, the formation of a sense of community is also part of the mix. Blokland (2017) wrote, "identity is a precondition for social life and, conversely, having an identity seems to be one of the most universal human needs" (p. 57). She went on to say, "We considered the connection between community and identity an analytical twin. Identity is a precondition for social life and vice versa" (p. 162). Blokland's work addressed formation of communities, which are frequently but not always place-based. Nonetheless, planners and placemakers must consider multiple and overlapping communities within places as well as a sense of community and attachment that forms around a place.

Expanding on the individual-place dynamic of identity development, Blokland (2017) saw individual identity and group or community identity as a conjoined twin. This suggests more of a triangulation of place, the individual, and a social dynamic. Portuguese psychology scholars Fátima Bernardo and José-Manuel Palma-Oliveira (2016) asserted that "place is conceptualized as an interchangeable relationship between the physical-spatial and human-social characteristics of space. In this sense, identity cannot not be understood without including both components" (p. 239).

Power and culture are also factors, as not everyone's experiences are the same. American forest service researcher Daniel R. Williams (2014) critiqued the cognitive analysis of Proshansky and others in environmental psychology "for lacking any serious discussion of how power and social and cultural processes influence the experience, meaning, and relationship to places" (p. 78).

While bodies of research on place attachment, place identity, and behavior have grown since the 1980s, they remained relatively thin. Importantly though, much of it crosses disciplines between geographers, psychologists, sociologists, and the hybrid fields of environmental psychology and community psychology. While designers and architects have weighed in on the topic, academic literature, as well as practice, presents scarce evidence of crossover with city planning.

Mixing Psychology, Art, and Space

In a 2018 visit to Bogotá, Colombia, I was treated to a week of interacting with and observing professionals and students involved in a program sponsored by the city's department of culture and sport that was working in numerous outer neighborhoods and inner-city social housing compounds. Led by the city's cultural agency, teams working in these communities were made up of an artist, an organizer, a planner or landscape architect, and a psychologist. In the outer neighborhoods, their task was to engage people in forming and activating small public parks where none existed. These neighborhoods were called "self-built communities" in that no city planning or municipal agencies were involved in their construction. Basic services such as water, sewer, power, and public transit had recently been installed, but public spaces were random at best and needed to be retroactively engineered.

In these cases, public spaces were identified, carved out, planned, and animated, not by edict or expert-driven process, but through a multifaceted and participatory organizing, planning, and design process drawing on creative talents and cultural practices of the people in the neighborhoods, especially the youth. The city was working to bring an organic process of community formation together with the sense of identity development and strengthen the sense of connection to place. In the social housing projects, similar teams worked to build social connections among diverse groups who had recently migrated to the city. Bringing artists, psychologists, planners, and organizers in team efforts to help communities form and create shared spaces and activities through collective action is not something I had seen in action before this. The developing sense of place attachment, stewardship, and connection to one another was palpable.

Drivers of Attachment

Place identity is generally derived from the meaning of place as it is perceived by those who occupy it. Individuals may or may not have language to describe it or have fully articulated what their place means. Nonetheless, most people have an intuitive sense of the identity of place or places important to them, as well as their place within it. Many authors in environmental psychology, including Bonnes, Lee, and Bonaiuto (2003) and Brown, Perkins, and Brown (2003) cited a groundbreaking study by Boston College psychology professor Marc Fried (1963) of the urban renewal (AKA, displacement of the poor) of Boston's West End during 1958 to 1961. Fried's study showed that residents had strong place attachments and community viability despite deteriorated housing conditions and other social conditions considered "deprived." At the same time, Brown et al. pointed out, the "Pruitt-Igoe public housing in St. Louis, which was physically sound initially, did not invite place attachments. Both examples, for different reasons, show the folly of equating good residential quality with strong residential bonds" (p. 260). The focus on quantifiable measures of "good" housing did not correlate with things that made people feel attachment. Of course, in both these cases residents were displaced and the housing demolished.

As a young homeowner and neighborhood activist on the south side of Minneapolis in the 1980s—the same neighborhood I still live in nearly 40 years later—I attended a neighborhood meeting to review a plan by a longstanding neighborhood plumbing and heating supply business that wanted to expand on its site. A city planner presented the plan that included vacating a residential street and taking out three or four duplexes to allow the business to expand its footprint and to have larger trucks service the business.

This was a difficult situation because the family-owned company employed neighborhood residents and had been on its site for a couple of generations. Without the ability to expand, they would have to move to a suburban location. Neighbors were strident on wanting to maintain the neighborhood's residential character and not displace any residents. The planner seemed more interested in getting his plan adopted and clearly not comfortable with public process, especially in our racially mixed, inner-city neighborhood. At one point in the meeting his frustration got the better of him and he said, "I don't know why anyone would want to live in this neighborhood anyway." Everyone at the meeting was stunned. Did this city planner just say that about *our* neighborhood? Those precise words have rung in my head for over 30 years. The planner underestimated the sense of attachment I and my neighbors had for the place where we lived, even if he saw a highest and best use as a more important driver.

For nearly 20 years after Fried's (1963) study in Boston, the notion of attachment was not included among environmental psychology research topics (Giuliani, 2003). It wasn't until the 1980s that place attachment, especially related to neighborhoods, became a topic of research. The idea of places as an extension of the self initially grew among psychologists. American marketing scholar Russell Belk (1992) observed that "to be attached to certain of our surroundings is to make them a part of our extended self" (p. 38). The extended self is involved, he wrote, "only when the basis for attachment is emotional rather than simply functional" (p. 38). Of course, it is not simple to determine where emotional connections originate and whether the simple functionality of place, which surely contributes to security and comfort that Tuan (1974) observed are part of forming connections.

Brown et al. (2003) described place attachment in a revitalizing neighborhood as follows: "Place attachments are positive bonds to physical and social settings that support identity and provide other psychological benefits" (p. 259). Security and comfort, in forms that are both social and material, surely provide psychological benefit. Beyond that, what is the role of aesthetics and experience? Giuliani (2003) asserted, "We have all experienced some form or affective bond, either positive of negative, pleasant or unpleasant, with some place or other—a place that can be related to our current or past experience" (p. 137).

These authors review numerous terms used to refer to affective bonds with places. These included rootedness, sense of place, belongingness, insided-ness, embeddedness, attachment, affiliation, appropriation, commitment, investment, dependence, identity, and others. This variety, Giuliani (2003) wrote, "seems to indicate not so much a diversity of concepts and reference models as a vagueness in the identification of the phenomenon" (p. 138). Because individuals and, surely, cultural or ethnic groups have tendencies to relate to or attach to place differently, it will be difficult for researchers to quantify and universalize such phenomena or behaviors.

The Miami-based Knight Foundation, together with the Gallup research organization, released results of an extensive survey on place attachment in 2010. They asked thousands of people in 26 different cities in the United States over the course of three consecutive years what conditions make them want to remain and invest in their communities. To the surprise of many, the three consistently highest-ranking factors were aesthetics and beauty (design and natural features), activities (things to do and to engage in), and openness (welcoming nature of people and institutions). Conditions related to traffic, crime, and schools also rated but not in the top slots. All three of these conditions are highly contextual and dependent on individuals' perceptions. What has aesthetic appeal or what feels welcoming to one may not be the same as to another. Nonetheless, the idea that people care so much about these "soft" elements of their community is instructive.

In her review of place attachment research, Giuliani (2003) found that "most empirical research concludes—in general on the basis of factorial analyses— that attachment is 'multidimensional'" (p. 150). She cited two primary factors: social bonding and behavioral rootedness. In my experience, these can vary considerably in proportion to how they contribute to a feeling of attachment. Aesthetics, which is rarely addressed in existing theories (except the abovementioned Knight Foundation study), rates quite high in my own experience and in balance to openness. Place attachment originates in varying degrees between environmental factors and the character of the individual. I have come to learn during extensive travel the past couple decades that I tend to form place attachments quickly—but only to some places.

Experience and Belonging

Bernardo and Palma-Oliveira (2016) observed that early authors addressing place identity "centered on an individualistic perspective, thus neglecting the social nature of the relations between individuals, identities and place" (p. 239). Bernardo and Palma-Oliveira defined place identity as "a component of personal and social identity, a process by which, through interaction with places, people describe themselves in terms of belonging to a specific place" (p. 239). Having a sense of belonging may or may not be a claim everyone makes, as some live in contested spaces or in places where they have suffered physical and/or psychological trauma. They may have no place they feel they belong. As Canadian psychologists Leila Scannell and Robert Gifford (2014) pointed out, "for some 'home' can be a place of abuse or oppression" (p. 27). For others, this writer included, White privilege allows them to have a sense of belonging to multiple places.

Bernardo and Palma-Oliveira (2016) emphasized that identity is "a dynamic process, that allows the person to use the identity that is most convenient depending on the context. The person can choose the scale of identity that most contributes to their positive distinctiveness and self-esteem" (p. 241). What these authors failed to recognize is that this is spoken from a position of privilege. They suggested this "convenience" can include identifying with a specific housing enclave, a neighborhood, district, city, county, state, or country, and to choose among them as seems appropriate for the circumstance. For instance, depending on context, I might say I live above the Midtown Global Market, or in the Phillips Neighborhood, or in Minneapolis, or in Minnesota, or in the United States. The privilege of belonging—or feeling that one belongs in a given place, or a number of places—is not enjoyed by everyone. American cultural activist and writer Roberto Bedoya (2013) put the right to belong in the context of renewed social battles over women's rights to control their own bodies, LGBTQ rights, assaults on immigrants, and economic displacement through gentrification—not to mention exploding populations of homeless people who find belonging anywhere a daily struggle. He wrote, "before you can have places of belonging, you must feel you belong" (para. 3).

My own relationships to places are, no doubt, different than those of most—although surely not unique. These relationships cause me to ponder concepts of attachment and belonging, as well as my own White, male American privilege. The majority of my work life has involved considerable travel that has accelerated as the years progress. I find myself developing a feeling of attraction if not attachment to multiple places—sometimes unexpectedly and for reasons I have only begun to process.

Having spent varying degrees of time in perhaps a couple hundred small towns and large cities across North America, Europe, Asia, and South America, a few pique my interest. I find myself attracted to an unusual mix of places. In some I experience a strong connection with people, in others I connect more to the aesthetics, energy, and activities of the place. What fosters a feeling of attachment, for me, is not a simple formula.

For a period of 20 years, I have maintained two homes—a primary residence in Minneapolis and a second in Miami Beach. I feel very different connections with each. The attachments are complex, although aesthetics are especially key in Miami. Minneapolis has less appeal aesthetically, but 40 years of continual residence, myriad professional and community activities, and a domestic partner of 20 years create personal bonds, in addition to a sense of agency in my neighborhood and city, and thus a sense of security. Tuan (1974), who at the time he wrote *Sense of Place* and *Topophilia* was living and teaching in Minneapolis, described the phenomenon as "being completely at home—that is, unreflectively secure and comfortable in a particular locality" (as cited in Sixsmith, 1986, p. 294).

In Miami Beach, the aesthetic appeal is considerable. However, I have no "strong ties," as in close relationships, there—typically of family or longtime friends—only "weak ties" as described by Granovetter (1973, 1983). He associated weak ties with professional and social networks that may be wide but not deep. Aesthetic qualities, such as palm trees, beaches, Art Deco design, walkability, and people from all parts of the world, provide strong appeal.

Early research on place attachment evolving from psychology assumed that attachment was primarily social and that people developed bonds with other people to cement their attachment to places. My experience is different. In their concept of place attachment as rooted in experience, Giuliani (2003) offered one possible explanation:

> It must be underlined that, although the identity functions of territoriality play a central role in this framework, the development of an attachment bond is not derived from the salience of a place in the structure of one's own identity, but from the actual experience with a place.
>
> (p. 154)

For me, experiences, largely driven by the aesthetic, a sense of being welcome, and a feeling of safety, positively impact my sense of security and comfort, and my sense of belonging and attachment. Again, I am a White man and an American, a privileged position that comes with entitlement to feel I belong wherever I choose. This is different for people not fitting that description.

By recognizing the centrality of culture in human-environment relations, American anthropologist Edward Hall (1966, as cited in Gieseking & Mangold, 2014a) pointed out that place meaning is different for people with different experiences and backgrounds. Hidalgo and Hernandez (2001) expressed the need for research to "find out whether the different types of attachment to place vary depending on sociodemographic characteristics such as age, sex, and social class" (p. 275). They do not reference other types of cultural backgrounds.

Women tend to form greater place attachments than men, Hidalgo and Hernandez (2001) found in their research. Hispanic ethnic groups in a Salt Lake City neighborhood study formed greater attachment than Whites in similar areas according to Brown et al. (2003). Cultural and aesthetic dimensions and their impacts on the formation of place attachment need to be more fully explored. Some researchers have looked at "highly mobile populations," referring to refugees or migrants, for their relationships to a home country versus adopted new homes. Many researchers try to "universalize" findings or to be "colorblind" in examining research subjects and have not had opportunity to ask such questions, although scholars, including Asian American architectural design scholar Jeffrey Hou (2013), have written extensively about the ways different ethnic groups tend to use and design shops and public and private spaces differently. Deeper cultural awareness of such patterns of use is much needed in the practice of city planning.

From Place Aura to Placelessness

Over thousands of years, place-based communities formed in their own unique ways with infrequent contact with other areas of the world. Various modes of transportation facilitated greater contact at greater speeds as time progressed. By the early 19th century, rail travel brought about a transformational connection between places. In a historical perspective on the evolution of place identities, German-born American cultural historian, Wolfgang Schivelbusch (1978/2014) examined how railroads and the synchronized time zones they necessitated impacted place identity. He observed in the building of rail networks,

> the landscapes, joined to each other and to the metropolis by the railways, and the goods that are torn out of their local relation by modern transportation, share the fate of losing their hereditary place, their traditional here-and-now, or as Walter Benjamin sums it up in one word, their aura.
>
> (p. 296)

Cities maintained unique time zones as well as products and ways of doing things. The unique aura they developed began to be impacted by the sped-up process of movement of people between places and resulting cultural exchange. Schivelbusch continued, "the places visited by the traveler become ever more similar to the commodities that are part of the same circulatory system. For 20th-century tourism, the world has become one big department store of landscapes and cities" (p. 297).

In this department store of cities, a general assumption of globalization has been a homogenization of places. And, indeed, strip malls with chain stores and drive-through restaurants can be seen across the landscape in car-dominated cities, suburbs, and small towns, creating what Canadian geographer Edward Relph, among others, described as *placelessness* (as cited in Seamon & Sowers, 2008). Notions of homogenization, however, have been cast aside by some scholars and planners. British planning scholar Patsy Healey (1998) asserted that the seeming contradiction in globalization is that the distinctiveness of each city and neighborhood actually takes on greater significance. She wrote, "In a world where integrated place-bounded relationships are pulled out of their localities, 'disembodied' and refashioned by multiple forces which mould them in differ-ent directions, the qualities of places seem to become more, not less, significant" (p. 1531). In cultural planning, the identification of unique qualities and charac-ter of place is increasingly a central focus.

Addressing such patterns in city planning and design, Healey (2010) sub-sequently argued that generalizations based on cultural assumptions of what constitutes the "good life" result in formulaic design principles and public poli-cies that have resulted in disastrous outcomes. Such practices, she said, represent "major mistakes that twentieth century planners and policy experts tended to make" (Healey, 2010, p. 32). These must give way to more culturally and place-sensitive approaches, she argued. Qualities of place are more than an image or assemblage of distinctive assets. Healey added, "Place qualities are generated and maintained by complex inter-relationships between people in diverse social worlds, which potentially connect them to all kinds of other places and times in dynamic and unpredictable ways" (p. 35).

Constructing Authenticity

To address the danger of a city getting lost in a homogenized world, British urban theorist Kevin Robins (1993) observed that "as cities have become ever more equivalent and urban identities increasingly thin, it has become necessary to employ advertising and marketing agencies to manufacture such distinctions" (p. 306). A boom in place branding and marketing has produced new global industries. International cities, smaller cities and towns, and even neighborhoods within larger cities all seek to distinguish their unique identity. Some suburban communities are also increasingly seeking to distinguish themselves. Whether that identity is grounded in the reality of local residents or bolted on by a marketing firm devising clever slogans may represent the difference between a successful or failed identity.

Cultural planning seeks to locate, find consensus, and elevate place identity. As Bianchini and Ghilardi (2007) pointed out,

> Places that did not "stay true" to their history, social dynamics, economic background and distinctive heritage and urban features tended to struggle with maintaining a new identity and brand over time while those that adopted a more "organic" and joined-up approach to identity building were more successful.
>
> (p. 284)

This statement must be taken in a nuanced and contextual way, as it could contradict arguments about places becoming more welcoming and inclusive of difference. Simply replicating the history is unlikely to serve a community well. Future visions should be recognizable, building on or "staying true" to their history while reframing that history in sensitive and strategic ways. Such is a key task in cultural planning. Authenticity is a socially constructed concept, one that requires agreement on its meaning in a given place and time. Wholesale replacement of people, history, meaning, and physical infrastructure—as attempted in American-style urban renewal schemes—left considerable social, economic, physical and psychological damage (Fullilove, 2003, 2016). Assessing which values, stories, and physical assets are retained or even expanded upon and which are let go is the sacred quest. Articulating place identity and meaning and engaging key stakeholders in doing so is one of the pursuits of cultural planning.

Left to market forces and in the absence of sensitive planning, community identities will serve some interests to the neglect of others. Collins (2018) warned that, "such strategies of place marketing and cultural urban revitalization benefit tourists and wealthy residents rather than improving the well-being of the local public" (p. 3). In some urban enclaves with clearly identifiable or compelling cultural identities, Collins argued, "business owners have recognized that they can profit from the commodification of place, even if they themselves do not share the same heritage as the neighborhood's brand" (p. 3). Los Angeles neighborhoods he studied such as Korea Town, Thai Town, Little Armenia, and others, have capitalized on an ethnic identity, even though not all of their residents and businesses are of these respective groups. What these efforts and others reflect are a search for meaning and distinctiveness, a sense of identity to which residents can feel a part with the hope of improving the quality of life along with improving local livelihoods.

Collins (2018) wrestled with his observations that culturally defined urban districts are on the one hand expressions of cohesion and efforts to collectively promote economic wellbeing for members of the community, yet, on the other hand, these efforts open communities to exploitation by property speculators, developers, or even civic leaders. This, he said, leaves planning scholars in a perplexing place. "While the marketing of culture by immigrant communities *can* half improve the local quality of life, it can also fuel gentrification and displacement and establish static place identities that are contested by new residential populations" (p. 3).

From a planning perspective, Collins (2018) wrote,

> There is enormous tension here: For some ethnic champions, neighborhood designation opens new possibilities to preserve and support the culture of the community. For others, community designation is part of a scheme to attract more capital, visitors/shoppers, and development to the area and increase land values and personal gain.
>
> (p. 9)

Collins also stated that "for community development practitioners working in such areas, it is therefore important to understand how community stakeholders themselves define their neighborhood and its cultural assets" (p. 4). This is what cultural planners are best equipped to do and an area city planners often neglect.

Changing Places

What places mean to people emerge and evolve over time. Williams (2014) described how meaning is often expressed through stories that are "historical or other narrative accounts of peoples and cultures that have occupied or otherwise experienced these places" (p. 76). Such narratives evolve, sometimes are forgotten, and can be replaced by new stories. Conflicts may play out in short-term, violent change or through gradual changes over years, decades, or centuries. Again, Winston Churchill's aphorism applies: these narratives and the people who inhabit and shape them work both ways. Williams continued, "Places typically have multiple, often conflicting histories that shape and define cultures and individual identities" (p. 76).

Part of the complexity for city planners and placemakers are the multitude of ways places change, how changes impact feelings of place attachment, and the weighty responsibility they have for playing a role in making changes. Proshansky et al. (1983) wrote, "Physical settings themselves may change radically over long or relatively short periods of time, and thereby no longer correspond to existing place-related cognitions that serve to define the self-identity of the individual" (p. 79). These changes may be demographic and environmental. They continued, "The result of economic, political, and social impacts may have important consequences for the place-identity of the person" (p. 79). City planners plotting changes of place bear responsibility for all of these consequences.

The psychological wellbeing of individuals and groups within neighborhoods or areas of a city may be profoundly impacted based on planned or realized changes. Proshansky et al. (1983) cited other factors impacting attachments, including "the intrusion of unwanted groups, the evidence of crime in the area, and beginning signs of physical decay, may all precipitate stronger emotional attachments to one's home and neighborhood" (p. 79). Of course, such changes might also negatively impact attachments more for some people than others. What several researchers have cited is that changes threatening previously stable environments push residents to see and attach themselves to characteristics they had taken for granted and/or had not previously articulated.

Examining place attachment in a revitalizing neighborhood, Brown et al. (2003) reflected, "Place attachments are nourished by daily encounters with the environment and neighbors, seasonal celebrations, continued physical personalization and upkeep, and affective feelings toward and beliefs about the home and neighborhood" (p. 259). Nourishing a sense of place attachment is often an important concern of cultural planners, placemakers, and community development professionals.

Summary

No single theory can explain place attachment, and it may not be within the capacity of city planners, designers, and placemakers to sort that out. What is possible to understand and explore through planning, placemaking, and design is that there are cultural differences in how and why people relate to and form bonds with place. It is essential to appreciate how powerful those bonds may be. Contrary to the APA bulletin discussed earlier (Morley, 2018), which advocated for a focus on objective measures to identify the characteristics of place, emotional factors cannot be excluded from the conversation.

Cultural planners sometimes find a creative challenge in the process of discovering and building consensus around place character and identity, yet it becomes increasingly complicated in an age of rapid globalization. City planners, who often need to think in concrete terms, may find this process frustrating. Identification of common ground, shared values, and a vision for desired future characteristics of place challenge planners and placemakers of all kinds. The experience and comfort level cultural planners bring to this process represents another way cultural planners can contribute to city planning.

Cultural planning works to identify and enhance place meaning, looking for shared cultural practices and commonalities as well as historical and contemporary conflicts and ways to productively engage people in dialogue around the evolution and future of that identity. In cultural plans, these may come together around collective activities such as festivals, use of public space, and economic development strategies that employ the unique mix of creative practices, skills, locally identified products, and tourism.

Homogenization of places resulting from cut-and-paste city-planning practices may have wittingly or unwittingly been employed as a strategy to dilute or dissolve place bonds—or maybe to simply make every place feel the same for everyone. These are not productive strategies. Instead, it is critical that city planners listen to residents and work with cultural planners to identify characteristics of place and identity valued by residents and then formulate ways to constructively build on the positive dimensions of place attachment. In cities with rapidly changing populations, including those willing to take in climate refugees and other migrants, it is important that place identity not be rigid and that the process of discussing it remain open.

Stevenson (2014) described how cultural planners explore identities of place and try to articulate them:

> Place and the emotional climates associated with them are also comprised of the 'traces of memories of different social groups who have lived in or pass through' a particular place ... Sometimes layers are evident but more often they lie beneath the surface awaiting excavation or relocation—a task that cultural planning is frequently charged with performing.
>
> (p. 43)

Can exploring and nourishing a sense of place identity and attachment also be part of the agenda of city planners? In the next three chapters, I describe some ways to approach these challenges. These include artist-led public engagement, processes for cultural mapping, and engaging in the ongoing work of seeking meaningful design and aesthetic qualities of places. These are some ways the work of city planners and cultural planners can complement one another.

References

Bedoya, R. (2013, February). Placemaking and the politics of belonging and dis-belonging. *Grantmakers in the Arts*. Retrieved from https://www.giarts.org/article/place making-and-politics-belonging-and-dis-belonging

Belk, R. W. (1992). Attachment to possessions. In I. Altman & S. M. Low (Eds.), *Place attachment: Human behavior and environment* (pp. 37–62). Boston, MA: Springer. doi:10.1007/978-1-4684-8753-4_3

Bernardo F., & Palma-Oliveira, J.-M. (2016). Urban neighborhoods and intergroup relations: The importance of place identity. *Journal of Environmental Psychology, 45*, 239–251. doi:10.1016/j.jenvp.2016.01.010

Bianchini, F., & Ghilardi, L. (2007). Thinking culturally about place. *Place Branding and Public Diplomacy, 3*(4), 280–286. doi:10.1057/palgrave.pb.6000077

Blokland, T. (2017). *Community as urban practice*, Cambridge: Polity Press.

Bonnes, M., Lee, T., & Bonaiuto, M. (2003). Theory and practice in environmental psychology – An introduction. In M. Bonnes, T. Lee, & M. Bonaiuto (Eds.), *Psychological theories for environmental Issues* (pp. 1–26). Abington: Ashgate.

Brown, B., Perkins, D. D., & Brown, G. (2003). Place attachment in a revitalizing neighborhood: Individual and block levels of analysis. *Journal of Environmental Psychology, 23*(3), 259–271. doi:10.1016/S0272-4944(02)00117-2

Collins, B. (2018). Whose culture, whose neighborhood? Fostering and resisting neighborhood change in the multiethnic enclave. *Journal of Planning Education and Research*. doi:10.1177/0739456X18755496

Couclelis, H., & Golledge, R. (1983). Analytic research, positivism, and behavioral geography. *Annals of the Association of American Geographers, 73*(3), 331–339. doi:10.1111/j.1467-8306.1983.tb01420.x

Fried, M. (1963). Grieving for a lost home. In L. J. Duhl (Ed.), *The urban condition: People and policy in the metropolis* (pp. 151–171). New York, NY: Basic Books.

Fullilove, M. T. (2003). Neighborhoods and infectious disease. In I. Kawachi & L. F. Berkman (Eds.). *Neighborhoods and health* (pp. 211–222). Oxford: Oxford University Press.

Fullilove, M. T. (2016). *Root shock: How tearing up city neighborhoods hurts America, and what we can do about it*. New York, NY: New Village Press.

Gieryn, T. F. (2000). A space for place in sociology. *Annual Review of Sociology, 26*, 463–496. doi:10.1146/annurev.soc.26.1.463

Gieseking, J. J., & Mangold, W. (2014a). Introduction. In J. J. Gieseking & W. Mangold (Eds.), *The people, place, and space reader* (pp. xix–xxxiv). New York, NY: Routledge.

Gieseking, J. J., & Mangold, W. (2014b). Section 3 – Place and identity: Editors' introduction and suggestions for further reading. In J. J. Gieseking & W. Mangold (Eds.), *The people, place, and space reader* (pp. 73–76). New York, NY: Routledge.

Giuliani, M. V. (2003). Theory of attachment and place attachment. In M. Bonnes, T. Lee, & M. Bonaiuto (Eds.), *Psychological theories for environmental Issues* (pp. 137–170). Abington: Ashgate.

Granovetter, M. (1983). The strength of weak ties: A network theory revisited. *Sociological Theory, 1*(1), 201–233. doi:10.2307/202051

Granovetter, M. S. (1973). The strength of weak ties. *American Journal of Sociology, 78*(6), 1360–1380. doi:10.1086/225469

Gustafson, P. (2014). Place attachment in an age of mobility. In L. C. Manzo & P. Devine-Wright (Eds.), *Place attachment: Advances in theory, methods, and applications* (pp. 37–48). London: Routledge.

Hall, E. T. (1966). *Beyond culture.* New York, NY: Random House.

Hayden, D. (1995). *The power of place: Urban landscapes as public history.* Cambridge, MA: MIT Press.

Healey, P. (1998). Building institutional capacity through collaborative approaches to urban planning. *Environment and Planning A: Economy and Space, 30,* 1531–1546.

Healey, P. (2010). *Making better places: The planning project in the twenty-first century.* Houndmills: Palgrave Macmillan.

Hidalgo, M. C., & Hernandez, B. (2001). Place attachment: Conceptual and empirical questions. *Journal of Environmental Psychology, 21*(3), 273–281. doi:10.1006/jevp.2001.0221

Hou, J. (2013). *Transcultural cities: Border crossing and placemaking.* London: Routledge.

House of Commons. (1943, October 28). *House of Commons rebuilding.* Retrieved from https://api.parliament.uk/historic-hansard/commons/1943/oct/28/house-of-commons-rebuilding

Manzo, L. C., & Devine-Wright, P. (2014). *Place attachment: Advances in theory, methods and applications.* London: Routledge.

Morley, D. (2018). Measuring community character. *PAS QuickNotes,* No. 72. American Planning Association, Retrieved from https://www.planning.org/publications/document/9142842/

Pratt, G., & Rosner, V. (2012). Introduction: The global and the intimate. In G. Pratt & V. Rosner (Eds.), *The global and the intimate: Feminism in our time* (pp. 1–27). New York, NY: Columbia University Press.

Proshansky, H. M. (1978). The city and self-identity. *Environment and Behavior, 10*(2), 147–169. doi:10.1177/0013916578102002

Proshansky, H. M., Fabian, A. K., & Kaminoff, R. (1983). Place-identity: Physical world socialization of the self. *Journal of Environmental Psychology, 3*(1), 57–83. doi:10.1016/S0272-4944(83)80021-8

Qadeer, M. A. (1997). Pluralistic planning for multicultural cities: The Canadian practice. *Journal of the American Planning Association, 63*(4), 481–494. doi:10.1080/0194436970897594

Robins, K. (1993). Prisoners of the city: Whatever could a postmodern city be?. In E. Carter, J. Donald, & J. Squires (Eds.), *Space and place: Theories of identity and location* (pp. 303–330). London: Lawrence & Wishart.

Sandercock, L., & Forsyth, A. (1992). A gender agenda: New directions for planning theory, *Journal of the American Planning Association, 58*(1), 49–59. doi:10.1080/01944369208975534

Scannell, L., & Gifford, R. (2014). Comparing the theories of interpersonal and place attachment. In L. C. Manzo & P. Devine-Wright (Eds.), *Place attachment: Advances in theory, methods, and applications* (pp. 13–36). London: Routledge.

Schivelbusch, W. (2014). Railroad space and railroad time. In J. J. Gieseking & W. Mangold (Eds.), *The people, place, and space reader* (pp. 294–297). New York, NY: Routledge. (Original work published in 1978)

Seamon, D. (2014). Place attachment and phenomenology: The synergistic dynamism of place. In L. C. Manzo & P. Devine-Wright (Eds.), *Place attachment: Advances in theory, methods, and applications* (pp. 11–22). London: Routledge.

Seamon, D., & Sowers, J. (2008). Place and placelessness: Edward Relph. In P. Hubbard, R. Kitichin, & G. Valentine (Eds.), *Key texts in human geography* (pp. 43–51). London: Sage.

Sixsmith, J. (1986). The meaning of home: An exploratory study of environmental experience. *Journal of Environmental Psychology*, *6*(4), 281–298. doi:10.1016/S0272-4944(86)80002-0

Stevenson, D. (2014). *Cities of culture: A global perspective*. London: Routledge.

Tuan, Y. F. (1974). *Topophilia: A study of environmental perceptions, attitudes, and values*. Englewood Cliffs, NJ: Prentice Hall.

Williams, D. R. (2014). Making sense of "place": Reflections on pluralism and positionality in place research. *Landscape and Urban Planning*, *131* (November), 74–82. doi:10.1016/j.landurbplan.2014.08.002

Chapter 6

Artistic Intelligence
Creativity in Public Process

Strategy making in the planning field requires complex imaginative, intellectual, and technical work, involving a wide range of sources of understanding and imaginative power.

—Patsy Healey (2010, p. 188)

Artists are celebrated for their imaginative powers—creative inclinations and skills they act on and foster throughout their lives. To provide the power Healey called for in the quote above, some cities have enrolled artists in different aspects of city planning. In my work as a planning consultant, I've had the opportunity to bring artists into many planning processes. Their skills are applicable in virtually all aspects of planning, but the focus in the work I do, and in this chapter, is on how artists engage in and lead public participation processes.

Projects I have been involved with span 27 different U.S. states and have included artists from theatre, design, visual, and fabric arts, writers, choreographers, vocalist-songwriters, and others. While some artists take their work into other arenas of public service, and some cities have involved artists in many different areas of planning, the focus in this chapter is based on my experience in neighborhood and district planning, creative economy development, and cultural planning. In these settings, artists have worked as codesigners, facilitators, and collaborators in data collection and interpretation. Projects are carried out directly with municipal agencies as well as independent actors such as community foundations, chambers of commerce, or other service organizations. Sometimes we work on stand-alone plans, and sometimes on integrated plans side-by-side with city planners or other consultants with expertise in areas such as transportation, parks, and economic development.

In this chapter, I explore theory, history, and experiences related to the roles of artists in advancing these practices. While my work is not unique—and I will reflect on a few of its earlier practitioners—it is only slowly finding acceptance within the formal city planning profession.

Finding Joy in Civic Engagement

In his 100-year survey of urban planning, American planning historian William Rohe (2009) examined the evolution of local and neighborhood-based approaches citing important lessons. One of those was "that local social relations and networks matter greatly to people and should be given great weight in revitalization planning" (p. 216). Building, rebuilding, and maintaining social networks that are open, equitable, functional, and leave community members with a sense of fulfillment and even joy are essential for every community. I learned during the 1980s and 1990s, through my involvement in community-based arts, that artists can be highly effective organizers, problem-solvers, and literal, as well as metaphorical, builders of alternative social, organizational, and physical community networks. For over 20 years, I led an arts organization that served as ground for convening, conducting dialogue, forming partnerships, and staging action. There I learned about the capacities of creative processes and of individual artists to effectively assess group dynamics, identify solutions, and build bridges.

Conditions conducive to fostering positive interactions, activating imaginations, and facilitating deliberative practices critical in urban planning are precisely the conditions I have experienced through artist-led practices. Orchestrating or staging new and meaningful ways for people to be together and to share fulfilling experiences is exactly what theatre directors, choreographers, poets, muralists, musical conductors, and other artists do brilliantly. Canadian scholar-practitioner Steven Dang (2005) asserted that "as a means of conversation, the arts are often more accessible and inclusive than the standard town hall meeting or open house" (p. 124). My experience says that this is putting it mildly. They can be as different as night and day.

Creative environments are less intimidating, less judgmental, and often provoke a good degree of simple social enjoyment and a sense of satisfaction while addressing serious and complicated issues. Artists can bring skills to help those on the margins amplify their voice, especially important for individuals less skilled at verbal debate or reluctant to stand up in a community meeting.

"Art can be that important initial point of entry, transcending language and providing opportunities for residents to learn to work together on shared projects," wrote Dang (2005, p. 125). Techniques artists use employ a variety of participatory practices including visual arts, theatre, dance, music, and even writing as activities that draw out residents' ways of relating to, using, and envisioning their community spaces and experiences.

City Planning and Artmaking

With public sector resources squeezed, and while cities confront increasingly complex challenges, it is important to find ways to do more than one thing at a time in civic work. Expanding the imaginative capacities of the public sector, as Landry and Caust (2017) advocated, and promoting engagement in local democracy both present enormous challenges, especially in neoliberal political environments bent on dismantling people-centered institutions and policies. Creative engagement practices are among the contributions artists can make to city planning, community development, and civic institutions generally.

In normative city planning practice, planners are positioned as experts who formulate proposals to advance development or changes. Through public process, they inform residents and invite—although don't always really welcome—comment. Residents sometimes push back and disputes may ensue. Some advocates from within the planning field, such as Forester (1999, 2018), have urged planners to engage in more consultative processes, seeking ideas and deliberating their merits with residents. These have not become standard practice, nor have the imaginative powers of artists been enlisted, with rare exceptions.

Artist-led, culturally attuned creative practices, when applied to the public participation process in planning, can result in better outcomes. These include expanding the diversity of people involved, eliciting deeper local knowledge, and making participation more meaningful, enjoyable, productive, and less contentious. Well-planned and facilitated public processes can build social connections, gather data, approach challenges with fresh eyes, activate group imaginations, find common ground, lead productive codesign activities, reframe complex problems, and strengthen participatory democracy, among other things. These are tall orders, and not every artist is inclined or prepared to jump into situations calling for such outcomes.

Still far from mainstream, artist-led creative engagement represents a growing practice among cities. Over the past decade, Los Angeles, New York City, Boston, Portland (Maine), Minneapolis, and St. Paul are among two-dozen cities employing artists in various roles and departments including planning. These range from regional and comprehensive city planning to neighborhood and district planning to special topical plans including parks, culture, transportation, and so on. Projects have ranged from addressing repeated flooding in North Dakota, to multiple artists in the Minneapolis planning department working to increase public involvement. An artist-in-residence program in New York City, launched in 2015, engages artists across many city agencies. A similar program in Boston began in 2016, engaging seven artists to address racial equity across multiple city platforms. A year later, the Boston-based Metropolitan Area Planning Council, a regional planning agency, created an artist-in-residence position, successively bringing in a sculptor (Lewenberg, 2019) and then a theatre artist (Harmon, 2019) to help staff improve strategies for involving the public across the 101 towns and cities the agency covers (see also the program, "Animating Democracy" from Americans for the Arts, n.d.).

Artmaking involves repurposing raw materials to create value, beauty, and new meaning as well as to identify unique and different purposes for those materials. And artists don't limit themselves just to conventional materials. They work with sound, movement, color, objects, buildings, spaces, or neighborhoods to address place and design as well as relationships, sense of identity, or social systems, just to name a few. Applying artmaking or creative practices to such tangible and intangible assets and dimensions of a neighborhood or city can change the game and open new possibilities. Creative engagement can take stakeholders on symbolic or metaphorical journeys to engage in learning, change-making, and community-building together. This enables and empowers community members and public officials to learn more about each other and themselves. It can move them to a new level where they make things together, find new connections, form new narratives and relationships, and experience collaborative action.

Planning and Public Process

Public participation in city and community planning has its own complex history. After half a century working on public participation as an institutionalized part of municipal planning in the United States, planners are still seeking ways to more effectively engage residents. Working alongside city planners, it is evident that to some of them, mandatory public processes are perfunctory, annoying assignments; for others, they are an opportunity to "sell" their ideas to a skeptical or uninformed public. Some planners find public responses challenging, while others discover useful information to help iterate and improve plans.

Creative processes led by someone outside the formal municipal structure can take public participation to another level.

Baeker (2002) attested, "The tools of the artist are an essential part of how we imagine cities: through stories, images, metaphors, exploring possibilities as well as critiques" (p. 24). Tools range from techniques to find shared vision, exercise voice, articulate ideas through song and movement, share stories, and celebrate the collective making of something new, even if symbolically. Notable urban theorists of the late 19th and mid-20th century, including Geddes (1915/1949) and Lewis Mumford (1961), advocated citizen participation in planning before it was generally accepted in the practice. Mumford promoted civic exhibitions on urban and regional issues, surveys, and public input as important in the creation of planning alternatives or scenarios. According to Baeker, Mumford saw plans as, "instruments of communal education" (p. 23).

Early city planning demanded engineering and organizational skills to coordinate resources and materials to implement expert-designed schemes. In contemporary planning, it is now recognized that planners need social and political skills more than, or, at least, in addition to, technical skills. In her article "Just Planning," British scholar Heather Campbell (2006) wrote, "The recent history of planning thought has seen the replacement of the planner as instrumental rationalist by the planner as facilitator" (p. 103).

Conducting public engagement using routine settings and formats along with cut-and-paste solutions is sure to fulfill the definition of insanity often attributed to Albert Einstein. Studies related to creativity and innovation consistently cite play, experimentation, and risk-taking as critical for new discovery. Those are rarely described in municipal procedure manuals, although Landry has focused more recent work on opening municipal agencies and processes to creative thinking. (see Landry and Margie Caust's, 2017, *The Creative Bureaucracy & Its Radical Common Sense*).

New thinking doesn't come from the center or mainstream of any profession. German-born computer science scholar Gerhard Fischer (2005), teaching in the United States, suggested that the edges "are where the unexpected can be expected, where innovative and unorthodox solutions are found, where serendipity is likely, and where old ideas find new life" (p. 5). City bureaucracies are notoriously risk-averse, necessitating new ways of thinking in order to just open themselves to creative processes. This is another way that artists can be helpful. They tend to be comfortable on the edges, outside the mainstream, outside the box. Innovation, play, experimentation, and risk-taking are core to their practice.

Some urban planning literature touches on creative techniques but largely ignores partnerships with creative practitioners (AKA, artists). Forester, a long-time proponent of public participation and of planning as a learning and deliberative process, references theatrical and arts terms so often in his writing, it's surprising he doesn't advocate recruiting theatre professionals and visual artists. In his book, *The Deliberative Practitioner* (Forester, 1999), he described "the staging of deliberation in planning" (p. 236) and he stresses "creativity and finesse" as well the importance of improvisation. Like Campbell (2006), Forester called on planners to reframe part of their work as what he called "process managers" to engage people in idea-generation and problem-solving. He also wrote about "the power of the sketch, the power of visual inquiry" (p. 109) as a potent tool in public engagement. In more recent writing, Forester (2018) described planning as "real drama—drama no less powerful, no less moving, no less instructive, and no less illuminating for being set on the stages of our cities and neighborhoods" (p. 15). He continued, calling on planners to create environments conducive to productive idea generation, discussion, and deliberation of solutions to planning challenges—precisely the things artists do well.

The creative environments that artists facilitate can change not only the expectations of participants but how they relate to planners and to one another. In her ideas for "unlearning the colonial cultures of planning" (the title of her book), Porter (2016) argued that one step is to "place people in a different relation with each other: one of service, not of winning the argument" (p. 158). Planners, in their important role of process managers, wrote Forester (1999), "exert real influence … by shaping processes of inclusion and exclusion, of participation and negotiation" (p. 90). He described how some of the most productive community deliberations take place in meetings that "brought them all together, not abstractly by appealing to 'community building' or to some unitary public interest, but performatively—practically, interactively—over cards, drinks, music, camaraderie and dance" (2018, p. 606). For Forester, these cultural practices served only to form and lubricate social connections. Relationships and comfort levels are important dimensions of the work. However, the activities he described did not fully integrate creative thinking and practice and cultural difference into the *process* of gathering information, devising solutions, and deliberation. He simply observed how sociability greased the wheels for planners to move their plans forward.

Planning as Storytelling

Sandercock (2003), an articulate advocate of story and storytelling as integral to planning, sees creative narrative practices, particularly filmmaking, as ways to open planning processes to the increasingly diverse people and cultures inhabiting cities of all sizes. This brings threefold benefits: the expansion of practical tools, the sharpening of critical judgment, and the widening of democratic discourse. Supporting such a need for multivariate input and criticality in the planning process, Porter (2016) further called for planning to be "self-aware as well as world-aware and working in the service of intellectual *and* [emphasis added] emotional connection" (p. 158). Building connections between people on a human or cultural level may, in fact, be a core function of planning, not a serendipitous byproduct.

Borrowed from the discipline of anthropology, ethnography is a method of collecting stories and a way of bringing *local knowledge* into the planning process. Honoring local knowledge has emerged as a critical part of good planning called for by various planning scholars and best derived through story gathering, telling, and focused listening. Techniques of applied ethnography offer planners a way forward in achieving more effective community participation (Maginn, 2007).

Dang (2005) characterized artists as the storytellers of their communities. "They can provide a planner not only deep insight into a community, but ready-made and powerful means of communicating them" (2005, p. 124). Dang advocates that planning education should include mining the rich meanings in stories and cultural artifacts. Planners need to take advantage of their communities' story-collectors and storytellers.

Californian James Rojas is among those who make the case that data are not limited to things that can be counted. Referring to his experience among urban planning students at MIT, where he graduated in 1990, Rojas described how creative inclinations made him the "odd duck" (personal communication, January 9, 2019). He made models and analyzed space not through quantitative methods but as a creative visual practice. To him, the city "is a spatial, visual, and material culture that ignites memories, emotions, and aspirations" (personal communication, January 9, 2019). This, he said, has to be understood through storytelling. In Los Angeles in the early 2000s, while involved with the arts, Rojas developed his practice of putting model-making to work to help people tell their stories. In a 2018 blog he wrote, "storytelling increases public involvement in city planning, increasing awareness of how the built environment shapes people's lives and how they can shape it in return" (Rojas, 2018, para. 18).

Rojas estimated he had conducted over 500 workshops in cities across the United States and Mexico, yet his practice is far from embraced by mainstream planning. "I ask participants to collaborate in building their ideal community using familiar objects such as hair rollers, popsicle sticks, pipe cleaners, and other material" (personal communication, January 9, 2019). He considered this immersive storytelling that "allows participants the physical activity of reflecting, touching, moving, and playing with objects on imaginary maps" (personal communication, January 9, 2019). He explained that participants are able to "quickly inquire, discover, prototype, and experiment with solutions. They learn their city is occupied by thousands of stories, seen or unseen, and all these stories collectively have power to promote physical change" (Rojas, 2018, para. 15). People gain a greater sense of agency, common purpose, and shared vocabulary when they make something together than when they simply try to talk about it or respond to images presented by planners or developers.

Similarly, in his work on deliberative process and through his research with planners, Forester (2018) observed cases in which planners rendered informal sketches or concepts for community members to respond to. This encourages curiosity and play, what he called "interactions of inquiry before argument" (p. 595) in service of stimulating participants' imaginations of possible futures. Sketches, collages, sculptures, photographs, and other creations of participants in planning processes provide valuable data. Planners, however, are not trained to interpret or analyze them and as such are often inclined to dismiss them. Stories, sounds, and movements elicited in response to prompts or to community challenges, can also serve as valuable data as is common in sociological research.

How to best harvest and analyze such data in planning is an emerging practice—one rich in possibilities. Artists and planners can borrow a page from qualitative research, especially ethnographic and phenomenological methods, to systematically collect and code data—stories, interpretations of drawings, photographic images, movement scores—to find hidden meanings and patterns that can lead to meaningful findings and conclusions. Planners spend considerable time learning to read data expressed through statistics. Artists and art historians learn to work with different symbols. Ethnographers and dramaturgs find meaning in nuances of stories. There are many interpreters who can read more than one of these "languages". They are needed in city planning.

Creative Expressions as Data

Artists' training and discipline emphasize observation, listening, questioning, and intuiting the shape, meanings, stories, and symbols in their surroundings and in human actions, as well as possibilities in materials. Carter (2015) characterized city planners and designers as *dramaturgs* (p. 15). Dramaturgy is the practice of contextualizing, interpreting, and adapting story for the stage as a partner with playwrights and directors to give structure and representation of the key dramatic elements appropriate for the audience and context. City planners are not trained to approach their work this way, or to even value abstract or symbolic data revealed through creative processes. This is where extended dialogue between artists and planners can be beneficial. There is much potential for artist-generated data to have meaning for city planners, and such conversations are increasingly taking place.

Creative and culturally attuned methods employed or led by artists can offer needed dimensions in city planning, listening to and appreciating the nuances in diverse cultural traditions of residents. Such methods also help engage people of more diverse ethnic and economic backgrounds in public process and draw people more deeply into contributing to the analytical and visioning work of planning. Artists who are culturally attuned to, or, better yet, part of intersectional traditions, cultures, and ways of thinking can more effectively involve diverse communities who share geographic places in neighborhoods and cities in the co-creation of solutions to community challenges and engagement in devising more viable alternatives. As discussed in Chapter 2, because city planning grew from technical roots in engineering, architecture, and data-driven policy development, its practitioners have steered away from or resisted creative disciplines or working with artists as partners.

Creative Engagement: Setting the Stage

I am not the first to argue the merits of artist-led engagement practices in the planning arena or to reflect on such experiences. Among early documented practitioners who integrated creative disciplines with formal spatial planning were American avant-garde dancer Anna Halprin and her landscape architect husband, Lawrence Halprin. Based in the San Francisco Bay Area, their 1960s and 1970s experiments brought their respective practices together (Merriman, 2010). British geographer Peter Merriman (2010) described how the Halprins attempted "to rethink landscape architecture and dance through the understanding of the spaces of choreography and performance, and the performativities and choreographies of spaces" (p. 431). The Halprins not only tried new ways to conceptualize spatial planning, but also new ways to involve a wider mix of people in articulating spatial thinking. They combined their practices and progressive politics to democratize choreography and dance performance, to include people of color and other marginalized people in workshops to exercise collective creativity and democratize landscape and urban design. According to Merriman (2010), they developed and practiced community processes "grounded in principles of group therapy and an emphasis on participation, direct personal experience and play" (p. 439).

Australian planner Wendy Sarkissian began her creative practice in the 1970s, later publishing a reflective book, *Creative Community Planning: Transformative Engagement Methods for Working at the Edge*, with artist-planner Dianna Hurford and writer Christine Wenman (Sarkissian, Hurford, & Wenman, 2010). In summing up their experiences as creative planning consultants, Sarkissian et al. described their efforts "to meet at a place of creation that calls new, informed and meaningful ideas into existence through rationality, integration, community knowledge and experience" (p. 7). Their book traces a wide-ranging body of work in communities of all types and sizes across Australia. They experimented with performance, music, visual arts, and stories. They worked with local artists and activists, "listening to stories, identifying common goals and forming partnerships in action: this is creative community engagement—engagement that is as much about learning as doing" (Sarkissian et al., 2010, p. 154).

Since the late 1990s, Dang (2005) worked with communities in Canada in creative community engagement, using the artistic process to "tap the creative collective potential of participants" (p. 123). He further observed, "While the planning profession may be reluctant to engage in community cultural development work, community-based artists are hard at work in community planning" (p. 123). Dang's own work focuses on activating local artists and imaginations. He described gathering stories as well as images from local artists (artists defined broadly)—images that tell profound stories that illustrate community values. Dang categorized three ways to employ art in planning: "Art as Window," "Art as Dialogue," and "Art as Doorway" (pp. 123–125). In this construct, creative processes help participants see, discuss, and move to new ways of conceptualizing spatial design together.

Dang (2005) observed how "community-based arts practice often demonstrates community planning at its best: strengths-based, capacity-building, participatory, inclusive, communicative, reflective, innovative and adaptive" (p. 124). This work is also part of the wider "turn to community in the arts" described by Wyatt, MacDowall, and Mulligan (2013), as discussed earlier in Chapter 4. They described a trend beginning in the late 20th century, "a surge of new or renewed interest in the idea of community across all art forms" (p. 82). Multiple forces, they asserted, have contributed to this turn; one, they said, stems from "artists' attempts to bridge relationships between aesthetic and activist practices; a dissolution in the boundaries between cultural, social, political and economic domains; and the increasing instrumentalization of the arts" (p. 81).

Artists of many disciplines working in community settings since at least the 1960s have developed an extensive array of techniques and practices to foster community building and promote engagement in social issues and civic affairs. American cultural activists and writers Bill Cleveland (2000) and Arlene Goldbard (2006) have chronicled community-based arts and "community cultural development" through which artists across disciplines developed approaches in a variety of settings to activate engagement in community. They surveyed many of the ways artists impact individuals and communities in relation to spatial change and policy-making, and social network building and organizing around social justice issues. The work they described prepared the ground for much of the artist activism and artist involvement in planning and civic work of the current era.

Process as Product in Planning: Four Case Studies

Four brief stories follow based on some of my work involving artists in community planning contexts. The investment needed to include artists varied widely, from one-time facilitation activities to extensive 12- to 18-month involvements in conceptualizing, implementing public engagement, and harvesting relevant planning outcomes. Most of these artists had extensive backgrounds in community-based work and/or teaching and were eager and adept at welcoming and mentoring less experienced artists. Most of the city planners involved readily admit they learned much from the artists. One planner vowed he would never conduct community planning again without involving artists.

Community Building as Patchwork: A North Dakota Case

In the spring of 2015, our planning team, having been commissioned jointly by the City of Grand Forks, North Dakota, and a community foundation invited a local quilting artist to lead an eclectic group of over 80 community members through the steps of cutting and arranging fabric into small squares—one step in quilt-making and in a larger planning project. Invited to a community planning meeting, some participants were caught unaware, but all engaged constructively and ultimately appeared to enjoy the experience. This was 18 years after a massive flood and fire devastated this fiercely independent community. Residents had worked hard to put their city back together, yet early in our planning process, we sensed a piece was still missing. Residents had done the long and sometimes painful work of physical and economic reconstruction, yet they seemed to have lost the joy in building a community together. Along with quilt-making, a local music and dance group performed while residents assembled their squares into a large, collective patchwork on the floor. As the work came together, a shift was evident. Young and old passed the microphone to explain the meaning of their contribution to the quilt and how their piece contributed to the community. Without judging the artistic merit of any square, they applauded each other celebrating their creative achievement. Making artwork together under the guidance of an accomplished locally known artist, all while discussing their vision for the community's future, brought a critical element of joy in collective achievement back to community work.

Learning from Diversity in an Urban Center: A Minneapolis Case

A year-long Minneapolis district planning project I led in 2011–2012 was designed to engage a diverse mix of stakeholders in a variety of ways in accordance with the complex nature of the linear district known as downtown's Hennepin Avenue. The project was funded by grants and supported by the Hennepin Theatre Trust, operator of three historic downtown theatres, and by the City of Minneapolis. While the process began with explorations of local Indigenous history and leaned largely on local knowledge, it included outside expertise to push the boundaries of thinking and to inform the process. Visitors included American artist Candy Chang, creative city visionary Charles Landry, American urban geographer Don Mitchell, and Los Angeles community development leader Chanchanit Martorell. Set a month apart, their presentations keynoted parallel artist-led public participation workshops. Community engagement activities addressed long-term capacity-building by creating and/or strengthening relationships among stakeholders in the practice of problem-solving.

The project drew wide attention and discussion to both assets and challenges of the district and built understanding of how resources and creative energies of various institutions and businesses could be collectively employed to take on challenges from homelessness to street crime to unwelcoming urban design to the demonization of Black teenagers. A challenge facing the district was one of connectivity—connectivity between institutions, businesses, and a wide range of stakeholders. With a wealth of cultural assets and historic meaning, Hennepin is considered the city's 'main drag,' the heart of its nightlife.

Moving beyond physical assets to the collection of stories was an important step. For part of this work, the project engaged several youth organizations as settings for artists to work. Under artists' guidance, youth interviewed, videotaped, photographed, wrote poetry and music, and created radio spots highlighting stories of people in the district. Products were presented in numerous venues along the 1.5 downtown miles of Hennepin Avenue including the central library, art museum, office building atrium, and public high school, as well as through social media. Among the challenges with the project was devising public participation to involve the diverse mix of people who make the avenue their space. Stakeholders ranged from White suburban families attending the Disney *Lion King*, LGBTQ club-goers, homeless people, basketball fans from the adjacent arena, and teenagers hanging out. The district represents a kind of urban space and experience unfamiliar to many in the region.

To design and assess the activities, we conducted multiple meetings with four lead artists, urban designers, and architects, and each included regular input from three institutional project partners and a representative of the city. Artists included a theatre director, visual artist, choreographer, and vocal artist/song-writer. All the artists were African American. They used facilitation techniques attuned to diverse cultural sensibilities appropriate to this urban place. The challenge for the artist team, similar to that described by Sarkissian et al. (2010), was to create "spaces of trust for different kinds of stories to emerge and for people to express themselves in their own vocabularies" (p. 13). Activities exercised every voice singularly and in unison, practiced listening to others, moved in relation to others, and drew visions of the future to activate and bring forth a tapestry of ideas that were incorporated into the plan.

Testing the Limits: A Suburban Case

In a 2014–2015 project in the growing Minneapolis suburb of Bloomington, with a team of six artists, including three from the Hennepin Avenue project, we conducted multiple projects across 18 months. These included a seven-day charrette under a large tent in a centrally located park. Not a standard charrette, it was more of a festival of artist-led discovery and planning. Activities included walking and bike tours, an idea competition, and dialogues with historians, planners, and developers, in addition to food, music, dance, ice cream socials, and more.

One small project within the larger effort responded to the municipality's articulated desire to incorporate creative placemaking and public art in new developments and existing neighborhoods. This mini project tested the local government's permit review procedures vested in their Design Review Committee (DRC). This group included city planners, fire marshal, police, economic development officials, risk manager, and others. We selected several projects proposed by community artists for a mock review by the DRC on the stage of a small auditorium with an audience.

The most revealing and simple artist proposal was to place a soapbox—a small raised platform—in a public space to be used at will by members of the public with something to say. Multiple members of the DRC found significant problems with the proposed soapbox. Citing existing regulations and public safety concerns, the DRC declined the proposal. This did not bode well for the potentials of a public art program. Nonetheless, the city has gone on to create one of the most active and adventurous such programs in the region. This semi-staged theatrical exercise shed light on the gap between desired ends and existing policies.

Finding Stories of Place: A Rural Midwest Case

The story circle is a vehicle long employed by community-based theatre practitioners. It served as a useful tool for a 2012 project covering an 8,000-square-mile rural watershed area spanning parts of Wisconsin and Minnesota. The area, known as the St. Croix River Valley, was identified by leaders in the region for the possible formation of a U.S. Park Service National Heritage Area—a locally managed network of cultural, educational, and touristic resources organized around a meaningful historic or cultural theme. A foundational task was to identify whether people across the region shared a substantive connection—a shared story—that was meaningful, well-supported by existing historical assets, and relevant to the region's future. With oversight of a stakeholder steering committee representing the vast geography, our team was invited to help identify that critical story. The heritage project was more than a simple listening tour and required core artists and teams of volunteers to conduct 11 gatherings in a consistent fashion. Considerable care went into devising a methodology and preparing the teams. This enabled the process to engage people more deeply through participation in story circles and careful listening with systematic documentation of each story.

In each of the 11 counties in the region, community members attended workshops that resulted in 438 discrete stories grounded in an accumulated 10,000 years of experiences. One of the warm-up activities employed at each gathering was to ask each of the roundtables, populated by six to eight participants, to add up their total years living in the region. This allowed some to claim many years of experience and others to claim the freshest perspectives—all valued equally. The next stage involved distilling data from the 438 stories to identify the four most prominent themes for further consideration.

We then chose a process that represented some risk and had at least one vocal skeptic. A youth theatre troupe based in one of the small towns in the region was engaged to work with an area playwright to turn each of four emergent themes into five-minute scenes. The youth troupe acted out each of the prospective themes at four strategically located subregional gatherings.

Rather than a presentation by a historian or economic development specialist, teenagers illustrated the themes through theatre. As a clear majority of participants in all the workshops and summits sported gray hair, this brought fresh thinking as well as participation from a new generation. The response was phenomenal. Theatre brought the ideas to life in wonderful ways simple words or PowerPoint images could not. The cross-generational relationship-building added a critical dimension not only to the planning but to the meaning of the prospective Heritage Area.

Summary

Unlike city planners, artists are not experts in the technical details of planning, nor do they often have direct access to the levers of decision-making in municipal government. As such, they provide an ideal complement to city planners as they focus on the human interactions, deeper meanings, and problem-solving processes. Artists draw on local knowledge and how it can be relevant to the questions at hand. They are inquisitive and deconstruct things to reframe issues and bring participants on a journey together to new ways of understanding the challenges their communities face. Artists can't provide answers to all the challenges city planners and communities face. They can be potent collaborators and facilitators to help communities and planners work together to devise solutions.

Through my more recent years as a community and cultural planner, I've come to see how creatively activating people can help stakeholders better tap their thinking and use multiple expressive forms, feel part of a group, and create a more constructive or positive "vibe" around public process. I've come to appreciate that *how* planning is conducted significantly influences the outcomes. And, I learned that every community activity *must* include food and beverage for participants to share!

At the same time, it's worth noting that artists' efforts, participatory processes, and even food for community members can be a smoke screen. For those involved, these activities can become something planning critic Samuel Stein (2019) referred to as *cover*, "designed to make them feel good about losing" (p. 190). He described how major real estate interests have inordinate control of city governments and how planners find themselves boxed in with few options but to serve the interests of capital while trying to soothe losses endured by residents. To maintain credibility with their community, planners must be sure the work of artists and the participation processes are genuine, meaningful to the planning, and not a smoke screen.

It is imperative, therefore, that city planners and their creative partners also understand this work as long-term capacity-building for communities to exercise grassroots democracy, as the next two chapters describe. Together, city planners and artists can work towards helping diverse people in their communities find common ground, build their imaginative and collaborative muscles, learn how the wheels of government work, and find joy in working together with neighbors—so they're more likely to want to do it again!

References

Americans for the Arts. (n.d.). *Animating Democracy*. Retrieved from http://animating-democracy.org/collection/artists-working-and-within-municipal-governments

Baeker, G. (2002). Beyond garrets and silos: Concepts, trends and developments in cultural planning. Department of Canadian Heritage. Ontario Ministry of Culture, Quebec Ministry of Culture and Communications.

Campbell, H. (2006). Just planning: The art of situated ethical judgment. *Journal of Planning Education and Research, 26*(1), 92–106. doi:10.1177/0739456X06288090

Carter, P. (2015). *Places made after their stories: Design and the art of choreotopography*. Crawley: UWA Publishing.

Cleveland, William (2000). *Art in Other Places: Artists at Work in America's Community and Social Institutions*. Oakland, CA: New Village Press.

Dang, S. R. (2005). A starter menu for planner/artist collaborations. *Planning Theory & Practice, 6*(1), 123–126. doi:10.1080/1464935042000335029

Fischer, Gerhard (2005). *Distances and Diversity: Sources for Social Creativity*. University of Colorado, Center for LifeLong Learning and Design (L3D), Department of Computer Science, 430 UCB, Boulder, CO.

Forester, J. (1999). *The Deliberative Practitioner: Encouraging Participatory Planning Process*. Cambridge, MA: MIT Press.

Forester, J. (2018). Deliberative planning practices without smothering invention: Practical aesthetic view. In A. Bachtiger, J. S. Dryzek, J. Mansbridge, & M. E. Warren (Eds.), *The Oxford handbook of deliberative democracy* (pp. 595–611). Oxford: Oxford University Press.

Geddes, P. (1949). *Cities in evolution*. London: Williams & Norgate. (Original work published 1918)

Goldbard, Arlene (2006). *New Creative Community: The Art of Cultural Development*. New Village Press: Oakland, CA.

Harmon, E. (2019, February 14). *Q & A with Hortense Gerardo*. MAPC's New Artist-in-Residence. Boston, MA: Metropolitan Area Planning Council (MAPC). Retrieved from https://www.mapc.org/planning101/qa-with-hortense-gerardo-mapcs-new-artist-in-residence/

Healey, P. (2010). *Making better places: The planning project in the twenty-first century*. Houndmills: Palgrave Macmillan.

Landry, C., & Caust, M. (2017). *The creative bureaucracy & its radical common sense*. Gloucestershire: Comedia.

Lewenberg, C. (2019). A reflection from MAPC's first artist-in-residence [Blog post]. *Americans for the Arts.* Retrieved from https://blog.americansforthearts. org/2019/05/15/a-reflection-from-mapc's-first-artist-in-residence.

Maginn, P. J. (2007). Towards more effective community participation in urban regeneration: The potential of collaborative planning and applied ethnography. *Qualitative Research, 7*(1), 25–43. doi:10.1177/1468794106068020

Merriman, P. (2010). Architecture/dance: Choreographing and inhabiting spaces with Anna and Lawrence Halprin. *Cultural Geographies, 17*(4), 427–449. doi:10.1177/1474474010376011

Mumford, L. (1961). *The city in history: Its origins, its transformations, and its prospects.* New York, NY: Harcourt, Brace & World.

Rojas, J. (2018). Let me tell you a story! storytelling to enhance urban planning engagement [Blog post]. *Planetizen.* Retrieved from https://www.planetizen.com/features/97224-let-me-tell-you-story-storytelling-enhance-urban-planning-engagement

Porter, L. (2016). *Unlearning the colonial cultures of planning.* Abingdon: Routledge. doi:10.4324/9781315548982

Rohe, W. M. (2009). From local to global: One hundred years of neighborhood planning. *Journal of the American Planning Association, 75*(2), 209–230. doi:10.1080/01944360902751077

Sandercock, L. (2003). *Cosmopolis II: Mongrel cities in the 21st century.* London: Continuum. doi:10.5040/9781472545527

Sarkissian, W., Hurford, D., & Wenman, C. (2010). *Creative community planning: Transformative engagement methods for working at the edge.* London: Earthscan.

Stein, S. (2019). *Capital city: Gentrification and the real estate state.* New York, NY: Verso.

Wyatt, D., MacDowall, L., & Mulligan, M. (2013). Critical introduction: The turn to community in the arts. *Journal of Arts & Communities, 5*(2/3), 81–91. doi:10.1386/jaac.5.2-3.81_1

Chapter 7

The Maps Strike Back
From Empires to Equity

City planners would be lost without maps, and yet, maps don't tell the whole story. In fact, maps can divide and tell a very limited story, a story that may exclude most of the people and voices they might purport to encompass. Historically maps were used to control narratives, political power, and economies, as well as shape identities. Most are still used to those ends. Maps can limit thinking, separate people, and misrepresent or mischaracterize identity. Mapmaking, as an act, is an exercise in power. At the same time, mapmaking can be a process to promote democracy and inclusion. Maps can help people find themselves and find their place.

As French social philosopher Michel de Certeau (1988) eloquently suggested, "What the map cuts up, the story cuts across" (p. 129). Stories and storytellers can bridge divides and include people. Likewise, maps, and the process of creating them, have the potential to empower people, express their sense of identity, and connect them to place.

This chapter looks at maps, participatory mapmaking, and the application of creative practices to mapping processes as tools to identify community assets and build community engagement and cohesion. As a form of storytelling, maps can serve as bridges. While no narrative or map will ever tell the whole story, mapmaking, like storytelling, when practiced as a process in which people feel in control of their narrative, can accrue a variety of benefits. Used as a verb, the word *map* suggests an endless variety of techniques and processes. Virtually anything, tangible and intangible, can be mapped. That said, *how* mapping is done as well as *who* is doing it is indicative of where power lies. Appreciating mapping as a *process*—one practiced in the spirit of democracy—becomes even more important in efforts to build more just, equitable, and inclusive communities.

Cultural planning practitioners and scholars, including Baeker (2002), Mercer (2006), and Stevenson (2014), described cultural asset mapping as a widely accepted foundational step in cultural planning. Stevenson (2014) explained mapping as "about place and tracing the intersection of place and meaning" (p. 39). As pointed out earlier, however, cultural asset mapping has not been consistently practiced in cultural planning in the United States. I advocate that it should be and that, as a practice, it can bring great value to city planning.

Mapping Everyday Lived Experience

Participatory asset mapping, a related practice emerging from the field of community organizing, allows people to discover previously invisible or underappreciated resources at their disposal as well as to learn about varied and shared stories of their community. Such mapping processes spark conversations and build greater understanding between people by helping them find common ground among things they value about their communities. Cultural asset mapping brought together with participatory mapmaking focus on meaning and shared values while building social bridges. Mapping memorable elements of everyday lived experiences can uncover symbolic, historic, and real present-day dimensions that can connect or divide people. When part of a participatory process that fosters dialogue, such mapping activities serve to heal as well as to empower.

As the previous chapter might suggest, I advocate artist involvement and leadership in planning processes, and this includes participatory cultural asset mapping. An emerging practice in many parts of the world, artists are bringing valuable tools to the task of finding deeper meanings and creating a greater shared sense of place through mapping processes. Canadian cultural scholars Nancy Duxbury and W. F. Garrett-Petts, with New Zealand artist Alys Longley, are leaders in writing about creative cultural mapping. In their recent book, *Artistic Approaches to Cultural Mapping* (Duxbury, Garrett-Petts, & Longley, 2019), they assign artists a rather exhaustive and dynamic job. Artistic approaches, they said, can

> transform the process of cultural mapping by challenging more instrumental approaches, by animating and honouring the local, by giving voice and definition to the vernacular, by recognizing the notion of place as inhabited by story and history, by slowing down the process of seeing and listening, by asserting and embodying the aesthetic as a key component of community

self-expression and self-representation, by championing inclusion and experimentation, by exposing often unacknowledged power relations, by catalyzing identity formation, and by generally making the intangible both more visible and audible through multiple modes of artistic representation and performance.

(p. 18)

Are city planners equipped to expand their mapping practices while incorporating Lefebvre's (1974/1991) third dimension of *everyday lived experience*? Rather than beginning with maps of land use and built forms, can city planners map places of meaning and stories of people and events that mark the landscape with joy, hope, trauma, and pain? Better appreciating variations in how the ways of life of residents, workers, and visitors are embedded in place helps develop a cultural sense of place and city plans more in tune with residents' feelings. This goes deeper than the outlines representing built and physical landscapes that city planners work from. Can city and cultural planning work together to make places more welcoming and accommodating to a wider range of people and their cultural practices?

Creative maps and mapping help planners, and the communities they work with, better understand the character and meanings of place, the feelings and/ or attachments people have, and relationships they may not have known existed. Further, and perhaps more importantly, participatory processes mobilize and empower people to feel a greater sense of belonging and agency. Community members sharing stories and taking charge of the narrative is part and parcel an exercise in democracy. At the same time, it's important to appreciate this kind of mapmaking as a process and a dimension or activity of democracy (as will be discussed in Chapter 8) rather than fixed maps that assign place meaning exclusively to the hands of an existing group of people. Can we find joy in hearing new stories and adding layers to place meaning remaining be open to new arrivals as well as lifelong and multigenerational residents?

Maps and Power

How people understand maps is also an important dimension to the power of maps. Maps are "often regarded as neutral, scientific, and accurate reflections of the world," wrote British geographer Heather Winlow (2020, p. 312). However, as she pointed out, maps are constructed from and express the values and beliefs of their authorizers. To best interpret and analyze their cultural, political, and economic context, it must be understood who is making them, how they are making them, and for what purposes, as well as who and what are included and left out and why.

A recent story in the Thompson Reuters Foundation's *Places* described objections of neighborhood leaders to the de facto renaming and redefining of their communities by Google Maps, an entity that is literally redefining the world. Real estate developers, Airbnb, Starbucks, and others with financial interests in directing people to certain places supply data to what is now the world's largest mapmaker. Thus, these maps do not always honor long-held place histories but represent visions that serve those profiting from those places (Bachi, 2019). While the technology and players are new, this is not much different from how maps have come about and have been used historically.

Scholars and activists alike question the motives of mapmakers. American geographer J. Brian Harley (1988) asserted, "As much as guns and warships, maps have been the weapons of imperialism" (p. 131). Maps characterize, and in some cases vilify or erase people. By the mid-19th century, Winlow (2020) wrote, "The whole globe, excluding the polar regions, had been explored, ordered, and cartographically reproduced. Myths of fantastic peoples had been dispelled but ideas of moral and physical difference remained" (p. 310).

For instance, after 150 years, the notion of Africa as "The Dark Continent" lingers. Its alleged mysteries and savagery were described under that title by British explorer and writer, Henry Morton Stanley during the latter half of the 19th century (Stanley, 1890). Popular media continue to perpetuate the existence of savage and mystical forces, reinforcing contemporary racism and bolster White supremacy. Winlow (2020) described how "ethnocentric assumptions about moral and physical differences were applied to contemporary populations" (p. 310). She added,

> Alongside this erasure of ethnic groups from the landscape, there has been a separate history of racial cartography that has involved the deliberate portrayal of difference within the map text, a form of mapping that has also served to reinforce notions of "otherness."
>
> (p. 309)

As to the power of maps to claim territories, Porter (2016), in her work on the colonial history of planning, wrote,

> Critical re-reading of maps exposes how maps are instead a technique of power, of the power/knowledge nexus, where the authority to represent

the world resides in the (colonial) power producing the map and claiming its truth. Maps helped perform discovery and in doing so, helped perform dispossession.

(p. 70)

Maps have long erased Indigenous peoples and the identity and meaning of places. Maps represent the known and the unknown, establish the familiar and ignore what the mapmaker prefers to remove, to make desirable or undesirable. As Winlow (2020) explained, "Behind most maps is a patron; historically, the monarchy, the government, and the church have all initiated mapmaking schemes" (p. 312). American geographer Brenda Parker (2006) cited a text by a Mayan mapmaker with the slogan, "map or be mapped" (p. 472). Maps continue to be a tool or device for cutting up the physical world into territories, ownership, and uses. While they are handy for planners to delineate zoning or for travelers to find their destinations, the symbolic history of maps betrays them, especially when members of a community see their own places misrepresented, as in the Google Maps story.

From Illusion to Tool

The idea of maps as a purely objective product of science has long been debunked. Redaelli (2019) agreed, writing, "it is an illusion that the map is a mirror of reality" (p. 51). Maintaining this illusion serves as part of the exercise of power. Citing an influential and long-used cartography textbook, *Elements of Cartography* by Arthur Robinson (1969), American geographer Jeremy Crampton (2001) described how the textbook perpetuated the myth of mapping as science. Decades passed, Crampton wrote, before "an 'epistemic break' between a model of cartography as a communication system, and one in which it is seen in a field of power relations" (p. 235). Regardless of how planning schools now teach mapping, the myth that they represent a neutral science also lingers.

In the present neoliberal era of global capitalism and high technology, corporations and big data have the greater power to create maps and define places, thereby redefining people and identity in those places. Global capital has made considerable investment in maintaining the illusion that maps represent an objective reality. Harley's (1988) unconventional thinking about maps in the 1980s helped turn a corner in mapping scholarship and practice. The power of maps became more transparent and was challenged. He and others began to contemplate ways to democratize maps and the process of mapping. "If maps are tools of power for the elite," asked Parker (2006), "then can mapping help others claim such power?" (p. 477).

Tracing the evolution of the purpose of maps from the user point of view, Crampton (2001) described how maps came to be understood first as storage mechanisms for spatial data, then as a medium of communication, and more recently, at least among scholars, as social constructions that do not represent scientific fact. They have, in real ways, become multidimensional. Scholars of maps advocate questioning their patrons or authorizers, contents, production methods (and by whom), media used to express content, as well as the interface or how users experience maps, including through dynamic interactivity. Shifting power relationships represents one of the potentials of cultural mapping. Porter (2016) argued that "'compartmentalizing culture' in this way is an act of power, because it enables authority over what can and cannot be considered valuable in environments and for whom" (p. 110).

Most city planners today have at their disposal sophisticated mapping tools along with databases representing social and economic phenomena that can be displayed in informative and sometimes dynamic graphic layers over representations of geographic places. Layers may represent household incomes, property values, automobile traffic flows, footfalls on sidewalks at different times of day, climate patterns, and walking-shed. The list is endless. In digital form, maps can be dynamic or interactive so they reflect different times of day, week, or season, or so that different layers can appear and disappear to illustrate relationships. What city planners rarely have are significant data on the cultural dimensions of their cities and historical and contemporary meanings of places.

Locating Culture

Cultural mapping aims to capture stories, to identify places of meaning, and to describe intangible aspects of community life as part of informing the development of plans that support community values and aspirations. Places of meaning identified by residents, however, may or may not conform to officially or institutionally accepted place meanings and uses. Besides the obvious cultural organizations or formal gathering places, fine-grained data on tangible and intangible cultural and creative assets is thin or nonexistent. Places and practices that have significance in everyday life—especially for Indigenous people, communities of color, and immigrants—are not recorded in government databases. Meanings reside in the memories and daily life patterns—the everyday lived experiences—of residents and visitors.

Approaches to mapping by city planners and cultural planners differ in that the former typically base their maps on the jurisdictional, natural, and built elements of physical space. Cultural planners begin with mapping cultural practices of people, place meaning, and important activities to understand the creative, historic, organizational, visual, and symbolic dimensions of places—who uses them, how, when, and why. Doing so using the best practices of civic engagement advances dialogue and community-building processes. The *what* that cultural planners map should be both tangible and intangible. Asking people about their daily experiences and places of meaning doesn't always yield expected results.

In the summer of 2019, I supervised 10 teams of university students in Beijing in cultural planning exercises to investigate different neighborhoods around that huge Chinese city. In observing activities and talking with residents, multiple teams reported corner stores as critical and meaningful places of meeting, information exchange, and informal cultural activity. A few months later in Massachusetts, working with a group of cultural activists, a local grocery store similarly surfaced as a key cultural asset—a meeting place and place of information exchange. These businesses, and the functions they perform, are less traditional yet essential cultural resources. This came as a surprise to those collecting data.

As part of cultural planning work in the city of Providence, Rhode Island, in 2011, I worked with Craig Dreeszen to inventory formal and informal public and private gathering places within several known creative hot spots. These data were added to the planners' base maps so future planning could accommodate and foster cultural and creative vibrancy. With the Rhode Island public transit agency and the city, we also mapped character and meaning along four key transit corridors into the downtown. Combining historical research, documenting existing cultural assets and activities, conducting neighborhood surveys, and community focus groups, we produced character of place reports.

In one case, Elmwood Avenue, built over trading pathways used by the Narragansett and Wampanoag, was identified as the "Gateway to Opportunity," distinguished as a tree-lined trolley car suburb that symbolized the American Dream for new immigrants. It was laid out as a greenway to Roger Williams Park that was named for the colonial dissident who was banished from Massachusetts for speaking out against religious intolerance and the taking of Indigenous lands. In another case, Chalkstone Avenue was singled out for "Honoring Providence's Workers." Long populated by working people, it was built with workers' housing and a trolley to accommodate the workforce for Providence's 19th-century factories and mills.

These and other character reports informed public art commissions designed to enhance the identity around key stops and ultimately increase use of transit services. Such fine-grained mapping, as well as citywide mapping of place meaning, serves to make planners more attuned to what and why people feel attached to places. They are thereby able to avoid mistakes of a symbolic nature that may explode beyond what a "rational" city planner may see as important. This also gives planners a better idea of long-term patterns of use, especially related to gathering and conducting events or small-scale activities that have meaning in the everyday life in a neighborhood or community.

Seeing Community Assets: A Foundational Concept

Before discussing the *what*—the things to identify that constitute cultural assets—and the *how*—the processes to engage in asset mapping—it's important to review the idea of assets, what they mean for communities, and why a focus on mapping assets is important. Identifying and then mapping cultural assets also has to begin with defining what those two words represent: culture and assets. Culture is addressed at length in an earlier chapter, although below I provide guides to identifying tangible and intangible cultural assets. Here, I reflect on ideas related to assets and why this way of thinking is important in planning and community-building contexts.

What exactly are community assets? Where do we find them and how do we put them to work? If they're not cash, real estate, natural features, or equipment, how are they useful? In all manner of social change and community-based work since the 1990s, there has been a turn to identifying and mobilizing assets— human, organizational and community strengths, relationships, resources, and capacities. This represents an intentional shift, especially in under-resourced communities, away from what had been a debilitating emphasis on problems, deficits, and shortcomings.

In 1993, John McKnight and John Kretzmann published *Building Communities From the Inside Out: Towards Finding and Mobilizing a Community's Assets*. This emerged from their research and organizing in resource-poor and marginalized communities. They endeavored to articulate and practice community building strategies based on assets rather than exhaustive inventories of deficiencies. The McKnight and Kretzmann (1993) book provided practical approaches and tools. This way of thinking and conducting community work begins with an analysis of assets, strengths, and capacities—to uncover and identify sources of power within people, organizations, and communities—and to see change as something that most appropriately begins and is driven from within. This approach goes beyond people making do with what they've got. It's an important fore-runner and tool in organizing communities.

During a 2015 visit to Buenos Aires, I was hosted by a group of community arts activists doing wonderful work in economically distressed, disenfranchised neighborhoods. These included a shanty town—a self-constructed village with no municipal water, sewer, electricity, or plotted streets. A tour of the village was both heartbreaking and inspiring. Conditions were not good. However, I saw residents had found ways to work together, to dispose of waste and to comman-deer nominal water and electricity through a network of hoses and wires strung overhead. Of course, there was little security or safety in these makeshift systems. Made of scrap metal, bricks, and other found materials, homes were spartan but people created private spaces, and in a few cases, small courtyards and areas to retreat. Occasionally, a small window revealed a tiny shop with soft drinks, snack foods, and some basic canned provisions. Neighbors watched out for children wandering through the narrow, winding pathways between homes. Mutually supportive efforts were palpable.

My hosts hoped to provoke my sympathy for the poverty and my anger at the government for not providing basic services. My inadequate efforts to express the positives were not well-taken. They wanted me to see what they saw—the deficiencies. Later during this visit, I spoke to a group of educators and art-ists working in these communities. Again, I felt I didn't adequately convey the asset-based theories and how the strengths present in the makeshift community provided a basis for organizing and self-advocacy. The group resisted my ideas, seeing the only solution as outside intervention.

At a later time during the same visit, I met with a woman who had devel-oped a program working with women in shanty towns to recycle plastic waste to make furniture and other useful items. Funded by the city's waste removal service, the program helped women learn skills and apply creativity to reduce waste, make useful items, and generate small supplemental incomes. Asset-based thinking was squarely in her vocabulary. Of course, important in the equation of long-term change, the plastic recycling work needs to be part of ongoing organizing and capacity building.

Concurrent with building on assets within and among individuals, organi-zations, and communities, learning to wield the power to leverage and guide resources from outside is equally important. This serves both to build capacity from within and is an anti-colonialist approach to fight exploitation and wealth extraction. Asset-based strategies developed in contrast to a focus on deficien-cies, something that individuals and communities internalize, perpetuating the sense that they lack power and are dependent on outside intervention, resources, and problem-solvers. Mapping assets and learning to leverage them are a part of asset-based organizing and capacity-building leading to empowerment and advancing social, cultural, and economic equity.

Decades before McKnight and Kretzmann articulated these ideas, community-based arts practitioners engaged in similar approaches, recognizing, and raising up important and otherwise unheard stories and talents to build individual and group power often as part of social-justice and social-change efforts. Such community-based work requires creativity to identify and highlight resources and capacities that are present and to use those to leverage more: building on strengths to overcome shortcomings. Mapping assets and devising strategies to employ them is where such work begins.

Community Mapping and Participatory Asset Mapping

"Community mapping is not mapping for or of a community, it is mapping by the community of their values, assets, and visions for the future," wrote Canadian community activist and educator Maeve Lydon (2003, p. 4). Community maps, produced collaboratively by residents, highlight local knowledge and resources. Community maps claim power by visibly displaying community authorship. Community maps affirm local knowledge (Parker, 2006). Self-representation by a community represents a change in social and power relationships and procedures as well as serves capacity-building. An operative question Parker (2006) asked was, "Can community mapping help produce egalitarian or socially just cartographic representations of place?" (p. 471). She widely cautioned that such maps have limited potential to make change in the absence of ongoing efforts as well as in the face of political interventions. She went on to warn that "even projects with subversive aims can be misappropriated by powerful interests" (p. 481). As noted in Chapter 6, Stein (2019) cautioned that such efforts can be "cover" to distract people from ways they're being exploited. Thus, it is critical to appreciate the totality of such empowerment strategies.

As I have found in my mapping work, and Parker (2006) affirmed, "how participants work together and negotiate issues of place and representation is as important as the map itself" (p. 472). The *way* mapping is practiced is critical. A 2012 toolkit from a Los Angeles-based group known as Advancement Project (a group dedicated to fostering equity and healthier communities; see Burns, Paul, & Paz, 2012) provided a helpful definition of key terms:

> *Participatory Mapping* is the process of creating a tangible display of the people, places, and experiences that make up a community, through

community members themselves identifying them on a map. *Asset Mapping* is the general process of identifying and providing information about a community's assets, or the status, condition, behavior, knowledge, or skills that a person, group, or entity possesses … *Participatory Asset Mapping*, a process where community members collectively create asset maps by identifying and providing the information about their own community's assets on a map.

(Burns et al., 2012, p. 6)

The Advancement Project advocated mapping as part of community organizing in any context. Their process was designed to support strategic efforts by building on existing community strengths, most importantly people and their capacity to act together on their convictions. Mapping helps people work together to build cohesion and visualize networks of service and advocacy organizations, neighborhood associations, and other services existing or envisioned.

Enter Cultural Asset Mapping

Canadians Murray and Baeker (2006) asserted,

Patrick Geddes got it right, stressing the need for planners to "map before you plan." Cultural mapping is the first step and defining feature of cultural planning. It is a tool for deepening understanding of local cultural systems and engaging communities in this process.

(p. 16)

Mercer (2006) recommended that in the process of cultural planning, "we must excavate the layers of our city downwards into its earliest past … and thence we must read them upwards" (p. 5). Cultural mapping, he described, involves, "tracing people's memories and visions and values—before we start the planning" (p. 5). It is also important to reflect on and map, as best as possible, all the different kinds of *places* people occupy, as discussed in Chapter 5.

Progressive designers trying to better understand and engage with their communities take a similar approach. American environmental design scholar, David de la Peña et al. (2017), described it this way:

The tenacious designer knows that efficacy requires understanding the political, economic, and cultural contexts in which projects proceed or are scuttled. It means mapping out not only neighborhoods, watersheds, and bus routes but also power hierarchies and community networks, schedules, and stories that resonate.

(p. 4)

Landscapes and structures resulting from the work of city planners and designers both enable and limit activities in physical space, but also impact the cultural, social, and political dimensions, as discussed in Chapter 5. Cultural asset mapping includes both tangible and intangible assets of a community or place, and, when done well, reflect a wide array of local *and* expert knowledge. Cultural mapping provides an understanding of cultures, histories, and a community's unique identities as well as intensities of feelings about those places, stories, and characteristics. Used at the beginning of any community development or planning project, such mapping work also generates an inventory of potential partners and other community resources that may be instrumental in achieving the goals of any plan, and, alternatively, those that may present obstacles.

Finding Authenticity: The "What" of Asset Mapping

Because cultural mapping serves different purposes in different places, it is important to ask what should be mapped or included. This question must be addressed by each community engaging in cultural mapping and/or planning based on local values, conditions, ways of working, and aspirations. What is to be mapped or "counted" is a challenging question in such a wide-ranging endeavor as asset mapping. As Redaelli (2019) pointed out, for researchers this can be daunting.

> Given that the cultural sector has not acquired a standardized definition yet, cultural mapping is characterized by a complexity and fragmentation that requires one to define *what* is included every time people engage in an exercise aiming to capture and represent culture.

(p. 60)

Her use of the qualifier "yet" suggests an anticipation that a standard definition may someday be agreed upon. Unlikely and undesirable. But, the value in defining what is to be mapped comes as much, or more, through the discussion as it is in the map itself.

Different people see different assets based on values, experiences, and current needs. A rural community, urban community, or wealthy or poor community will see different assets. The same is true for an older Black community, a newly established urban Latinx community, or a suburban White community. Given increasingly diverse communities in the United States, defining what is to be mapped becomes even more important. Accepting that every community is unique and may benefit from an understanding of what makes it so, this becomes a positive exercise for planners and communities alike.

Highlighting values is one reason that mapping belongs on the front end of planning (Redaelli, 2019). By virtue of deciding what to map and who to engage in the process, a community or its leaders make a strong statement of values. Parker (2006) described how, in community mapping, one can see the "reproduction of power relations is constituted in its practice" (p. 470). An operative question then is how does the content and process of mapping change or reinforce existing power relationships? Redaelli (2019) suggested a two-part framework:

> Tangible assets include cultural organizations, public art, natural and cultural heritage, architecture, people, artifacts, and other material resources. Intangible assets consist of values and norms, histories and memories, traditions, rituals, and other immaterial factors that determine a shared sense of place.
>
> (p. 60)

As most maps manifest in a visual form, another dimension—and one that could be interpolated for each of the five senses—begins with mapping soundscapes. Australian architectural design scholar Kelum Palipane works with place-mapping techniques based on what she called "sensory ethnography." She wrote, "The process includes noise mapping to identify sound sources and their relationship to urban activities and discerning meaning through various qualitative methods such as surveys and interviews" (Palipane, 2017, p. 58). Recognizing that people have different dominant senses and ways of understanding and appreciating place, Palipane recommended a participatory methodology using photo surveys, soundwalks, and interviews to collect information on perceptions of the community. Her research was designed to "enable architects to produce designs for urban regeneration that reflect the diverse sociality of the existing demography" (p. 56). While most architects operate in the visual realm, she points out, people develop attachments to place that can be based on other senses. She cites the works of American urban theorist Kevin Lynch who blew open thinking and practice in how cognitive mapping is constructed. Regarding his book, *Image of the City,* Palipane wrote how this "explores the 'imageability' of cities, a method comprising of mapping a category of elements used in the cognitive delineation of the city by consulting many users" (p. 57).

Tangible and Intangible Cultural Assets

Figures 7.1 and 7.2 represent ways to identify tangible and intangible cultural assets. Mapping the tangible is easier. These are readily documented through physical location, dates and places of activities, and economic data on various industries. Intangible assets, outlined here, must be mapped from data provided by people with knowledge or experience of the place, people, and stories. Such mapping is less concrete and more subjective. Participatory practices from social science research, including forms of Action Research and Phenomenology, can be called upon to identify, harvest, and document appropriate qualitative data through participatory activities. Like any data, including demographic and economic data collected by government agencies, they are not perfect. Their lifespan has limits. Refining, updating, and finding meaning in the data are also necessary steps. That said, it's essential to appreciate and make the most of the process of data collection as well as its community-organizing dimensions.

Figure 7.1, used, courtesy of Greg Baeker (2019) and developed through his decades of cultural planning in Canada, addresses tangible assets with places and events that are easily added to a geographic map and database. Figure 7.2, which I drafted, represents a set of intangible assets and identifies ways to find meaning and connectivity towards a purpose of developing greater social cohesion and civic capacity.

Finding Authenticity: The "How" of Asset Mapping

Each mapping effort requires different tools for data collection, analysis, and articulation in a map form. Data collection techniques can include focus groups, breakout groups, interviews, surveys, community walks, online mapping software, Wikimapia and secondary data. Because asset mapping can yield extensive qualitative data that doesn't fit on a two- or three-dimensional map (such as experiences, stories, or perspectives relayed by community members), it may require multiple forms, some of which may be dynamic. Nonetheless, the Advancement Project, referenced above, recommended mapping activities that result in a tangible visual representation of the community that participants can collectively celebrate. Databases and other three-dimensional forms are critical to include as needed, but, in my experience as well, an object that lends itself to an unveiling party remains essential. The social dimensions of maps and map-making also hold power.

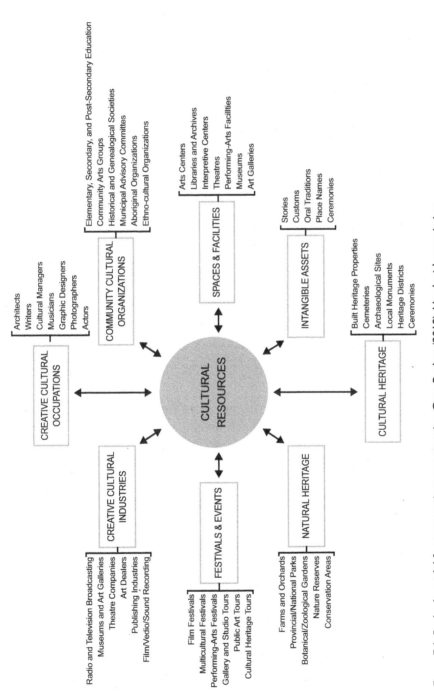

Figure 7.1 Baeker's model for community asset mapping. Greg Baeker (2019). Used with permission.

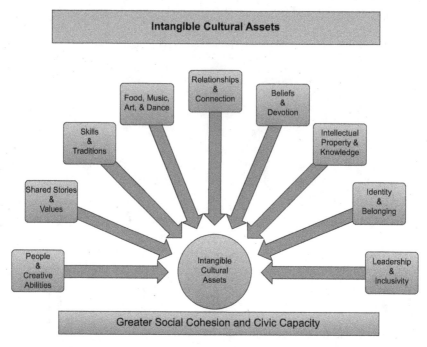

Figure 7.2 Intangible cultural assets.

Cultural planners who conduct mapping through existing databases or by involving only representatives of the professional cultural sector may be reinforcing existing power hierarchies and doing little to democratize or decolonize culture or planning. Cultural asset mapping can and should be a participatory process that builds networks among people and connects a variety of assets found in communities. This process allows people to discover resources that contribute to their unique environment and to more clearly see distinctive and valued qualities of place.

Cultural assets are best recognized by a combination of members of an area together with outsiders who bring different perspectives. Assets cannot be fully gathered by one individual or organization, nor only by insiders or outsiders, no matter how rigorous the effort. Mapping carried out using any number of techniques should always focus on approaches that serve to build community through shared identity, collaborative work, and dialogue. The process itself, when robustly carried out, has equal or greater value than the resulting map or inventory of assets that might be generated.

Ways cultural mapping engages people throughout the entire endeavor remain critical. Cultural mapping can be a stand-alone effort but usually takes place at the beginning of a planning process and should be part of ongoing organizing and community-building efforts. To understand places beyond their physical characteristics, theorists in the formation of social communities, such as Blokland (2017), have asserted that "it makes sense to apply the idea of community as an experience, not as a place" (p. 26). Mapping of experiences are subjective and creative, and not always easy but important.

Participatory methods, described above, address the general framework for cultural asset mapping. However, ways of approaching and addressing culture add a layer to the process. Designing a participatory process for any specific place—from an organization to a neighborhood to a city—requires attention to both scale and understanding the people and cultures of that community so the process itself resonates and does its best to not conflict with or offend cultural sensibilities and sensitivities in that place.

In the design of any planning process, one size does not fit all. In an agricultural area, processes that build on metaphors and include steps referencing planting, seasons, and harvests might resonate best. Alternatively, people in a postindustrial city might relate to ways of repurposing skills and spaces. With any cultural or ethnic groups, the ways of doing things that go more with the grain and not against may be more successful. Designing a community planning process has many nuances and larger cities and multiethnic communities of all sizes require a variety of opportunities to participate, each tailored to groups within the community.

Understanding and planning with a community is, however, an iterative process. Mapping can, and generally should, be part of the process of discussing the meaning and parameters of the culture of a community. Beginning with the broad definition of ways of living together, defining or interpreting these for a local context should be an early part of a planning project—a prerequisite to mapping, which is in turn a prerequisite to strategic elements of planning.

Summary

Engaging a community in participatory cultural asset mapping can promote both diversity and equity. Simultaneously it can build community identity and social cohesion and support sustainability. It can also produce an inventory and/or representation of the community's practical cultural assets useful for planners. Each of these outcomes underscores the importance of mapping as a participatory practice and informs how a resulting map may be used within and by a community. This includes fostering collaboration and finding shared values and goals, as well as building a sense of community ownership of and responsibility for the tangible and intangible assets people value. The essence of cultural mapping comes through articulating and sharing information about the community and encouraging active participation by a broad group of stakeholders while working to identify what is shared.

One way to build a framework for both cultural flexibility and sustainability is to see that a community's culture is defined through such participatory processes and that assets are defined by members of the community. This requires a broad range of people to be part of mapping, community planning, and decision-making. Acknowledging shared values, diversity, and differences within the community leads to the creation of a community's unique identity. When many individuals are part of this process, it builds on a sense of ownership.

Building place-based identity, or placemaking, within a geographic region is an outcome of many cultural mapping projects. Developing a map to highlight unique qualities of a place, including tangible and intangible assets, builds a network of stories that not only connect the individuals who tell them, but can also attract new residents and visitors through an atmosphere of openness and acceptance. Resulting maps can be used for advocacy, better-informed city planning, and local economic and community development.

The process strengthens a community's sense of pride and cohesion. Creating a space for open and honest dialogue about the cultural assets of a community is not easy but should be the driving force behind cultural mapping. Cultural mapping does not end when a map is plotted. Once the community has engaged in such collaborative projects, it is important to build on partnerships and momentum created. It must be continually fostered through collaborative and innovative activities that benefit the larger community. The mapping process provides one means of engagement; it should not be the end of it.

In the next chapter, I build on ideas of engaging residents in exploring various dimensions of their communities. I delve into how design and aesthetic qualities of place are potent signifiers of belonging or dis-belonging, and how processes of participatory democracy need to be employed for communities to be more inclusive.

References

Bachi, U. (2019, July 4). "Took away our identity": Google maps puzzles residents with new neighbourhood names. *Place*. Retrieved from http://www.thisisplace.org/i/?id=2d8d06e0-96c4-4e57-96f4-e89e2aa169ea

Baeker, G. (2002). Beyond garrets and silos: Concepts, trends and developments in cultural planning. Department of Canadian Heritage. Ontario Ministry of Culture, Quebec Ministry of Culture and Communications.

Baeker, G. (2010). *Rediscovering the wealth of places: A municipal cultural planning handbook for Canadian communities*. St. Thomas, ON: Municipal World.

Blokland, T. (2017). *Community as urban practice*. Cambridge: Polity Press.

Burns, J. C., Paul, D. P., & Paz, S. R. (2012). *Participatory asset mapping: A community research lab toolkit*. Los Angeles, CA: Advancement Project. Retrieved from https://www.communityscience.com/knowledge4equity/AssetMappingToolkit.p

Crampton, J. W. (2001). Maps as social constructions: Power, communication and visualization. *Progress in Human Geography*, *25*(2), 235–252.

de Certeau, M. (1988) *The practice of everyday life*. Berkeley, CA: University of California Press.

de la Peña, D., Jones-Allen, D., Hester, R. T., Jr., Hou, J. Lawson, L. J., & McNally, M. (Eds.). (2017). *Design as democracy: Techniques for collective creativity*. Washington, DC: Island Press.

Duxbury, N., Garrett-Petts, W. F., & Longley, A. (Eds.). (2019). *Artistic approaches to cultural mapping: Activating imaginaries and means of knowing*. London: Routledge.

Harley, J. B. (1988). Maps, knowledge, and power. In D. Cosgrove & S. Daniels (Eds.), *The iconography of landscape* (pp. 277–312). Cambridge: Cambridge University Press.

Lefebvre, H. (1991). *The production of space*. Oxford: Basil Blackwell. (Original work published 1974)

Lydon, M. (2003). Community mapping: The recovery (and discovery) of our common ground. *Geomatica*, *57*(2), 131–144.

McKnight, J., & Kretzmann, J. (1993). *Building communities from the inside out: A path toward finding and mobilizing a community's assets*. Evanston, IL: Center for Urban Affairs and Policy Research, Northwestern University.

Mercer, C. (2006). *Cultural planning for urban development and creative cities*. Self-published manuscript. Retrieved from https://www.kulturplan-oresund.dk/pdf/Shanghai_cultural_planning_paper.pdf

Murray, G., & Baeker, G. (2006, September). Culture + place = wealth creation. *Municipal World*, *116*(9), 13–14. Retrieved from http://stcatharinescultureplanningsubcommittee.pbworks.com/f/culture_place_wealth_creation.pdf

Palipane, K. (2017). Interrogating place: A socio-sensory approach. *Cities People Places: An International Journal on Urban Environments*, *2*(1), 55–69. doi:10.4038/cpp.v2i1.18

Parker, B. (2006). Constructing community through maps? Power and praxis in community mapping. *The Professional Geographer*, *58*(4), 470–484. doi:10.1111/j.1467-9272.2006.00583.x

Porter, L. (2016). *Unlearning the colonial cultures of planning*. Abingdon: Routledge. doi:10.4324/9781315548982

Redaelli, E. (2019). *Connecting arts and place: Cultural policy and American cities*. London: Palgrave Macmillan.

Robinson, A. (1969). *Elements of cartography*. New York, NY: Wiley.

Stanley, H. M. (1890) *In darkest Africa, or, the quest, rescue, and retreat of Emin, governor of Equatoria*. New York, NY: Charles Scribner & Sons.

Stein, S. (2019). *Capital city: Gentrification and the real estate state*. New York, NY: Verso Books.

Stevenson, D. (2014). *Cities of culture: A global perspective*. London: Routledge.

Winlow, H. (2020). Mapping race and ethnicity. In A. Kobayashi (Ed.), *International encyclopedia of human geography* (Vol. 8, 2nd ed., pp. 309–321). Amsterdam, Netherlands: Elsevier.

Chapter 8

Guardians of Democracy
The Right to Design the City

Deep democracy will not be created by a master plan, experts, or government officials, but rather by the small daily acts of engagement
—Patricia Wilson (2019, p. 232)

The City as Home

People fashion and fill their homes with things that reflect who they are and what they care about, things that make them comfortable. In making a space into a home, people often display evidence of their personal history, including their ancestors. Most like their homes to be welcoming to visitors. How can people fashion and furnish the cities in which they live in order to feel at home? Most people don't know who designs and builds their city or understand the economic, political, and social forces that shape the landscape. Conversely, planners, designers, architects, policymakers, developers, and builders fashion cities to reflect their experience, aesthetic understanding, and what makes them feel comfortable. What do they know about the people in cities, what they care about, and what makes them comfortable? Are cities welcoming to visitors? Do they honor those who have occupied them throughout time? Whose histories are reflected in the built environment?

Asking planners, designers, and others who shape cities to accomplish these things for the succession of different people who call, have called, or might call a city their home is a tall order. This chapter explores ideas related to spatial justice (Soja, 2010), aesthetic justice (Mattila, 2002), and how democratically infused planning and design of communities together with creative practices can shape communities to which more people of diverse backgrounds can feel a sense of connection. Advancing aesthetic inclusion as well as participatory, deep, deliberative, or grassroots democracy (Forester, 1999; Green, 2004; Wilson, 2019) is a central responsibility of planners, designers, and the others who shape the built environment. Building on the processes discussed in Chapters 6 and 7, this chapter explores practices that weave more broad-based participation, deliberation, and democratic principles into city planning.

Finnish planning scholar Hanna Mattila (2002) argued that the *aesthetics*, or look and feel of a place and how that resonates with its occupants, should be included in the pursuit of justice along with social, economic, and political aspects. In terms of where design and aesthetic values originate, these are also cultural matters. In her groundbreaking article, "Aesthetic Justice and Urban Planning: who ought to have the right to design cities?", Mattila (2002) urged city planners and designers to not simply employ aesthetic and physical forms as a tool to solve problems, but to see aesthetics for its social and moral importance. Defining aesthetically good urban form, she contended, is a political matter, not simply a task to be left to professionals. Escobar (2017), building on these connections, wrote, "Design is about creating cultural meanings and practices, about designing culture, experience, and particular ways of living" (p. 2).

In the pursuit of aesthetic justice and the roles city planners play in promoting democracy, it is important to not reduce democracy to the idea of one-person-one-vote or making planning and design choices through a majority-rules electoral process. Ideas in this chapter related to democracy lie in the complexities of *deep democracy* that Wilson (2019) described: the empowerment of each individual, ensuring they have a voice and that voice matters.

Creative planning and design bring many voices and hands into the process of building cities through participatory strategies and activities, while at the same time building the practices and grassroots structures of democracy. This chapter looks at the inclusion of local knowledge and everyday lived experiences in planning and how they manifest through aesthetic choices and built forms. Building on the discussion of place attachment in Chapter 5, I explore how design reflects, or doesn't reflect, the cultures of people in cities. Approaches to aesthetic justice are described in the context of how the practices of city planning and design can build on principles of participatory democracy.

The Production of Space

It is useful to reflect again on Lefebvre's (1974/1991) "production of space," related to how cities are formed and to whom they belong. Along with his three interconnected elements—the perceived, conceived, and everyday lived experience—Lefebvre's work also provoked thinking about "the right to the city." Who shares those rights, and what are the extent of them? People's everyday lived experiences are often undervalued and barely reflected in the perceived or conceived dimensions. Displacement of intuition and feelings from city planning, recommended by the American Planning Association (Morley, 2018), illustrated this (see Chapter 5).

While the physical, economic, legal, and political elements are well-represented and addressed by any number of professions and institutions, who takes into account everyday lived experiences in shaping cities? To be fair, some city planners and designers recognize and incorporate local knowledge and, to varying degrees, listen to residents and see them as experts on their community. Healey (1998) argued that the knowledge of planners cannot be automatically assumed to be superior to the local knowledge of inhabitants or other stakeholders. Some planners tap this knowledge to inform and complement their own expertise, and it may also influence designers, engineers, and policymakers. However, planning and design practices as a whole have been slow and even resistant to give local knowledge weight on par with the assessments and ideas of professionals.

Lefebvre (1974/1991) and others, including Mitchell (2003), described cities as contested spaces. Corporate and other private interests, along with governments that too often are not acting in the best interest of the public, make cities places where people, especially the poor and those who are not part of a dominant cultural or economic class, feel they don't belong (Bedoya, 2013). In fact, they are sometimes not allowed to belong, as in the criminalization of homelessness (Mitchell & Heynen, 2009). Lefebvre posed the fundamental question: Who has the right to the city? Mitchell and others have contemplated this central and sticky question. Taking it further, for example, does the right to have a smoke-free public space trump the rights of smokers? Or, do the rights of the homeless person to simply survive or sleep interfere with another's right to a perception of safety? Acting out against the rights of others took center stage at the time of this writing with a spate of so-called "Karen" incidents in the United States in the media daily. These were situations in which White women called police on Black men simply because they felt frightened, or they lashed out to object to others' actions with which they didn't approve such as wearing a face mask during the COIVD-19 pandemic.

Cities and Their Personalities

For a city to feel like home to all its inhabitants, their everyday lived experiences need to be baked into its physical fabric. In almost any space over time, and within a modicum of permissive governance, people will make their homes, stores, businesses, streets, and public spaces reflect their cultures, aesthetic preferences, and/or personalities. I take great pleasure in traveling to cities in various parts of the world to experience and photograph eclectic neighborhoods and business districts where adornments to public and private spaces include interesting and colorful objects, products, works of art, and plantings extending from homes and shopfronts. Some residential neighborhoods reflect wide diversity in architectural styles in the homes. Others have remarkable uniformity. In talks, I present images of how people make the exteriors of their homes and storefronts reflect their personalities, as well as images of the homogenized sameness within gated, highly controlled communities. I ask audiences, "how do these reflect the personalities of residents and shopkeepers?"

The personality that a city or neighborhood develops initially and projects over time is an important consideration in whether a city makes residents and visitors feel as though they belong and are welcome. Intuitively, most people understand the personality of their city or neighborhood and how it makes them feel, although they can't always articulate it. They may be less aware of how they might contribute to that personality. One can also ask if the personalities of these places are healthy in the psychological sense.

The psychology of cities is a recent interest of Charles Landry and Chris Murray (2017). In their book *Psychology and the City*, they wrote, "being in a city is a two-way psychological process. The city impacts upon our mind—our mental and emotional state impacts upon the city" (Landry & Murray, 2017, p. 5). They build on Churchill's statement cited earlier. Similarly, addressing unfortunate 20th-century directions in city planning and design, Andres Duany, Liz Platter-Zyberk, and Jeff Speck, in their work, *Suburban Nation*, also riff on Churchill's idea, writing, "we shape our cities and then our cities shape us" (Duany, Platter-Zyberk, & Speck, 2000, p. 83).

I made similar observations about the personalities of places through my own work in community and cultural planning over the past two decades. Some communities clearly have low self-esteem, some high. I've sensed some with deep feelings of abandonment, helplessness. Alternatively, some have a sense of empowerment, a can-do attitude, or even entitlement. More than a decade ago, an insightful community leader in a small community where I was working looked at me during one of our conversations and said, "so, you're like a community therapist"—something I had not considered. With no psychological training, it was, in fact, a mantle I was reluctant to take on. Nonetheless, planners, designers, architects, and others involved in placemaking need to acknowledge they make a significant impact on how people feel about places as well as about themselves. Landry and Murray opened up a valuable discussion of these ideas. Building on the field of architectural psychology, however, more thought and research in this arena is called for, especially in helping planners gain greater awareness of their impacts.

Finnish architect Juhani Pallasmaa succinctly described the impacts of the design of physical structures: "A building is not an end in itself. A building conditions and transforms the human experience of reality ... it frames, structures, articulates, links, separates and unites, enables and prohibits" (as cited in Escobar, 2017, p. 39). Escobar asserted that buildings possess this power through "a tectonic language" (Pallasmaa, as cited in Escobar, 2017, p. 39), something we interact with using our body and senses.

Including psychology in the mix of tools for understanding and improving cities seems a no-brainer, something the Bogotá cultural agency, cited in Chapter 5, understood. Landry and Murray (2017) went on to question the psychological state of some architects, designers, and developers who have inordinate influence over the built environment.

> The psychology of the architect or property developer can clearly impact on the people they design for, and, using the principles of psychology to investigate the effects of design judgments, we can ask whether they in fact actually like people.
>
> (p. 53)

Landry and Murray described how some buildings and urban environments may be compensating for damaged egos or other psychological trauma experienced by their planners, designers, and architects, the vast majority of whom were men. Cold, unwelcoming, or inhospitable places, Landry and Murray said, originate in the psychological makeup of the designer and thus become part of the personality of the city.

Cities are living systems built by and for those with wealth in spite of the pockets of poverty they often contain. City plans and designs primarily reflect the culture of a privileged class with aesthetic choices made by (mostly male) professionals—some of whom, as Landry and Murray (2017) pointed out, may themselves lack healthy psychological balance, or they simply imbue designs with toxic masculinity. Where, then, do people, especially women, people of color and low-income, and immigrants find themselves and their stories in these environments?

A Toxic Built Environment?

Citing more than 40 years of research, the American Psychological Association in 2018 declared "toxic masculinity" as harmful, not just to boys and men, but to those around them. They cite masculinity traits such as stoicism, competitiveness, dominance, and aggression. What have long been accepted male behaviors include what the American Psychological Association (2018) report described as a "constellation of standards that have held sway over large segments of the population, including: anti-femininity, achievement, eschewal of the appearance of weakness, and adventure risk and violence" (p. 2). In city planning and design, professions long dominated by men, these marks of masculinity surely found their way into the design of buildings, public spaces, and cities. Might some buildings and public spaces, even urban plans, then be considered toxic?

Several decades ago, Dolores Hayden asked—and provided examples of— what a non-sexist city would look like. She pointed out how dominant design patterns isolate women and "set the stage for the effective sexual division of labor" (Hayden, 1980, p. S172). She described how "dwellings, neighborhoods, and cities designed for homebound women constrain women physically, socially, and economically" (p. S171). As the design professions responsible for the design and construction of America's cities at that time were almost exclusively men, is it any wonder that toxic masculine characteristics and psychological traits have been baked-in much of the built environment?

Escobar (2017) held little back, labeling modernist design as utterly arrogant and pretentious in claims of being universal. He asked, "Are these masculine imaginaries of creation—design imaginations for sure—really universal, or unavoidable, as their fathers pretend?" (p. 17). And, not only have the design and visual art worlds been dominated by men, but by *White* men. Escobar related,

> There are few social spaces more unrelentingly white than the art and design studio. … This unreflective whiteness in design territories is unable to excavate the racist and sexist ideologies embedded in Bauhaus-derived aesthetics that constitute good design for many.
>
> (p. 47)

Do these ideologies, as well as toxic masculinity, show through dominant design choices and impact people so profoundly? The current state of global politics might suggest they do. A draft presidential directive, proposed at the time of this writing in the United States, would require new federal government buildings to use classical Greek and Roman design architecture to evoke power (Rogers & Pogrebin, 2020).

While everyone is being shaped by the designed and built environments surrounding them, what opportunities do they have to shape those environments? Escobar (2017) advocated radical approaches to design that can bring about a more just and sustainable world, one that is informed and actively shaped more by people's everyday lived experience. He wrote,

> Sustainability is a cultural process rather than an expert one... We should all acquire a basic competence in the shaping of our world. ... For too long we have expected the design professions to bend an inert world into shape.
>
> (Escobar, 2017, p. 44)

The Right to Design the City

To find ways to reflect cultural diversity and a healthy, functional psychology into urban design, city planners must go above and beyond bringing more women and people of color into the profession. They must examine their own biases, develop greater cultural competency, and incorporate local knowledge and the *everyday lived experience* of inhabitants centrally to ensure that a multitude of voices are engaged in substantive ways. Further, it is important that efforts be made for this to be a joyful process, as described in Chapter 6, rather than dour or contentious. A plan or design derived through a contentious process wrought by anger will likely result in a contested space and built environment that, in turn, reflects anger and passes it along to those experiencing the space. Will a design created through a joyful process reflect and bring joy? In the 19th century, Nathaniel Hawthorne wrote, "If cities were built by the sound of music, then some edifices would appear to be constructed by grave, solemn tunes—others to have danced forth to light, fantastic airs" (Hawthorne, 1839/1972, p. 183).

Aesthetic choices always reflect someone's culture, whether these choices are made for museum exhibitions, building designs, or urban spaces. Do they reflect the culture and personality of the city planner, designer, architect, developer, policymaker, or artist? Perhaps they reflect the culture of the dominant economic class or even so-called "majority culture" in a given city or neighborhood. What, then, of the many so-called "minority cultures" present, who are no longer in the minority in most American cities? How are these cultures represented or reflected? The lack of equitable cultural representation in design and the built environment Mattila (2002) described as *aesthetic injustice*. Is it possible for members of all these communities or subcultures to see themselves in the built environment? The faulty notion of universal good design or aesthetics ignores cultural variations and preferences and suppresses the cultural identities of those outside economic and cultural elites, thus Escobar's use of the term "pluriverse" (see Introduction). Equitable distribution of so-called good design, as Mattila argued, advances injustice rather than reduces it.

Mattila endeavored to find another option besides the idea of equity planning (planning and designing for justice) and the idea of planning and design as an artistic practice (as in a singular vision). She asked how physical environments can equitably reflect the different cultures and different everyday lived experiences present. This is especially challenging in multiethnic or multicultural cities. Like homes, can cities reflect the personality and cultures of their inhabitants, what they care about, and what makes them and their visitors comfortable? In complex urban environments, is this even possible?

One solution modernism advanced was aesthetic education—essentially teaching everyone the merits of dominant cultural aesthetics. Often, this approach makes no pretense of equitably representing the aesthetics, histories, and cultures of diverse peoples. This solution, Mattila (2002) asserted, is a manifestation of cultural imperialism. Considering a dominant group's experience and culture as *universal*, she said, "produces practices that the non-dominant groups experience as oppressive" (p. 135). Observed Soja (2010), "Once spatial injustice is inscribed into the built environment, it is difficult to erase" (p. 41). Another modernist solution is grounded in a distributive model, or the idea of equal distribution of an aesthetically good environment. Some assert that in attempts to do so, modernism delivered consistently bad design from which mostly the poor were supposedly to benefit.

However, giving everyone the choice to determine community aesthetics outside their own home or building front is obviously problematic. Mattila (2002) wrote,

If we were able to distribute an aesthetically good environment to each according to his or her own taste, then we could in this way increase aesthetic welfare and distribute it more equally. But this is not possible since everyone experiences the same public space in the urban environment. This means that problems of aesthetic justice cannot be solved merely by distribution.

(p. 135)

An approach Mattila (2002) advocated is to conduct ongoing processes that involve people in decisions that shape their aesthetic environment. Dialogue and civic engagement around city design, she says, are the only way to work towards the ideal of *aesthetic justice*. "My contention," Mattila wrote, "is that aesthetic justice cannot be promoted within urban planning by leaning on the traditional idea of artistic autonomy, which would leave the designers with the power to define the 'aesthetically good environment'" (p. 137). She went on to say, "aesthetic justice within urban planning should not, then, primarily concern the fair distribution of aesthetically good urban form, but fair distribution of the rights to design the city" (p. 137). This must include access to these processes and a consciousness that the design of place includes social, economic, and cultural places along with the physical (see Chapter 5).

Picking up on Lefebvre's (1974/1991) and Mitchell's (2003) discussion of the right to the city and Mattila's (2002) assertions about aesthetic justice, de la Peña et al. (2017a) declared, "design is a political act" (p. 261). In *Design as Democracy*, these authors illustrated detailed ways to implement these concepts:

> The politics of design determine who gets what, from parks and housing to landfills and freeway pollution. The politics of design determines if a bench prevents a homeless person from sleeping or if a park includes facilities for all the neighborhood to enjoy. The politics of design determines whether land resources essential for a healthy ecosystem are enhanced or destroyed.
>
> (p. 261)

Can Aesthetics Be Democratized?

Towards these ends, I add the concept of *aesthetic democracy*, in the context of the democratization of the process of planning and designing urban environments. Mattila (2002) acknowledged that aesthetic justice is a continual work-in-progress. The realization of aesthetic justice comes through participatory processes and democratic practices applied to city planning and to aesthetic and design choices. It can only partially or incrementally be realized through actual physical structures and spaces.

In his book, *Aesthetic Democracy*, Thomas Docherty (2006), a British scholar of critical theory and cultural history, coined the term but with different meanings. He was addressing the important and symbiotic relationship between aesthetics and democracy but did not suggest the democratization of aesthetics—the meaning I use in this chapter. Docherty establishes profound links between aesthetics and democracy as "so intimate as to suggest that democracy is entirely *conditioned* by aesthetics as such" (p. ix). He continues:

> A polity that degrades or ignores the aesthetic, or sees it as an arithmetical add-on to a social formation rather than a fundamental geometry that shapes the very possibility of our being sociable and free at all, entirely misses the point; and the consequences of that is not only a degradation of the concept of freedom, but also a reduction in actual freedom.
>
> (p. x)

The democratization of aesthetics begins with the recognition of the significance of aesthetics and their relevance in a cultural context. Aesthetic choices in urban design are political choices. The *process* of making such choices must incorporate democratic principles and practices within city planning and design.

Cities, while amazingly resilient systems, have and will increasingly have people of diverse cultures with differing interests sharing space. In such places, argued Sandercock (2004), the politics of voice can become volatile. Who is speaking—and who is speaking for whom—are frequently asked questions. This growing struggle, said Baeker (2002), is rooted in social patterns of representation, interpretation, and communication, including cultural domination, nonrecognition, and disrespect. City planning and design professions have privileged some aesthetics, land uses, and ways of conducting civic dialogue over others. As such, some cultural or ethnic groups, who have the know-how to navigate, feel comfortable and welcome in the process, while others feel they don't belong. Growing nationalism in the United States and hostility towards immigrants and refugees make this increasingly real and volatile.

Mattila (2002) asserted that the complexities of cultural differences between races, sexes, ages, and so on, and their impact on the design and use of space generally go unnoticed in the theories of architecture and urban design. However, she found that "contemporary thinking within the field of public art, for example, has brought to the fore the need for artists to really get to know the 'varied cultural identities' for the members of their particular audiences" (p. 134). Can planners and designers, like these public artists, likewise get to know the varied cultural identities of the many different peoples and cultures inhabiting contemporary cities? And might they be able to find others, including artists, to help in this part of the work?

Artists as "Craftsmen of Participation"

As described in Chapter 6, bringing to the planning practice the tools of artists and decades of community-based arts practice offers opportunities to unleash imaginations, bridge cultural divides, build the efficacy of community members, and instill deep democracy. Healey (2004) described how artists and creative sector workers maintain the flow of intellectual capital in communities and refresh ways of thinking. Artists are boundary-crossers who bring an array of tools for building and maintaining intellectual exchange in communities. Deep democracy depends on such intellectual exchange, openness to different ideas, willingness to venture to unfamiliar places, and risk-taking.

> In whole systems approaches, that involve broadly based, participatory decision making and embrace a broad understanding of cultural resources, the tools of the artist are engaged by all who care about the collectively imagined public space in which they dwell.
>
> (Baeker, 2002, p. 24)

As mentioned earlier, artists in various parts of the world have evolved community arts practices as ways of connecting with and empowering residents in addressing issues of inequity in multiple realms of community life. These often include spatial and cultural inequities where residents can build agency in changemaking on a local level. A French team, Philippe Eynaud, Maïté Juan, and Damien Mourey (2018), studied the work of a civil society organization in Marseille over a period of years. While this work is far from unique, their analysis provides excellent insights into common strategies and challenges in the work. Eynaud et al. framed this work in the context of the right to the city and to observe how it enhanced residents' "capacity to mobilize and reappropriate the city" (p. 621). The authors described participatory artmaking that "echoes Lefebvre's call to explore and invent new ways of experiencing the city collectively in order to exercise the right to the city" (p. 623). Further, Eynaud et al. embedded this with "the right to reinvest the space we live in with new meanings, with our collective imagination" (p. 623). They described shared spaces as "being constantly (re)produced ... as a spatial resource that needs to be fairly distributed and preserved across a community" (p. 622). This work is urgent, they pointed out, "especially in underprivileged areas where the multicultural identity of immigrants has been repressed and devalued" (p. 623). Activities in Marseille neighborhoods described by Eynaud et al. were designed with and for residents as reflexive workshops "to give voice to resident-users and encourage them to become actors in the urban planning of their neighborhood, translating their say into feasible architectural proposals" (p. 628).

The practice of "commoning," or shaping shared spaces together, Eynaud et al. (2018) wrote, "requires artists to engage in a form of civil activism" (p. 622), which often pushes the recognized boundaries of artmaking. These approaches, they continued, "go against the idea of *haute culture* in a democracy to favor the idea of a cultural democracy where individual creativity can be nurtured within a collective artistic project" (p. 624). This, they argued, "turns artists into craftsmen of participation" (p. 634).

Eynaud et al. (2018) connected this artist-led work with strengthening democratic practices. They wrote, "the sociocultural reappropriation of urban spaces made possible by these new uses and experiences are reproductive of the local community and strengthen its empowerment" (p. 631). They went on to describe that through the process,

> the question of a more democratic split of responsibilities and rebalancing power relationships is at the heart of participatory art projects. It leads to the creation of new forms of territorial governance to enable citizens' participation in the production of urban space.
>
> (p. 631).

John Forester (1999) similarly observed that, "ordinary challenges of planning are actually quite extra-ordinary. They can teach us about the theory and practice of democratic politics, public management, and the public-serving professions more generally" (pp. 1–2). In the Marseilles case, city planners, artists, and community members essentially co-created shared spaces and inhabited a ground between the community and formal institutions to position themselves with greater agency. Eynaud et al. (2018) concluded that, "combined with participatory artworks, urban commons allow spatial justice to be challenged by giving more visibility to alternative forms of public action and more legitimacy to urban governance based on diversity and pluralism" (p. 636).

Design as Hands-on Democracy

Promising work in the design profession centers around participatory design as a means of gaining from and instilling practices of democracy. de la Peña et al. (2017a) described participatory design as "hands-on democracy in action … a continuous process of shaping and reshaping civic landscapes so they can be informed and inhabited by deep democracy" (p. 1). They detailed an array of democratic techniques in an extensive cookbook of practices collected from over 50 designers, artists, and scholars who have devised and employed them in a variety of community settings. de la Peña et al. (2017a) called for the design profession to actively contribute to deep democracy. They asserted that, "for participatory design to be truly democratic it cannot remain a standardized public process … it challenges designers to seek meaningful, ethical, and effective ways to design with communities" (p. 1). This provides a platform for local knowledge and everyday lived experience to be recognized and put to work. For de la Peña et al. (2017b), participatory design is "one of the most effective means in a democracy to create cities and landscapes that distribute resources and shape places to be sustainable, representative of diverse publics, well informed by local wisdom, and just" (p. 261). As with Eynaud et al. (2018) in the French example, de la Peña et al. described democratic design as transactive and political: "It facilitates a process of give-and-take between community members, designers, technical experts, and power brokers" (p. 2).

Among the benefits these design practices bring, according to de la Peña et al. (2017b) is that,

> Participants experience empathy as they learn to walk in each other's' shoes. Shared language is found as knowledge flows from the community, as local and outside technical expertise mix. Everyone gains knowledge beyond their limited experiences. … This initiates thinking multimodally across boundaries of discipline, race, and class. This empowers communities and sustains stewardship.
>
> (p. 2)

Through participatory practices, they stated, "we gain confidence, become empowered, or experience the joy of creating. When we finish, we may see our community, others, and ourselves differently" (de la Peña et al., 2017a, p. 3).

The question for city planners and designers is how to institute practices of aesthetic democracy and what does it look like? Tours of older cities almost anywhere in the world—ones that have evolved over time, block by block and building by building—reflect colorful, complex, sometimes messy urban spaces, spaces with multiple layers of meaning brought about by many people over time who have made the city their home. It's worth repeating here Talen and Ellis's (2004) eloquent description of cities as, "collective works of art unfolding through time" (p. 28).

City planners and designers engaging in participatory approaches also need to include conflict management in their list of skills as de la Peña et al. (2017a) argued,

> we must know how to cooperate, to negotiate, and to compromise, and how to do so constructively and effectively. But in many cases, confrontation and conflict are unavoidable. Democratic designers do not consider *conflict* a dirty word, but rather a time-honored means to honorable ends.
>
> (p. 4)

When they create successful spaces for deliberative processes, wrote Forester (1999), "planners and designers can do far more than chase after compromises: they can promote effective processes of public learning, practical and innovative instances of public deliberation, even consensus building in many parts of the larger planning process" (p. 61).

Viewing democracy as both a practice to use in the design process as well as an important by-product of participatory design, de la Peña et al. (2017a) wrote,

> As we design together to achieve our objectives, we build community capacity to act effectively, to work with allies, and to negotiate. ... We strengthen our democracy through what John Friedmann called "the radical openness required by dialogue".
>
> (p. 3)

More diverse ideas and ways of seeing ultimately enrich the process and the outcomes. de la Peña et al. (2017a) concluded, "participation makes cities and economies stronger, and that participation in design is not compromise but, rather enrichment" (p. 5).

Guardians of Democratic Process

According to American city planner William Potapchuk, "planners are often the guardians of democratic processes on the local level. They are often the key staff called upon for making public processes work, and yet they receive very little training in the area" (as cited in Forester, 1999, pp. 82–83). Deep democracy requires this reallocation of political power when it comes to decisions around city-planning issues and aesthetics. Distributing this power to people in their own communities can bring about a new sense of individual and group capacity. As communities evolve through these practices, de la Peña

et al. (2017a) argued that "groups previously marginalized may have better access to places that have become more welcoming and tailored to their
needs. The community's most deeply held values may be directly expressed in
the cultural landscape" (p. 3).

Forester (1999) called for planners to serve as guardians of many different
kinds of spaces for deliberation:

> We should keep alive two related conceptions of public space: those of the
> physical Newtonian spaces of plazas, parks, and avenues in which streams of
> diverse citizens typically pass each other by, and the argumentative public
> spaces of municipal offices, conference rooms, legislative chambers, school
> auditoria, living rooms, and small town meeting places like the firehouse or
> church basements in which community members jointly envision, criticize,
> and refine the design and redesign, the preservation and development, of
> our cities and towns.
>
> (p. 63)

He went on to assert that "if planners and architects focus only on physical
objects, they will hardly appreciate how they can weaken or strengthen deliberative public spaces through which they must do their work" (Forester, 1999,
p. 63).

Adopting collaborative approaches to emphasize ways of thinking and acting, city planners encourage discussion of the qualities of places and address
conflicts in nonthreatening ways (Healey, 1998). Setting deliberative spaces in
a nonhierarchical manner and facilitating greater interaction, Healey observed,
simultaneously builds capacity for problem-solving both in city planning and in
the community in general. In addressing such challenges, Healey (1998) wrote,

> This recasts the role of urban planning in a new form as an active social
> process through which the governance power to regulate and to distribute
> resources which affect the qualities of places is reshaped by a collaborative
> reflection on the ideas, systems of meaning, and ways of acting.
>
> (p. 1543)

As described in Chapter 6, artists working in community or social practice arts
can help disenfranchised community members find and amplify their voices.
Artists have also honed skills to deconstruct complex issues and to evoke poign-
ant personal and collective stories. de la Peña et al. (2017a) described how these
democratic design practices,

address oppression, exclusion, inequity, and inaccessibility because we understand that even in design of the smallest part, we are shaping the moral capacity of our living democracy ... We find a calming effect from exhuming and ordering new information together. We consider alternatives that are evoked by the process.

(p. 2)

Bringing together multiple points of view is central to deepening the knowledge planners can acquire—and the knowledge members of communities have about their own communities. "At stake is not just consensus building," wrote Forester (1999), "but the integration of acting and learning, relationship building and world shaping, that reaches far beyond narrow deal making to the creative practice of deliberative planning and design in the public sphere" (p. 84).

Summary

Building on practices of grassroots democracy, which is part of their everyday work, city planners, like all other public sector workers, have a responsibility to be guardians of democracy. Now, in the third decade of the 21st century, institutions, systems, and policies designed to ensure democracy are being undermined. In the ways city planners go about their work, are they strengthening these institutions and systems or contributing to their deterioration, if just out of neglect?

Inclusive planning processes, described in this chapter as well as in the previous two, represent real and symbolic moves towards participatory forms of democracy and the pursuit of justice, aesthetic and otherwise. Belgian planning scholar Louis Albrechts (2005) described how such processes result in "strengthening of the social tissue [and enhancing] social capital and political capital as citizens and local politicians [take] pride in 'their' city" (p. 16). American planning scholar Kathryn Howell (2016) described this as an empowerment approach to planning.

Like other forms of justice, aesthetic justice is a continuous pursuit, a conscious practice to be developed, critiqued, fine-tuned, and pursued again. The work of progressive urban designers, as well as best-practices of city planners (Forester, 2018) to bake democracy into their processes, provides many practical approaches. When combined with understanding the cultural sense of place, described in Chapter 5, and creative engagement practices discussed in Chapters 6 and 7, city planners have new tools, new ways of seeing, and new allies. The practice of aesthetic democracy—ongoing efforts to achieve aesthetic justice—draws on local knowledge and everyday lived experience together with the expertise of city planners, designers, and artists acting in the role of facilitators.

City planners, together with artists, designers, cultural planners, and cultural workers, can and must contribute to the advancement of democracy on a local and everyday level through *how* they approach their work. Open, creative, and participatory processes for deliberation, co-creation, and decision-making at the neighborhood and citywide levels are available for planners to incorporate in their work to advance aesthetic justice. Greater balance is also needed in how city planners, and other professionals, consider everyday lived experiences with equal importance as the perceived and conceived dimensions in the production of space. In doing so, city planners can more equitably reflect culture and humanity in planning and design. Cities can become more just, engaging, and welcoming homes for their increasingly diverse populations.

References

American Psychological Association. (2018). *APA guidelines for psychological practice with boys and men*. Retrieved from https://www.apa.org/about/policy/boys-men-practice-guidelines.pdf

Albrechts, L. (2005). Creativity in and for Planning. *Planning Theory, 4*(3), 14–25. https://doi.or/10.1080/02513625.2005.10556929

Baeker, G. (2002). *Beyond garrets and silos: Concepts, trends and developments in cultural planning*. Canada: Department of Canadian Heritage/Ontario Ministry of Culture, Quebec Ministry of Culture and Communications.

Bedoya, R. (2013, February). Placemaking and the politics of belonging and dis-belonging. *Grantmakers in the Arts*. Retrieved from https://www.giarts.org/article/placemaking-and-politics-belonging-and-dis-belonging

de la Peña, D., Jones-Allen, D., Hester, R. T., Jr., Hou, J. Lawson, L. J., & McNally, M. (Eds.). (2017a). Introduction. In *Design as democracy: Techniques for collective creativity* (pp. 1–8). Washington, DC: Island Press.

de la Peña, D., Jones-Allen, D., Hester, R. T., Jr., Hou, J. Lawson, L. J., & McNally, M. (Eds.). (2017b). Putting power to good use, delicately and tenaciously. In *Design as democracy: Techniques for collective creativity* (pp. 261–264). Washington, DC: Island Press.

Docherty, T. (2006). *Aesthetic democracy*. Palo Alto, CA: Stanford University Press.

Duany, A., Platter-Zyberk, E., & Speck, J. (2000). *Suburban nation: The decline of the American Dream*. New York, NY: North Park Press.

Escobar, A. (2017). *Designs for the pluriverse: Radical interdependence, autonomy, and the making of worlds*. Durham, NC: Duke University Press.

Eynaud, P., Juan, M., & Mourey, D. (2018). Participatory art as a social practice of commoning to reinvent the right to the city. *Voluntas, 29*, 621–636 https://doi.org/10.1007/s11266-018-0006-y

Forester, J. (1999). *The deliberative practitioner: Encouraging participatory planning process.* Cambridge, MA: MIT Press:

Forester, J. (2018). Deliberative planning practices without smothering invention: practical aesthetic view. In A. Bachtiger, J. S. Dryzek, J. Mansbridge, & M. E. Warren (Eds.), *The Oxford handbook of deliberative democracy* (pp. 595–611). Oxford, UK: Oxford University Press.

Green, J. M. (2004). Participatory democracy: Movements, campaigns, and democratic living. *Journal of Speculative Philosophy, 18*(1), 60–71. http://dx.doi.org/10.1353/jsp.2004.0005

Hayden, D. (1980). What would a non-sexist city be like? Speculations on housing, urban design, and human work. *Signs: Journal of Women in Culture and Society, 5*(S3), S170–S187. https://doi.org/10.1086/495718

Hawthorne, N. (1972). *The American notebooks.* Columbus, OH: Ohio State University Press. (Original work published 1839).

Healey, P. (1998). Building institutional capacity through collaborative approaches to urban planning. *Environment and Planning A, 30*(9), 1531–1546. https://doi.org/10.1068/a301531

Healey, P. (2004). Relational complexity and the imaginative power of strategic spatial planning. *European Planning Studies, 14*(4), 525–546. https://doi.org/10.1080/09654310500421196

Howell, K. L. (2016). Planning for empowerment: Upending the traditional approach to planning for affordable housing in the face of gentrification. *Planning Theory & Practice, 17*(2), 210–226. https://doi.org/10.1080/14649357.2016.1156729

Landry, C., & Murray, C. (2017). *Psychology and the city: The hidden dimension.* Gloucestershire, UK: Comedia

Lefebvre, H. (1991). *The production of space* (Trans. D. Nicholson-Smith). Oxford, UK: Blackwell. (Original work published 1974)

Mattila, H. (2002). Aesthetic justice and urban planning: Who ought to have the right to design cities? *GeoJournal, 58,* 131–138. https://doi.org/10.1023/B:GEJO.0000010832.88129.cc

Mitchell, D. (2003). *The right to the city: Social justice and the fight for public space.* New York, NY: Guilford.

Mitchell, D., & Heynen, N. (2009). The geography of survival and the right to the city: Speculations on surveillance, legal innovation, and the criminalization of intervention. *Urban Geography, 30*(6), 611–632. https://doi.org/10.2747/0272-3638.30.6.611

Morley, D. (2018). Measuring community character. *PAS QuickNotes 72.* American Planning Association, Chicago. Retrieved from https://www.planning.org/publications/document/9142842/

Rogers, K., & Pogrebin, R. (2020, February 5). Draft executive order would give trump a new target: Modern design. *New York Times.* Retrieved from https://www.nytimes.com/2020/02/05/arts/design/trump-modern-architecture.html

Sandercock, L. (2004). Towards a planning imagination for the 21st Century, *Journal of the American Planning Association, 70,* p. 133-141.

Soja, E. W. (2010). *Seeking spatial justice.* Minneapolis: University of Minnesota Press. https://doi.org/10.5749/minnesota/9780816666676.001.0001

Talen, E., & Ellis, C. (2004). Cities as art: Exploring the possibility of an aesthetic dimension in planning. *Planning Theory & Practice, 5*(1), 11–32. https://doi.org/10.1080/14649350420000185044

Wilson, Patricia A. (2019). *The heart of community engagement: Practitioner stories from across the globe.* New York & London: Routledge/Taylor & Francis.

Chapter 9

Downsizing
The Vernacular and the Creative Economy

For too long, creative enterprises have been overlooked by economic developers and public services that have consistently cast their nets for the big fish, rather than the more abundant—and ultimately more self-sustaining—schools of small fish.
—Stuart Rosenfeld (2004, p. 5)

Economic vitality and business conditions often sit high on the priority list for city planners and policymakers. Economics has also served—for better or worse—as the focus for the cultural sector when making its case for the value it brings to communities. The cultural sector is increasingly called upon, as described in Chapter 4, to take more active roles in such things as attracting skilled workforces, increasing tourism, catalyzing place-based regeneration, and improving livability and quality of life.

While the cultural sector has gained recognition among city planners and policymakers for its economic contributions, some activities, such as building flagship institutions or creative placemaking, have also stirred controversy. They are seen as progenitors of economic and socially driven gentrification that primarily benefit developers and the already well-heeled while displacing poorer residents and diminishing their cultural and creative contributions. Constructs such as the Creative Economy and creative cities, into which the cultural sector often fits, also get mixed reviews.

This chapter begins by looking at the phenomena of the Creative Economy and creative cities. I describe how these often embrace extractive or exploitive forms of economic development, emulating industrial era approaches that attempt to attract the "big fish," as American economic development authority Stuart Rosenfeld noted above. Economic development does not have to represent a zero-sum game of competition among cities for talent or to become the next Silicon Valley. I then argue that approaches based in nurturing vernacular creativity—found among the more abundant "schools of small fish"—can build more inclusive and sustainable economies from within.

City planners, city leaders, and the cultural sector can choose approaches that foster more equitable and sustainable development of local creative economies. I maintain that everyday or vernacular creativity, rooted in the people of a community, generate more equitable economic impacts, as well as contribute more to the social and civic health of communities. A focus on local talent, assets, and distinctive character that include more people of more diverse cultures in economic prosperity, runs counter to the dominant discourse of the Creative Economy and to global rivalries among cities. I conclude the chapter by describing eight small-scale, creativity-centered economic development strategies I've observed and used in helping communities build more equitable and sustainable economies by employing their human and creative capital and distinctive cultural assets.

Enter the Creative Economy

The term and concept of the Creative Economy came into widespread use in the 1990s as creative sector industries grew in the postindustrial era while cities struggled for new economic footing. Economic development specialists looking for the next growth engine saw it in media, design, and technology in particular. On behalf of the British Council (a public corporation in the UK that works on cultural relations and education), BOP Consulting (1998) articulated an early and influential definition: "Those industries which have their origins in individual creativity, skill and talent and which have a potential for wealth and job creation through the generation and exploitation of intellectual property" (p. 14).

Inclusive of both nonprofit and for-profit enterprises, what became known as *creative industries* typically includes advertising, architecture, computer games, design, fashion, film, jewelry-making, music, printing and publishing, television and radio, theatre, visual arts, and writing, as well as makers of handmade products from wood, ceramics, metal, glass, or other natural materials. In the arts and cultural sector, this includes production, presentation, and preservation through organizations big and small, as well as individual artists.

The British definition does little to change the game in terms of equity. It reinforces the division between wealth generation and job creation with the latter supporting the former. It also maintains the Western notion of individualism and of the artist as solitary genius. The British Council definition also nests the endeavor squarely in the Western colonial idea of property ownership—in this case, intellectual property—that it can carry across the globe and thus reinforces lasting visions of empire.

Since 2000 in the United States, creative communities, creative workforces, and other dimensions of the Creative Economy have also come into sharper focus but the country still lacks cohesive definition, strategies, or policy. That year, the New England Council, an association representing major regional business concerns, issued *The Creative Economy Initiative,* a report examining the nature of the emerging sector in that region. The report charted the relative size and pattern of growth of this newly defined sector and showed it outperforming most other industry sectors (The New England Council, 2000). The report also acknowledged the considerable contribution made by the arts and culture sector to "nurturing innovation, developing a skilled workforce, and helping businesses remain competitive" (p. 2).

Creative Economy proponents within the nonprofit cultural sector saw this broader definition as a way to elevate the significance of creative people and institutions and to gain greater favor from the powers-that-be in order to garner more financial support for the sector. This strategy to build a broader coalition inclusive of both nonprofit and for-profit creative industries employed aggregated economic data to illustrate the scale and rapid growth of this potent new sector.

Along with the Creative Economy, the more recently branded term *creative sector* (as distinct from the *cultural sector*) describes an agglomeration of production, distribution, and consumption activities that incorporate for-profit or sole proprietor enterprises along with the nonprofit arts into a cluster of *creative industries.* The U.S. Bureau of Labor Statistics recognizes 16 broad occupational types as part of this creative sector (Vilorio, 2015). These occupations are mostly nested within the industries listed above, although it is also important to recognize that manufacturers, retailers, and financial institutions, among others, employ designers, media makers, writers, and others who fall within creative occupations but often get counted within the industry type that employs them. Overall, this construct blurs the roles of and boundaries between artists and creative entrepreneurs as well as for-profit and nonprofit enterprises. Some in the cultural sector see this as a good thing, others do not.

The postindustrial or "new" economy—sometimes labeled the Knowledge Economy—within which the Creative Economy is a subset, considers information, creativity, human capital, and capacity for innovation as key economic drivers. These phenomena aren't new nor does the Knowledge or Creative Economy supplant the Industrial and Agrarian Economies. These older, once-dominant constructs are presumably enhanced and complemented by these increasingly recognized creative drivers.

A 2012 report by the National Governors Association expanded the discussion, describing some of the ways that arts, culture, and design assist states with economic growth (Sparks & Waits, 2012). These were:

1. "Provide a fast-growth, dynamic industry cluster
2. Help mature industries become more competitive
3. Provide the critical ingredients for innovative places
4. Catalyze community revitalization
5. Deliver a better-prepared workforce"

(Sparks & Waits, 2012, p. 1).

According to the report,

Globalization and the changing economy have affected individual states differently, but all are searching for ways to support high-growth industries, accelerate innovation, foster entrepreneurial activity, address unemployment, build human capital, and revive distressed areas.

(Sparks & Waits, 2012, p. 1)

Differing Approaches

The arts and cultural sector in the United States—what some called the *cultural economy*—became a bandwagon from as early as the 1980s (Redaelli, 2019). For others in the sector, either the Creative Economy or cultural economy represents a denigration of precious creative practices and dignified ways of life by treating culture and art as utilitarian commodities. These shifts in terminology are not uniformly embraced (Evans, 2009; Redaelli, 2019). Should these terms be considered a neoliberal push towards privatizing the arts in order to serve structures designed to concentrate intellectual property ownership, as in the British approach? Or, is the emergence of a broader creative sector a progressive recognition that creativity and creative work occurs and has value across cultures, sectors, and domains? Perhaps some of both. Either way, this relabeling has contributed to bringing this aggregation of arts, culture, and creativity more squarely into the sights of economic developers, policymakers, and city planners. While a new performing arts complex, creative district, or other such "hardware" have been on planners' radar since at least the middle of the 20th century (Ashley, 2015), the "software"—the process and less tangible products of the creative sector—remained largely invisible.

Some cultural planners, including myself, ventured into working with cities and small towns around cultural economy or Creative Economy development. I came to learn that there are significant and important differences in *how* it is approached. Critics saw such work as either diminishing artists and cultural practices or playing into a neoliberal trap to promote media, high-tech, marketing, design, and other intellectual property-based industries and their highly paid workers. However, I found there was no downside in helping creative individuals in communities of all sizes—whether self-defined as artists, tinkerers, or creative entrepreneurs—to earn a livelihood from their talents and skills, and to build that livelihood in synergy with the unique resources and/or identity of their geographic location. Artists, who are often self-employed, each constitute a small-business enterprise, whether they see themselves that way or not. This approach certainly does not fit a neoliberal or extractive capitalist agenda, and it honors creativity in all its forms, especially those outside Eurocentric art traditions.

My work promoted the development of renewable local assets, collective agency, and *vernacular creativity*—the small fish. This term is one I did not adopt until more recently and will be discussed more later. Briefly, it has been defined as "ordinary or everyday creative practice ... grounded in contextual specificity" (Burgess, 2010, p. 117)—in other words, things people make that have grounding in and relevance to the place where they are made. As so often, the devil is in the detail. And, while I cannot say my work in this area was free of unintended consequences, it gave me an opportunity to understand how it can be different from dominant economic development strategies based on industry and talent attraction.

The Creative Class and Cities in Transition

Cities and regions worldwide have struggled through postindustrial transitions. In this light, Creative Economy concepts, emerging in the 1980s and 90s, were explored and defined in the work of such authors as Australian economist David Throsby (1994), British-born American geographer Allen J. Scott (1997), and British scholar John Howkins (2002). However, these ideas gained wider popularity, and perhaps went off track, with the release of Richard Florida's 2002 book, *The Rise of The Creative Class*.

The theories and construct articulated by Florida spread rapidly as they synchronized with dominant economic development approaches. To be competitive in a global economy, he asserted, cities must attract well-educated, creative talent. Cultural sectors joined policymakers in many cities and eagerly took up an active role in doing so. Young, usually White, well-educated designers, software engineers, marketing executives, and the like became the golden children. In this zero-sum game, the nurturing of distinctive, local, creative talent took a back seat. Combined with neoliberal policies and trickle-down economics, the creative class craze left more and more people out of an economy that appeared to be performing well in the aggregate. In a later book, Florida (2017) offered an extensive apology for these unintended consequences.

Florida (2002) constructed an index for cities to test their readiness to be among the world's great creative cities in the form of the "three Ts": talent, technology, and tolerance. These became buzzwords for cities looking to join the global competition. Rivalries between cities grew, not for sports teams but for highly skilled workers. This quest for the creative class opened a doorway for the cultural sector to supply the kind of "cool" or bohemian urban environments Florida said "creatives" seek out. His work also promoted diversity through his Tolerance Index as a key to economic development. However, the cultural sector, as described in Chapter 4, has been resistant to fully embracing their role in advancing diversity, not to mention many cities also didn't understand or really value that "T."

One, perhaps positive, side-effect of Florida's work impacted the image of artists. In my early years working in the arts, "artist" was a dirty word among city leaders. Artists were characterized as social misfits who questioned or even offended authority. Alternately, they were seekers of handouts or seen as incessantly peddling peculiar wares or bizarre and obscene art projects. For city leaders, artists were pretty close to the bottom of the list of desirable residents—until 2002. Within a few years, I couldn't count the number of mayors, chambers of commerce, or other civic leaders in cities and towns of all sizes who asked me how they could get more artists to live in their communities.

The Rise of the Creative City

Consultants and scholars in the United Kingdom and Europe—notably, Landry and Bianchini (1995)— coalesced thinking around the creative, social, economic, physical, and policy issues that contribute not only to a thriving creative sector, but to the larger concept of creative cities. This concept was easily sold to planners and municipal officials, observed Canadian political economist Jamie Peck (2005), who critiqued the strategy as a "low-cost, market-friendly urban placebo" (p. 760). He argued that notions of the creative city would not be sweeping the globe if they ran counter to established business and political interests. "For the average mayor, there are few downsides to making the city safe for the creative class—a creativity strategy can quite easily be bolted on to business-as-usual urban development policies" (p. 760), Peck wrote.

Rather than celebrate unique local character, cities of all sizes leaned towards emulating a homogeneous aesthetic that could compete on an imagined national or international level. This is what Landry called the "Starbucks-and-stadiums" approach (as cited in Falk, 2007, p. 1). This added to the desire to check off boxes for arts and cultural assets. Carl Grodach and Anastasia Loukaitou-Sideris in their 2007 study of urban cultural policy in the United States observed, "It seems there is a baseline of things you must have to legitimize your city as a 'player'. Everyone must have a symphony orchestra, a ballet or other dance company and an art museum" (p. 20).

In my cultural planning work, it felt like a significant achievement to upend that thinking with client cities. I endeavored to turn their focus and pride to special amenities or characteristics that anchor their distinctive identity through which their city can stand apart. One thing I found is that it can be difficult for people who have spent most or all of their lives in their community to even *see* distinctive local qualities or to let go of the notion that to have value, their city must have the same things other cities have (including Starbucks and stadiums).

Across the globe, a Creative Cities Network was born of UNESCO in 2004. Cultural, creative, or arts districts (that had existed in one form or another, perhaps for centuries) and high-profile museum and performing arts complexes became greatly desired and key elements of regeneration strategies. These strategies were, of course, prompted or promoted especially by leaders of larger cultural institutions as a way to advance their interests and profiles. A few, like Bilboa, Spain, became iconic and are considered highly successful. However, as some cities found, they can be a Trojan Horse. Building them is the easy part. Subsidizing the operating costs and deficits over the long term is harder. Large landowners and developers are primary beneficiaries. City planners and civic leaders see these facilities as a strategy to boost tax revenues. Artists, lower-income neighbors, and small businesspeople found themselves priced out. As the Starbucks and stadiums move in, inequalities grow.

Creativity and the Rise of Inequity

The buzz around the creative city, creative class, Creative Economy, and creative placemaking has been generally embraced in city planning and in much of the cultural sector. In most cities, the creative sector, aligned with the cultural sector—including artists—is closely associated with Eurocentric practices and, in turn, middle- and upper-class White people. Growing majorities of people don't fall into those categories and find themselves off the map.

As scholars like American sociologist Sharon Zukin have long pointed out, the buzz thrives because it corresponds with municipal agendas related to economic and real estate development. This and the phenomenon of artists as harbingers or catalysts of gentrification were brought to light with Zukin's (1982) landmark book, *Loft Living*. Low-income residents, people of color, and immigrants are forgotten and often, in fact, are in the way of urban development. Later, Zukin (2006) accused city planners and policymakers of promoting urban amnesia, a practice of removing working class heritage and identity from their maps as part of creativity-based regeneration strategies (as cited in Edensor & Millington, 2010, p. 175).

The *creative sector* and Creative Economy may represent an expansion in thinking from "opera-house culture," and they are propelled in part as solutions to devastating postindustrial transitions. Cities in the United States are still recovering from massive disinvestment between 1950 and the 1990s driven by and exacerbating racial and economic segregation. To the degree creative- and culture-led strategies maintain Eurocentric imagery, values, and dominance, these approaches serve as another bulwark against the tide of people of color and immigrants who don't fit these frames. In the aftermath of these culture-led strategies, Stevenson (2014) asked whether "the result is fundamental cultural change and exchange or simply an expanded suite of food and consumption options" (p. 163). Critiquing Florida's (2002) creative class ideas, Stevenson went on to assert that "Florida's formula can readily be read as a prescription for gentrification and displacement" (p. 4).

Making city neighborhoods attractive and safe for the creative class as a municipal priority exacerbated deteriorating conditions for the poor—the "non-creative" classes. Florida himself, in his 2017 book *The New Urban Crisis*, traced the alarming parallels between "successful" creative cities and those with growing economic and social inequities. He admits promotion of the creative class played a role in these inequities.

The idea of creativity itself, argued British geographers Tim Edensor, Deborah Leslie, Steve Millington, and Norma M. Rantisi (2010), "becomes a discursive weapon to further problematize non-middle-class values and peoples" (p. 6). This, they said, represents a failure of planning and local policy to engage working-class communities. The focus on professional artists and bohemian environments excludes most people and their everyday creativity and further privileges metropolitan areas as sites of cultural production. These authors point out that individuals outside cities are no less creative, yet they also find themselves left off the map.

Edensor et al. (2010) went on to observe, "The champions of creative regeneration have fetishized these urban settings while ignoring forms of creative endeavor that emerge in rural, suburban, working-class, every-day and marginal spaces" (p. 11). These everyday acts of creativity in everyday spaces, wrote Evans (2005), "better represent cultural regeneration primarily through social and community-based projects" (p. 976). Community-based projects contribute more to regeneration, suggests Evans, because they employ everyday creativity and because they contribute more to the social capital of their communities.

Vernacular Creativity: Thinking Small in Big Ways

As some have observed, including one of the foremost thinkers on creativity, Hungarian-American psychologist Mihaly Csikszentmihalyi (1996), creativity cannot be divorced from its social context. In this sense, something of revolutionary value in one time or place may be folly in another. Grounded in endogenous resources, including local talents, Redaelli (2019) described the "situated character" of creative industries and asserted that they "are deeply rooted and embedded in their location" (p. 86).

However, in the competitive global cities frame based on industry-attraction strategies, global firms in design, high-technology, media, and software are privileged. As a form of hunting and gathering, these strategies leave locally grown and situated creativity off the map. Policy-driven approaches tend to give advantage to larger-scale forms of creative work over vernacular forms. However, vernacular forms—the small fish—have greater social, aesthetic, and economic merits. American urban redevelopment and historic preservation writer Roberta Brandes Gratz (1989) warned against what she called "big fix" or "grand plan" solutions. She cited successful projects where the key was "thinking small in a big way" (from her book's title). Not only do small projects have more equitably distributed economic benefits, she observed, but they retain and build on the threads of existing social fabric.

In another look at these less visible vernacular forms, Edensor and Millington (2010) challenged planners to reconsider what constitutes creativity. They asked, "If there is a *creative class*, then what about the *uncreative class*?" (p. 172). By elevating a creative class, a new hierarchy is promoted which, they argued, "problematize(s) social groups who are deemed to lack the necessary skills, cultural tastes and competencies to enter a circumscribed definition of the cultural or knowledge economy" (p. 172). Such hierarchical orderings, they claim, champion forms of urban development "in line with dominant class-based power relations" (p. 175).

Alternatively, vernacular cultural practices operate in ordinary spaces every day. Edensor et al. (2010) argued, "Creativity should rather be conceived as an improvisation quality that, across all forms of cultural activity, requires people to adapt to particular circumstances" (p. 8). This improvisation quality is one in which people and systems learn to be better problem-solvers and become more resilient, akin to asset-based capacity-building described in Chapter 7, rather than becoming dependent on outside or larger players. Burgess (2010) described vernacular creativity as "ordinary or everyday creative practice... [that] does not operate inside the institutions or cultural value systems of high culture or the commercial popular media" (p. 116). Similarly, Redaelli (2019) observed, "creativity and innovation are not characteristics that belong only to the creative industries" (p. 99). They belong in the everyday or the vernacular.

Vernacular cultural practices "encompass a wide range of activities that are distinguished by their expression of community values and their inclusion of many participants" wrote Markusen (2010). This, she says, stands in contrast to "the individualized and professionalized creation or reproduction of art or culture by experts detached from a community frame of reference" (p. 185).

The Creative Economy, and especially a vernacular Creative Economy, remain largely invisible in contemporary land-use planning and public-sector data collection practices. For the recent Minneapolis Creative Index study (Kayzar & Kayim, 2018), American urban geographer Brenda Kayzar mapped thousands of creative workers scattered across residential areas of the city who are off the radar of city planners and economic development professionals. They had little idea how to see artists as workers, let alone aggregate them or tap their potential contributions to larger development goals. Wrote Markusen (2010), "these artists and activities are thus not included in most definitions of the cultural economy that rely on statistics based on occupation or industry" (p. 186).

Clustering Creative Enterprises

In 2010, my consulting team was invited to help an artist- and neighborhood association-led effort in a mixed industrial, residential, and commercial district of St. Paul, Minnesota. The area faced a difficult transition, as construction was about to begin on a light rail line that was being inserted into an existing primary thoroughfare. One older industrial building that had housed studios for about 35 artists for nearly 30 years changed ownership. Artists were evicted for the development of luxury lofts—a classic story. Artists and community leaders feared more such evictions. Other investors had already repurposed other vacant industrial buildings for residential lofts marketed to creative workers and artists.

Using the station area as defined in transportation plans to delineate the district, we invited key stakeholder representatives to a six-month planning process. They ranged from a banker, real estate company manager, and loft developer to nonprofit arts and social service providers, artists, small business owners, residents, and the city council representative. Together they devised a strategic plan and adopted the name "Creative Enterprise Zone" (CEZ). Ten years later, the artist-leader continues to chair the board of the entity that is now a nonprofit, although the city has still not given the area an official designation. The self-managing district is highly successful in attracting and retaining creative enterprises. The appeal for artists, entrepreneurs, and nonprofits to be part of the CEZ is strong and developers still see plenty of fallow "old economy" real estate still to convert into creative spaces. Long-standing zoning that favors industrial uses, keeps at bay momentum to scrape and rebuild the district for large-scale residential and commercial development seen elsewhere. The CEZ has documented the numbers of jobs (as in artists/creative entrepreneurs) to push city policymakers to further protect this valuable economic engine.

New Constructs, Old Tools

In the 10 years since the naming of the CEZ, I've been approached by people from several other cities looking for the secret sauce. Given the formality of the district's name, they expect some imaginative municipal policy construct. I explain the CEZ is first, an old industrial area; second, has an interesting-sounding name; and third, that well-organized activists, artists, and neighborhood folks who are good at telling their stories have taken leadership roles.

The formal ring of the CEZ name was intended to incorporate old and new industries together, sharing common purpose—to maintain appropriately zoned and priced real estate and to have the city utilize tools typically reserved to attract and retain manufacturers on behalf of creative entrepreneurs. The city's development and investment policies did not see these newer industries (AKA artists/creative entrepreneurs) as anything other than placeholders for underutilized buildings until they could be reactivated for higher use. The CEZ's efforts have made visible the scale and growth of creative industries and their aggregated value as employers and economic generators. To attract a manufacturer offering 100 jobs, the city would do somersaults. However, a cluster of buildings with 300 artists and microenterprises that don't fit familiar industry types is barely on their radar. Policy tools to retain and grow these "jobs" remain slow to emerge because the enterprises themselves are still not well understood.

Municipal policy interventions that typically assist in the development of districts like the CEZ were the subject of a global policy survey by Evans (2009). He found "over 80 cities/city-regions produced some explicit policy or strategic plans in the creative city/industries field—whether headlined as such or as sectoral strategies—within 35 nation-states across all major continents" (p. 1010). Evans observed that city planners and policymakers are relying on old policy frameworks and tools that lack in responses to vernacular creativity. He found six typical policy interventions to support Creative Economy initiatives. In order of their frequency of use, they were,

1. securing/providing property
2. business support services
3. grants and loans
4. fiscal/tax schemes
5. infrastructure—physical and soft (broadband, etc.)
6. education, training, and support of networks and marketing

Such support systems, when successful, make it possible in a global environment for "small-scale producers [to] become global players themselves," asserted Bas van Heur (2010, p. 110), meaning they become exporters to potentially wide markets.

To make this work additionally beneficial, a study of economic impacts of artists by Markusen and David King (2003) found connections between the presence and influences of thriving artist communities and successful industries of all types. They argued that standard economic impact studies underestimate the full contribution of an artistic community to a regional economy. Markusen and King countered the parochial view of the arts as a consequence of, or even a parasite on, a successful business community. They make the case that productivity in a regional economy rises in correlation to the number of artists within its boundaries, producing what they call an "artistic dividend." In other words, an abundance of artists may be more cause than outcome in a healthy, homegrown economy.

Gardening as Anti-Gentrification Strategy

Many city planners may be familiar with the term *economic gardening*—systematic efforts to grow local economies from within. This is in contrast to the competitive strategy of business or industry attraction that remains the dominant strategy, pitting cities and towns against each other to surrender land, taxes, infrastructure, and other resources to the most aggressive companies with the biggest promises. Illogically, this remains the operative strategy in Minneapolis and St. Paul, a relatively small metro area home to 16 homegrown Fortune 500 companies in 2019 (and this does not include Cargill, the largest privately held company in the United States, or several hometown companies that were acquired or relocated elsewhere in recent years but keep significant operations there).

The term economic gardening, and its explicit practices, were made known in the 1980s in Littleton, Colorado, now home of the National Center for Economic Gardening. This network of practitioners and champions promotes efforts to encourage and nurture local, small start-ups. This is intended as a balance to the still dominant strategies in most cities characterized as hunting and gathering. Is this another manifestation of how traditionally male-oriented competition and the work of hunting and gathering takes precedence over traditionally female-oriented focus on collaboration, nurturing, and gardening at home?

Locally owned enterprises add more value than simply employing people. Some, like those in Minnesota, grow to become global exporters and infrequently extract nonrenewable resources. Local businesses tend to invest more in their communities—including in philanthropy, volunteer work, and civic leadership—and source locally. Growing locally and gardening are more than metaphors. Interesting parallels can be drawn between different forms of gardening. In terms of culture, food that is grown, prepared, and shared locally is the bedrock of culture and cultural experience.

Community gardening, in the agrarian sense, supplies useful lessons that play out in economic gardening. An interesting story by British social geographer Paul Milbourne (2010) described this other form of gardening as a tool for equitable regeneration, and thinking small in big ways with multiple benefits. Gardening represents what he sees as "more 'ordinary' forms of culture and creativity" (p. 153) that are integral to community gardening. In a disadvantaged northern English city with high levels of poverty, his research found that gardening produced different but equally important forms of vernacular creativity contributing to community reinvention and regeneration. Milbourne highlighted ways that community gardening transforms the social and cultural, as well as physical, attributes of space. Projects remade physical places while creating new forms of sociability and working relationships. He argued the need to recognize such vernacular creativity as a tool to fend off the repetition of gentrification patterns.

Place-based studies of poverty, Milbourne (2010) reflected, "have begun to highlight the ways in which the degraded state of the local environment contributes to processes of social exclusion" (p. 143). Degraded environments reinforce negative stereotyping, reduce quality-of-life, and compound feelings of disempowerment or low self-esteem. The social structures of community gardening have long been recognized to extend beyond the horticultural to incorporate cultural and creative activities packed full of meanings and social interactions. Milbourne argued that community gardens combine "the best of environmental ethics, social activism and personal expression" (p. 144). Their presence brings both direct and indirect benefits.

Creativity Goes to Work: Eight Small Approaches

A diverse and balanced natural environment, and relationships to it rooted in agrarian activity, is a healthier one. Similarly, a diversified economy, rooted in a community's assets and in tune with the identity of place, provides a more stable base, retains more of the wealth generated in the local economy, and contributes to civic infrastructure. In this section, I offer eight distinct, though sometimes overlapping, approaches that both draw from and promote vernacular creativity and more balanced local economic and social development outcomes. I have observed and employed these in working with communities across the United States over the past two decades. They are derived from 10 strategies illustrated in *The Creative Community Builder's Handbook* (Borrup, 2006) with some updates.

Strategy 1: Creative jobs. Artists and other creative entrepreneurs are generally overlooked as job creators. Each is a for-profit, tax-paying enterprise. Artists generate their own livelihood, often through multiple activities and sources in the "gig" economy equivalent to at least one job. The nonprofit arts and culture sector had not previously been considered a major contributor to the United States economy, but multiple studies have shown otherwise. In 2016, the nonprofit arts and culture sector represented over $800 billion in economic activity, accounting for 4.3% of the country's GDP (National Endowment for the Arts, 2019). And, this does not include individual, for-profit artist entrepreneurs who also bring other benefits. These entrepreneurs create unique products, services, and events that additionally contribute to quality-of-life and the identity of place. They tend to work in place and invest in both the social and civic vitality of their neighborhoods, cities, and towns.

Strategy 2: Shape and enhance identity. Developing civic pride and stewardship through community building and collaborative practices enhances a community's identity and self-esteem, engages residents, and welcomes visitors. Creative products and services, often based in distinctive foods or raw materials or are related to the natural environment, help every community form, uncover, and/or celebrate its distinctive identity. In the process of finding and reinforcing this identity, community members learn the importance of customs, traditions, and natural resources in their midst. A strong identity helps build stewardship of place and this, in turn, adds value to products created there. Connecting businesses and cultural groups around this identity and sense of pride builds clusters of activities and fosters cultural exchange, which can lead to more active and welcoming places—perhaps historic or arts districts, Main Streets, and distinctive neighborhoods.

Strategy 3: Stimulate trade and tourism. A strong identity and related mix of products and services creates favorable conditions for cultural or heritage tourism and exporting locally grown or made products. Well-managed marketing and tourism improves quality-of-life, builds pride, and enhances the capacity to work together. Good examples are found in every type of community, from inner-city immigrant neighborhoods to small towns in rural regions. Success requires cooperation across government, business, and nonprofit sectors, and often leads to even greater collaboration and enhanced capacity for problem-solving on all levels.

Strategy 4: Provide space to generate creative enterprises. Regenerating or building more sustainable and flexible economies begins with existing assets that can also attract investment. Creative entrepreneurs, chief among them artists, often make use of vacant real estate, such as underused warehouses, mills, and factory buildings, to jump start economic-development efforts. Legendary urbanist Jane Jacobs (1961/1965) said, "New ideas must use old buildings" (p. 201). While postindustrial and other transitional cities have old buildings in abundance, the changing face of retail and economic collapse of 2020 opened spaces in former malls, strip centers, and downtowns. Creative entrepreneurs seem to be in no short supply either. Matching them and creating a nurturing environment for creative enterprises is something city planners do.

Strategy 5: Diversify economies from within. The more legs an economy has to stand on, the more resistant it is to changes in any one sector and the more exchange takes place between sectors. Nurturing the creative potentials of multiple vernacular assets generates new enterprises and helps others reinvent themselves. Successful communities bring together the cultural, business, and civic sectors to create interdependent economic networks. They combine the natural environment, proximity to other resources, and cultural strengths. In what he calls, "intertwinement," van Heur (2010) argued that clusters "are dependent on networks for their emergence and development, but networks also rely on clusters for their own reproduction and transformation" (p. 106).

Strategy 6: Improve quality-of-life. In taking raw materials and creatively enhancing them or adapting them to other uses, artists and creative entrepreneurs enhance value and change meaning. Artists sometimes apply their skills to home construction or rehabilitation, enhancing the aesthetic qualities of public and private places. They also generate interesting activities that attract people and commercial trade. By bringing more energy and generating interesting things, artists enliven communities and enrich the quality of life. They often teach children and people of all ages dance, music, theater, visual arts, and other creative and traditional practices. When artists are part of a community, as opposed to merely visiting entertainers, they tend to tap into cultural traditions and help people feel more connected.

Strategy 7: Build trust, social capital, and community capacity. Participation in civic and cultural activities are major factors in a community's capacity to generate and support the success of new business and social networks. These are qualities to be purposefully nurtured. As American political scientist Francis Fukuyama (1996) observed, "The most useful kind of social capital is often not the ability to work under the authority of a traditional community or group, but the capacity to form new associations and to cooperate within the terms of references they establish" (p. 27). Economic success, he found, depends on the kinds of trust nurtured, a capacity he called "spontaneous sociability" (p. 10). That process can begin with neighbors shopping side-by-side or exchanging goods in the marketplace. It can grow through volunteering to produce community theater, participate in a holiday parade, or visit an event at a neighborhood art center, church, or school. Considerable evidence supports that cultural practices nurture and build on spontaneous sociability and social capital.

Strategy 8: Retain wealth. "Buy Local" has become a catchphrase in recent decades, promoting a practice that has proven to be one of the quickest and most effective ways to contribute to community revitalization (Markusen, 2007). Such campaigns encourage residents and tourists to buy locally grown or made products. It can also involve visiting a local theatre or music venue rather than a traveling road show. This not only reduces economic and environmental costs of long-distance transportation, but allows a community to keep dollars recirculating in the local economy. Developing appreciation of local creativity, food, arts, and the handmade encourages others to participate in growing their own creativity.

Summary

A vernacular Creative Economy—perhaps well-characterized as a mash-up of Creative Economy and economic gardening—brings greater value to a community in multiple ways. Instead of attracting outside talent and industries and thus supporting wealth-building for big investors, as in Florida's (2002) approach, a vernacular focus mines local assets for locally owned development and job and wealth creation.

"Big box" solutions in whatever form, or industry-attraction—importing solutions from outside a community, often costing communities in giveaways or direct subsidies—tend to become long-term problems. Their impacts are inequitable, unbalanced, and unsustainable, whether the business is a manufacturing plant, big-box retailer, major sports facility, or performing-arts complex. Development brought to a community through hunting and gathering or industry-attraction strategies inordinately depend on outside capital, labor, goods, and cultures. Because they require major investment, they ultimately extract more wealth. Profits go elsewhere, furthering wealth disparities. They often damage the environment, overshadow the unique identity of place, and diminish the integrity and value of the people and cultures of that community.

Community success is reflected in sustainable local economies based on distinct assets, particularly the people and cultural resources that enhance its identity and character. Energies are best devoted to sustaining and growing the local and the vernacular. Who wouldn't want to grow enterprises that emanate from and reflect local creative talents, generate satisfying work, are environmentally friendly, and give back to their community's civic, social, and cultural life? Identifying vernacular creativity requires asset-mapping, building on positive place identity and attachment, and engaging creative people in everyday life to work together to shape their communities.

References

Ashley, A. J. (2015). Beyond the aesthetic: The historical pursuit of local arts economic development. *Journal of Planning History*, *14*(1), 38–61. https://doi.org/10.1177/1538513214541616

BOP Consulting. (1998). *Mapping the creative industries: A toolkit*. London, UK: British Council. Retrieved from https://creativeconomy.britishcouncil.org/media/uploads/files/English_mapping_the_creative_industries_a_toolkit_2-2.pdf

Borrup, T. (2006). *The Creative Community Builder's Handbook: How to Transform Communities Using Local Assets, Arts, and Culture*. St. Paul, MN: Fieldstone Alliance.

Burgess, J. (2010). Remediating vernacular creativity: Photography and cultural citizenship in the Flickr photo-sharing network. In T. Edensor, D. Leslie, S. Millington, & N. M. Rantisi (Eds.), *Spaces of vernacular creativity: Rethinking the cultural economy* (pp. 116–126). London, UK: Routledge.

Csikszentmihalyi, M. (1996). *Creativity: Flow and the psychology of discovery and invention.* New York, NY: Harper Collins.

Edensor, T., Leslie, D., Millington, S., & Rantisi, N. M. (Eds.) (2010). Introduction: Rethinking creativity: Critiquing the creative class thesis. In *Spaces of vernacular creativity: Rethinking the cultural economy* (pp. 1–16). Abingdon, UK: Routledge.

Edensor, T., & Millington, S. (2010). Christmas light displays and the creative production of spaces of generosity. In T. Edensor, D. Leslie, S. Millington, & N. M. Rantisi (Eds.), *Spaces of vernacular creativity: Rethinking the cultural economy* (pp. 170–182). Abingdon, UK: Routledge.

Evans, G. (2005). Measure for measure: Evaluating the evidence of culture's contribution to regeneration. *Urban Studies, 42*(5/6), 959–983. https://doi.org/10.1080/00420980500107102

Evans, G. L. (2009). Creative cities, creative spaces and urban policy. *Urban Studies, 46* (5/6), 1003–1040. https://doi.org/10.1177/0042098009103853

Falk, N. (2007). Review of the book *The art of city making* by Charles Landry. *Journal of Urban Regeneration & Renewal, 1*(1), 1–3.

Florida, R. (2002). *The rise of the creative class.* New York, NY: Basic Books.

Florida, R. (2017). *The new urban crisis: How our cities are increasing inequality, deepening segregation, and failing the middle class—And what we can do about it.* New York, NY: Basic Books.

Fukuyama, F. (1996). *Trust: human nature and the reconstitution of social order.* New York, NY: Simon & Schuster.

Gratz, R. B. (1989). *The living city: How America's cities are being revitalized by thinking small in a big way.* Oakland, CA: New Village Press.

Grodach C. & Loukaitou-Sideris, A. (2007). Cultural development strategies and urban revitalization: A survey of US cities. *International Journal of Cultural Policy, 13*(4), 349–370. https://doi.org/10.1080/10286630701683235

Howkins, J. (2002). *The creative economy: How people make money from ideas.* London, UK: Penguin.

Jacobs, J. (1965). *The death and life of great American cities.* Harmondsworth, UK: Pelican. (Original work published 1961)

Kayzar, B., & Kayim, G. (2018). *The Minneapolis Creative Index 2018: Understanding the scale and impact of Minneapolis' Creative Sector.* Minneapolis, MN: Office of Arts, Culture and the Creative Economy. Retrieved from https://mcad.edu/sites/default/files/page/wcmsp-216598.pdf

Landry, C., & Bianchini, F. (1995). *The creative city.* London, UK: Demos.

Markusen, A. (2007). A consumption base theory of development: An application to the rural cultural economy. *Agricultural and Resource Economics Review, 36*(1), 9–23. https://doi.org/10.1017/S1068280500009412

Markusen, A. (2010). Challenge, change, and space in vernacular cultural practice. In T. Edensor, D. Leslie, S. Millington, & N. M. Rantisi, (Eds.), *Spaces of vernacular creativity: Rethinking the cultural economy* (pp. 185–199). Abingdon, UK: Routledge.

Markusen, A., & King, D. (2003). *The artistic dividend: The arts' hidden contributions to regional development.* Minneapolis: Project on Regional and Industrial Economics, Hubert H. Humphrey Institute of Public Affairs, University of Minnesota. Retrieved from https://www.giarts.org/sites/default/files/The-Artistic-Dividend.pdf

Milbourne, P., (2010). Growing places: community gardening, ordinary creativities and place-based regeneration in a northern English city. In T. Edensor, D. Leslie, S. Millington, S., & N. M. Rantisi, (Eds.), *Spaces of vernacular creativity: Rethinking the cultural economy* (pp. 141–154). Abingdon, UK: Routledge.

National Endowment for the Arts (2019). Latest data shows increase to U.S. economy from arts and cultural sector. Retrieved from https://www.arts.gov/news/2019/latest-data-shows-increase-us-economy-arts-and-cultural-sector

The New England Council (2000, May). *The creative economy initiative: The role of the arts and culture in New England's economic competitiveness.* Boston, MA: The New England Council

Peck, J. (2005). Struggling with the creative class. *International Journal of Urban & Regional Research, 29*(4), 740–770. https://doi.org/10.1111/j.1468-2427.2005.00620.x

Redaelli, E. (2019). *Connecting arts and place: Cultural policy and American cities.* London, UK: Palgrave MacMillan.

Rosenfeld, S. (2004, September). Crafting a new rural development strategy. Paper presented at *Conference, Knowledge clusters and entrepreneurship,* Minneapolis, MI. Retrieved from https://q.bstatic.com/data/bsuitewf/43d7844c311578bcc90f6f75ca44504a132050b6.pdf

Scott, A. J. (1997). The cultural economy of cities. *International Journal of Urban & Regional Research, 21*(2), 323–339. https://doi.org/10.1111/1468-2427.00075

Sparks, E., & Waits, M. J. (2012, May), *New engines of growth: Five roles for arts, culture and design.* National Governors Association. Retrieved from https://www.giarts.org/sites/default/files/New-Engines-of-Growth.pdf

Stevenson, D. (2014). *Cities of culture: A global perspective.* London, UK: Routledge.

Throsby, D. (1994). The production and consumption of the arts: A view of cultural economics *Journal of Economic Literature, 32,* 1–29.

van Heur, B. (2010). Imagining the spatialities of music production: The co-constitution of creative clusters and networks. In T. Edensor, D. Leslie, S. Milslington, S., & N. M. Rantisi, (Eds.), *Spaces of vernacular creativity: Rethinking the cultural economy* (pp. 106–115). Abingdon, UK: Routledge.

Vilorio, D. (2015, June). *Careers for creative people.* U.S. Bureau of Labor Statistics. Retrieved from https://www.bls.gov/careeroutlook/2015/article/creative-careers.htm

Zukin, S. (1982). *Loft living: Culture and capital in urban change.* New Brunswick, NJ: Rutgers University Press.

Zukin, S. (2006). *Naked city: The death and life of authentic urban places.* Oxford, UK: Oxford University Press.

Final Thoughts
Cities on the Edge of Tomorrow

Within the developing framework of this new urban regional political economy, there has been a shift of emphasis that has had the effect, often not consciously intended or desired, of opening up the field to an acceleration of the cultural turn.

—Edward Soja (1999, p. 69)

This book has addressed the power and multiple impacts of culture in both the substance and process of city planning in the face of accelerating demographic and climate changes. I called for city planning and its younger cousin, cultural planning, to find ways to work together that advance more sensitive, participatory, and just practices to shape more equitable, welcoming, and sustainable communities. Soja (1999) wrote extensively on ideas of spatial justice, recognizing the increasingly critical role of culture in shaping more just communities. In this book, I built on calls by other practitioners and scholars from city planning, cultural planning, and other fields, and I offered some of my own experiences to put *people*—their cultures or ways of life, and their ways of living together—at the center of planning, designing, and building communities. And, by putting people at the center, I mean going beyond simply putting them foremost in the consideration of planners, but to work creatively to bring more people into the process.

   The proposition I advanced is that bringing critical practices of cultural planning into city planning can create a new whole I think of as *just planning*. This does not mean *merely* planning, but planning with social, cultural, environmental, economic, and aesthetic justice at its heart. Together, I believe these practices can help planners constructively engage a greater diversity of people as well as help individuals and rapidly changing communities find ways of living better together.

City planning, as well as the cultural sector, suffer from subconscious forms of "immunity to change" (Kegan & Lahey, 2009), described here in Chapter 2. Meanwhile, shifts in global populations, politics, and climates are on course to deliver devastating outcomes. City planners bring considerable skills and experience working with communities and understanding interconnections between physical, political, and economic systems. At the same time, they've inherited a practice that does not always serve the best interests of residents (see Stein, 2019, as discussed here in Chapter 2), and that carries significant DNA from top-down, colonialist approaches to impose built forms and systems on communities, but not often with them (Escobar, 2017; Porter, 2016). Whether or not planners own up to how they have already impacted the culture and cultural dimensions of their cities, they must add culture to the list of systems they understand and knowingly impact. They need to address culture mindfully, constructively, and in its integral relationship to the many other challenges they address.

Cities Looking Forward

Depending on a city's geographic location, concerns around sustainability practices and the impacts of climate change are top of the list for planners or are somewhere in the top five. If not, they soon will be. In Miami Beach, where most of this book was written, climate change and sea-level rise are in the news and civic conversations daily. Ironically, welcoming people from all parts of the world to visit and to live and work there is not a problem, as it has proven to be in many other parts of the United States. Tourists come and go daily, of course, but the resident population is also global and dynamic. Census estimates in 2019 placed the foreign-born population of the City of Miami Beach at just over 50%, similar to that of the larger City of Miami. These are probably low estimates, as undocumented residents are numerous and even some recent legal immigrants avoid census-takers and make themselves invisible. Meanwhile, the area is often seen as ground zero for sea-level rise (see Goodell, 2017), even though some smaller, lesser-known communities in the United States have already been displaced.

In most other parts of the country, in the face of escalating negative rhetoric about immigrants, the need to accommodate more and different people living together, sharing space and resources is rising along with the sea and heat. Will American cities and towns on more stable ground accommodate a million Floridians, many of Latin American descent, who will need to relocate within a few decades? How about tens, if not hundreds, of millions more from South Asia, the Pacific Islands, Central America, and the Texas and Louisiana coasts, just to name a few? In a speech in the spring of 2019, then American President Donald Trump declared the United States "full" (as cited in Irwin & Badger, 2019), with no more room for anyone else to enter (unless they have significant financial wherewithal).

Meanwhile, divisive White-supremacist forces have escalated resentments and violence against people from Latin America, Africa, and the Middle East as well as other new and long-standing immigrant groups, people of color, and Indigenous peoples. Racist and xenophobic forces have set in motion a wave of reactionary politics based in White nationalism and hatred. City planners must find new ways to constructively contribute to the cultural issues discussed in this book. I hope it has made clear that these issues are integral to and part and parcel of their work in ways that are often invisible and mostly unspoken.

Organizing for Capacity and Inclusion

I advocated in this book creative approaches that support community organizing, building stronger cross-cultural connections, and capacity-building within communities. While this characterizes my approach to community and cultural planning, I realize not all city planners see organizing as helpful to their work. As described here in Chapter 5, "average citizens," as the American Planning Association has characterized residents involved in local planning matters (Morley, 2018), bring feelings and attachments relative to the character of place and thus to planning discussions that are not always welcomed by planners. In fact, communities that are more organized can present planners more obstacles, especially planners trained in rational, engineering, and data-driven solutions.

In the early 2000s, a young colleague, fresh from a prestigious graduate school of planning, was working for a nonprofit community development group in a historically Black neighborhood in Miami. I arranged a visit and tour to learn about their work. During the visit, I made observations about how I thought they could leverage community assets to help the community organize—something I assumed would be consistent with the nonprofit's goals and beneficial to residents. My friend looked at me puzzled and said, "I'm not sure how organizing the community would help us achieve our goals."

Planners are long-term thinkers and creative problem-solvers, and I trust they appreciate that communities with greater internal capacity will ultimately achieve more and be more resilient. Of course, as I pointed out earlier, the devil can be in the detail. *How* planners work and *how* communities organize make a big difference. Communities can and have organized to keep others out. They've also organized to prevent the demolition of historic buildings and the incursion of major highways through pristine or long-standing residential areas, changes many planners championed. Wisdom does not automatically or reliably lie with planners or with residents. Balance in this often-lopsided equation depends on the presence and acceptance of local knowledge. Especially in communities of color and poorer communities, the capacity to be at the table and bring that knowledge is often lacking. When not organized, those communities continue to get the short end of the stick.

In helping communities organize, planners have a responsibility to set an inclusive tone while building their own cultural competency and opening to culturally attuned planning processes and creative ways of thinking and working. In other words, they need to commit to decolonizing planning while simultaneously working with residents to devise just and sustainable solutions that address everyday changes along with enormous shifts in populations and climate conditions. Helping communities work better together and putting in place and rebuilding infrastructure are long-term work. These take time and ultimately have profound impact. Ways of living with the earth that are bringing about catastrophic environmental impacts did not emerge in just the past few decades, nor will they change within a few decades.

A Charge for Educators

Those with at least one foot in the academic sector, such as myself, must also ask how educational institutions can better prepare planners and designers—as well as cultural planners and those in leadership roles in the arts and culture sector—to better balance the *perceived, conceived*, and *everyday lived experience* that Lefebvre (1974/1991) described. Planners, designers, and cultural workers need to gain cultural competencies, learn to listen, observe, and engage people from a wide mix of ethno-social backgrounds in all elements of planning, design, and cultural work. For both city planning and cultural work, it is critical to let go of ideas of cultural scarcity, that there is value in homogeneity, and the righteous dominance or superiority of some cultural values or practices over others.

City-planning schools grown from engineering, design, and/or architectural traditions focus on the *perceived*. Others, based in social sciences, economics, and/or policy fields, focus more on the *conceived*. Do any focus on *everyday lived experience*? Similarly, arts and cultural management schools, often grounded in limited frames of reference such as nonprofit administration, marketing, and fundraising, rarely lift their heads from these limited functions. Are there any schools that bring all three elements of the production of space into balance? And, do any teach and practice how to integrate deep democracy in planning, design, institutional operations, and community leadership practices? Do any do so in ways that promote feminism and anti-colonialism, along with the spread of good humor?

It is critical for planning and cultural management education to help students develop their cultural competencies and awareness of their own biases and ways of being and working. They need to gain a comfort level working in areas of difference and open themselves to continual learning from, about, and with others. This includes how a complex mix of people and groups function as a larger system and find better ways of living together.

Just Planning

While it may seem unfair to load city planners with all these issues, their role is substantial and critical in helping cities adapt to and undergo unprecedented changes. They have unknowingly had great and mostly negative impacts on the cultures of their communities. Their capacities for long-term and systems thinking are urgently needed, as well as their ability to connect the organization of physical space and means of movement with social, cultural, economic, and environmental sustainability in ways that reflect and foster a just society.

While a marriage of cultural planning and city planning may not be around the corner, the complexity and diversity of urban populations and growing efficacy of creativity and culture in economic, civic, and social life signal greater urgency that the practices move closer together. In doing so, it is important to not put another "mouth to feed" at city planners' tables, but to find ways that culture and creativity are complementary and facilitative, adding value, deeper purpose, and more effective outcomes to the broader enterprise of city planning. The "marriage" proposed at the 1979 San Antonio gathering, referred to in Chapter 2, where policymakers, city planners, scholars, and arts administrators convened and might have brought different genetic materials together to bear a healthier offspring. It is not too late.

More than 40 years later, cultural planning must move to the next level of helping city planners better understand the cultures of their communities, to find more ways to build bridges, create more welcoming, inclusive, and equitable cities. If carried out as discrete, specialized plans, as they usually have been, cultural plans need to evolve in scope and quality, be inclusive, and serve as bridge-building vehicles across the many cultural or ethnic and racial communities within cities. Moreover, city planners need to adopt more culturally informed practices and to incorporate key techniques from cultural planning, such as those described in this book, into the center of their practice. Synergy between the two planning practices has gotten little attention in the United States, although cultural plans have begun to broaden their scope and impacts, especially in economic and physical regeneration of towns and cities. Their differences, described in Chapter 2, have stood in the way.

This book is a hopeful exercise in bringing together critical elements of what have been separate professional planning practices towards the goal of more effective planning and more sustainable cities. It is my hope I have made a contribution to the tools and ways of thinking for city planners to better understand people and places in a cultural sense in efforts to foster greater cultural equity, social justice, and sustainability in communities of all sizes. For city planners and cultural planners who might otherwise work in parallel but rarely together, I hope to see them build on each other's efforts and experiences in renewed practices resulting in more just planning.

What used to be metaphorically referred to as "glacial" change is no longer meaningful nor relevant at a time when glaciers are crumbling at a remarkably quick pace. Exponential cultural changes prompted by globalization (mobility, technology, and migration) are also happening faster than we can comprehend. Hopefully, efforts by institutions and professional practices to change cannot afford to remain within the old definition of glacial. Efforts to address both climate and cultural changes have been massively inadequate with potentially devastating results. How institutions, professional practices, and individuals respond to these changes represent the largest, most complex, and critical challenges facing the 21st century.

References

Escobar, A. (2017). *Designs for the pluriverse: Radical interdependence, autonomy, and the making of worlds.* Durham, NC: Duke University Press.

Goodell, J. (2017). *The water will come: Rising seas, sinking cities, and the remaking of the civilized world.* New York, NY: Little, Brown.

Irwin, N., & Badger, E. (2019). Trump says the U.S. is "full." Much of the Nation has the opposite problem. *New York Times.* Retrieved from https://www.nytimes.com/2019/04/09/upshot/trump-america-full-or-emptying.html

Kegan, R., & Lahey, L. L. (2009). *Immunity to change: How to overcome it and unlock the potential in yourself and your organization*. Boston, MA: Harvard Business Press.

Lefebvre, H. (1991). *The production of space* (Trans. D. Nicholson-Smith). Oxford, UK: Blackwell. (Original work published 1974)

Morley, D. (2018). Measuring community character. *PAS QuickNotes 72*. American Planning Association, Chicago. Retrieved from https://www.planning.org/publications/document/9142842/

Porter, L. (2016). *Unlearning the colonial cultures of planning*. Abingdon, UK: Routledge. https://doi.org/10.4324/9781315548982

Soja, E. W. (1999). In different spaces: The cultural turn in urban and regional political economy. *European Planning Studies*, 7(1), 65–75. https://doi.org/10.1080/09654319908720501

Stein, S. (2019). *Capital city: Gentrification and the real estate state*. New York, NY: Verso.

Index

Page numbers in *italics* refer to figures.